Advance Praise for *Patagonian Road*

"Oh, what a stunning and gorgeous book this is, and one I can't wait to gift my daughter when she's ready. The story of a young woman's year-long trip through the long and winding highways, foot-paths, city streets and dusty back roads of Central and South America, *Patagonian Road* reminded me of my own journeys and made me pine for the ones I never had. It also expanded my understanding of what the journey is—McCahill's rich and vivid and complex tapestry of landscape, culture, geography, ecology, and economics, shows us, lyrically and with great tenderness, how the individual is part and parcel of a much larger whole, and how we can't find ourselves without finding the world outside ourselves. I lived and breathed every place this book touched down and when I turned the last page my heart ached for the journey's end."

—Robin MacArthur, author of *Half Wild: Stories*

"Kate McCahill is a blues traveler, singing for citizens of the world who have no public voice. She depicts beauty within despair, allowing us to hear a comforting melody in an unsettling breeze and see the gorgeous colors within a bruise. If a feeling of loneliness pervades her essays, so do feelings of wonder and pleasure. It's simply impossible not to share her joyful and frequently bewildering sensations of travel."

—Sascha Feinstein, author of
Black Pearls: Improvisations On A Lost Year

"The world may be growing smaller in this technological age, but our need to understand it has not diminished. Kate McCahill embarks on her journey across Latin America with a classic heroine's mix of anticipation and trepidation. The patron saints of her journey include writer Paul Theroux, known for his engagement in the face of discomfort. The other is the author's Finnish grandmother, whose inner strength makes her bold immigration journey possible.

Elegantly written and beautifully observed, McCahill's journey takes her across mountains and cities, into the reaches of culture and history, and into the self. Much of this is experienced from the seat of a bus, surrounded by a sea of humanity, both part of and an observer of the passing scene. A love affair is lost, new ways of being are found, and the adventurous McCahill turns herself not just into an intrepid traveller but into a fearless writer.

McCahill is a fresh new author—bringing a perspective as both a woman and as a member of the current generation to emerge into a complex world and make it theirs. By turns charming, scary, vivid, and reflective—*Patagonian Road* is a treat for the reader who need not buy a ticket but only open its pages to be transported."

—Miriam Sagan, author of *Black Rainbow* and
Searching For A Mustard Seed: One Young Widow's Unconventional Story

"With her *Lonely Planet* guide in one hand and Paul Theroux in the other, Kate McCahill backpacks from Guatemala to Buenos Aires losing love and finding a whirlwind assortment of ex-pats, aid workers, travel junkies, and locals. *Patagonian Road* is a millennial's adventure story, roughing it in the age of Skype and cell phones, through a Latin America still in recovery from decades of revolution, American meddling, and authoritarian misrule."

—Douglas Glover, author of *Elle*; publisher and editor, *Numéro Cinq*

"'When you're traveling, you bloom,' says one of the many fascinating characters in this memoir, and it's true, both of McCahill and of the reader who travels with her. What a pleasure to move between tropical forests, deserts, moutaintops, and city grit, bearing witness to open curiosity and intelligent reflection. *Patagonian Road* offers the steady, fragrant blossoming of a life well lived and of a writer making her home on the page."

—Michele Morano, author of
Grammar Lessons: Translating a Life in Spain

"Kate McCahill is a fearless explorer, and in her travel memoir *Patagonian Road* she leads us on a long and alert path through Central and South América, describing people and places that she encounters and that, fortunately, we as readers would otherwise never meet. The narrative tension of this beautifully written book is the taking in so much of the world while fighting forgetfulness. Forging a supple language of remembrance, McCahill announces: 'You are alive, a voice inside me says, and the words fill me.' Her words fill us as well, on this journey that unfolds as a series of unexpected gifts."

—Philip Graham, author of
The Moon, Come to Earth: Dispatches from Lisbon

"Wonderfully vivid, insightful, and occasionally painful, Kate McCahill's closely observed memoir is more than a travelogue documenting a yearlong trip through Latin America; it is a clear-eyed examination of what it means to connect, to seek, and to become fully oneself. A beautiful debut."

—Kirstin Valdez Quade, author of *Night at the Fiestas*

KATE McCAHILL

to Katie,
Reese, Rio and
Zebediah,
Happy Reading!

PATAGONIAN
ROAD

A YEAR ALONE THROUGH LATIN AMERICA

♡ Kate M Cahill

sf**WP**)

sfwp.com

Library of Congress Cataloging-in-Publication Data

Names: McCahill, Kate, 1984- author.
Title: Patagonian road : a year alone through Latin America / Kate McCahill.
Description: Santa Fe, NM : SFWP, 2017.
Identifiers: LCCN 2016028264 | ISBN 9781939650542 (trade paper : alkaline paper) |
    ISBN 9781939650559 (PDF) | ISBN 9781939650566 (ePub) |
    ISBN 9781939650573 (MOBI)
Subjects: LCSH: Latin America—Description and travel. | McCahill, Kate,
    1984—Travel—Latin America. | Women—Travel—Latin America. |
    Americans—Travel—Latin America. | Travel—Psychological aspects. |
    Solitude. | Self-actualization (Psychology) | Latin America—History, Local. |
    Latin America—Social life and customs. | BISAC: BIOGRAPHY &
    AUTOBIOGRAPHY / Women. | TRAVEL / Central America.
Classification: LCC F1409.5 .M36 2017 | DDC 918.04—dc23
LC record available at https://lccn.loc.gov/2016028264

Published by SFWP
369 Montezuma Ave. #350
Santa Fe, NM 87501
(505) 428-9045
www.sfwp.com

Find the author at www.katemccahill.com

In memory of my grandmothers,
Elizabeth Batcheller McCahill and Helmi Lillqvist Sipila

Leave the door open for the unknown, the door into the dark. That's where the most important things come from, where you yourself came from, and where you will go.

—*Rebecca Solnit*, A Field Guide to Getting Lost

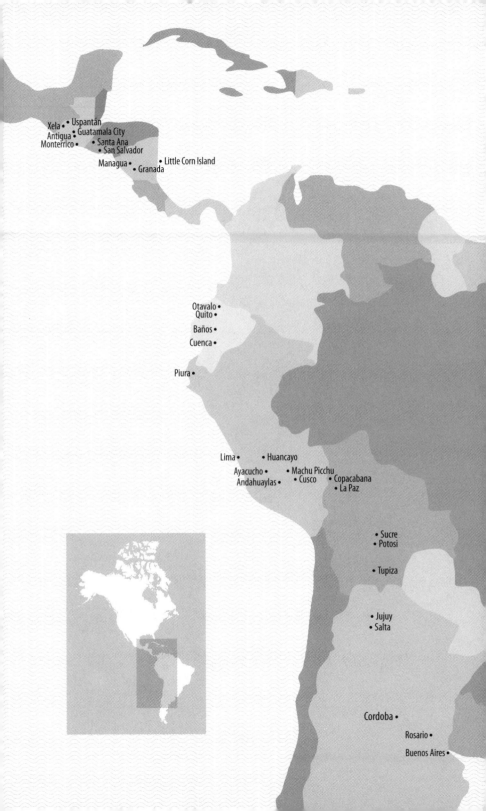

CONTENTS

PROLOGUE 1

PART 1: WINTER

Guatemala City, Guatemala 13

Xela, Guatemala 21

Antigua, Guatemala 43

Monterrico, Guatemala 55

Uspantán, Guatemala 67

Santa Ana, El Salvador 83

San Salvador, El Salvador 91

The Road 95

Granada, Nicaragua 99

Little Corn Island, Nicaragua 115

PART 2: SPRING

Quito, Ecuador 121

Santa Fe, New Mexico 149

The Road 157

Otavalo, Ecuador 159

Baños, Ecuador 163

Cuenca, Ecuador 177

Vilcabamba, Ecuador 189

Lima, Peru 195

Huancayo, Peru 207

Ayacucho, Peru 219

The Road 233

Cusco, Peru 241

PART 3: SUMMER

Machu Picchu 251

Puno, Peru 259

Copacabana, Bolivia 263

La Paz, Bolivia 275

Sucre, Bolivia 279

Potosí, Bolivia 285

Tupiza, Bolivia 291

The Road 295

PART 4: FALL

Buenos Aires, Argentina 303

The Road 331

Buenos Aires, Argentina 339

PROLOGUE

I take the bus to the end of the line. The 152 runs all along the Rio de la Plata, and today the sky is a faultless blue. Young mothers with little children ride the bus at this hour, and I have a seat to myself. All the windows are open, and the Rio's salty, grimy wind blows in.

The last stop is the university parking lot, and the driver eases his seat back for a nap as we trundle off. Students shuffle to class, ear buds blocking out the sounds of northern Buenos Aires in springtime: birdsong, cars coming and going, a woman calling out to a friend. Someone is strumming a guitar.

Through the open doors of the student center, there's a protest going on, cardboard signs and a murmuring crowd. I've heard there's a commune just past the university, tucked in the woods and wetlands there. I have to remind myself that this is Buenos Aires, too, though how different it feels from the wild city I've come to know. On my street in downtown Buenos Aires, romantic curls of molding on buildings and ancient, elegant sycamores conceal layers of grime and urine-stained walls. The city is always alight, cafés waking up at midnight, *milongas* running on into sunrise. When I'm wandering and take the wrong road too far, men click their tongues from where they stand in the garages of their mechanic shops. Fear arrives, sharp and quick enough to make my fingertips hum, yet by now it's also oddly familiar. I know that if I walk faster and don't look over, I'll probably be okay.

In this Buenos Aires at the end of the line, the wind smells of water and grass. The Parque de la Memoria stretches along the Rio. I enter by way of an unlocked, unmanned gate. A small sign: *Monument to the Victims of State Terrorism*. A series of more signs march beside a walkway. Slowly, I read each one, stumbling over words I don't recognize. I get my out pocket dictionary.

The first signs describe the years between 1950 and 1975, when members of Latin American militaries were sent off to martial schools funded by North America. There, they learned to torture, interrogate, and kill. They learned how to make someone disappear, the word used for those captured, detained, and often killed.

A breeze blows in off the water, rippling through the longish grass. There's no one else around.

The trained militants returned to their home countries, their value systems altered. Now, they were convinced that the right thing to do was to kill their countrymen.

In Buenos Aires, the disappearances began in the late 1970's. Anyone considered left-leaning—skeptical of the corrupt government, critical of entrenched systemic elitism—was at risk. Many Disappeared found their final resting places here in the Rio, often dropped in by air.

One sign pictures the Ford Falcon, the sedan outlined in black against a bright yellow square. The image is an ominous one for Buenos Aires, because it's the vehicle known for stealing people off the streets and disappearing them. One sign says that there were many pregnant women at the time of the detentions, but being pregnant didn't stop them from experiencing torture. The women were often disappeared, and the babies were sometimes left in the hands of the military officers and their wives.

One sign pictures white outlines of bodies, and beneath it a number: 30,000.

One round sign looks out over the water. It shows a crowd in the street and over that a thick red line, stamping the people out. Beyond the sign, the sky gleams clear and blue, the water breeze-rippled.

This is still Buenos Aires, I realize, and there is a different kind of wildness here: something deep and tragic, an ordered memorial for much lost.

In the winter of 1978, travel writer Paul Theroux boarded a train at Boston's South Station and rode for four months, traveling through Mexico, Central America, and South America. He rode trains through Guatemala and Panama, Colombia and Ecuador, Peru and Bolivia, all the way to Argentina. He wrote *The Old Patagonian Express*, an account of his journey by train, and thirty years later, I read it.

Theroux was a man traveling in a man's world. He spoke decent Spanish, had adequate funding, and enjoyed the privilege and respect that his race and status garnered. Yet what stood out to me most about Theroux's journey was that he never stopped to take in any place, for the trains were his real destinations. As a result, his perspectives of countries are fleeting, sensory, and hilarious. Each encounter is brief and dialogue-rich. Yet he never stopped to teach, or lecture, or even, it seemed, to write. He was a tourist first and foremost, and he never seemed to let himself get emotionally involved. I couldn't imagine traveling like that, not stopping to savor a beach, a neighborhood, a friendship, or a trail in the woods. Theroux never stayed anywhere long enough to fall in love with it.

Yet his map planted a seed in my mind. After college, I worked odd jobs at hotel front desks and restaurants until I'd saved up enough for a round-the-world plane ticket. For six months I backpacked in Asia alone. Words flowed from my hands in the evenings, sloppy cursive in water-stained journals. There was so much to write about, then.

When I returned to the States, everyday life quickly snapped me up again. I moved to Boston and went to dozens of interviews, finally landing a thirty-thousand-dollar salary, ten days vacation paid, at a small publishing house. I was thrilled to have the job, to have *a* job; the housing bubble was beginning, messily, to burst. There was never enough money or time, and I apologized away events that slipped past: weddings, dinners, baby showers. I was always running late. Still, there was emptiness, despite how the hours filled. I started to apply for fellow-ships, writing proposals in the hours before and after work, imagining a dream trip I'd take if only I had the money. I would learn to become a teacher, a profession I'd always wondered about. I would write, this time a book. I would draw the trip out into a year, and I would go by myself. I kept coming back to Paul Theroux, retracing his route through Latin America in my proposals and budgets and letters of intent. I printed application materials at the office, sneaking them past my boss.

And in the afternoons, while snow fell outside my window and onto the Mass Pike, I imagined the places I'd go: Guatemala, Hon-duras, Ecuador, and Argentina. Before Theroux, I couldn't even point them out on a map, and yet now the road seemed at once inconceiv-able and accessible. Planes and buses and taxis, my research proved, could get me to where I wanted to go. I started reading books only by Hispanic or Latin American writers, and I enrolled in Spanish classes at the adult education center in Cambridge. I mailed my fellowship applications. I waited.

About a year later, one of the fellowship committees called me in for an interview. Three months after that, someone else called to tell me I'd been granted enough money to travel for a year.

"What?" I remember saying, rudely, into the phone. And then I burst into tears, and the woman on the other end of the line laughed and asked me if I'd be all right.

A few days before I boarded a plane to Guatemala City, my mother and I spent one night at my grandmother's house in Connecticut. She's ninety-seven and lives alone. She emigrated from Finland seventy years ago when she was twenty-one. It was her older sister Eva who was supposed to come, whose name was printed on the ticket, but at the last moment she lost her courage and passed her ticket to my grandmother, who took it without hesitation. My grandmother was working on her family's dairy farm at the time. For a while, my mother told me once, my grandmother worried someone might come knocking on her door. Mail still comes to her addressed to *Eva* sometimes, but by now so many years have passed that it doesn't matter anymore. That night for dinner, we had a roast with homemade bread, mashed sweet potatoes, and green beans. For dessert we had apple pie that my grandmother heated in the toaster oven. She'd prepared two full days for the meal.

That night, my mom and I pushed our twin beds together so they touched. I could hear my grandmother's light snore in the other room. The house ticked and settled itself to sleep, the wood creaking in the attic and the water heater murmuring from the basement. I didn't sleep that night, barely even closed my eyes. Instead, I stared at the white lace curtains. Breezes through the cracked window blew them gently back and forth. Sometime just before daybreak, I felt my mother's hand reach with urgency toward me, felt her pat my body and then press her hand against me for a moment before drawing it back. She was checking to make sure I was there.

There's a woodprint hanging by the front door of my grandmother's house. It's a Finnish scene: a farmhouse, an apple tree, a mournful woman and a weeping man saying goodbye to another man wearing a backpack. He is walking away from them while they moan, his hand raised in a wave but his back turned and his head down. There was so much grief in that print, I always thought, and wondered why my grandmother displayed it so prominently all these years. On the morning I left, though, I knew: the permanence of a ship's journey back then, and for that sacrifice, this: a morning together, a trip I am taking, a life my grandmother chose for the rest of us.

My mother saw me staring at the woodprint.

"That's you," she said, nodding at the man with the backpack. We looked at each other for a moment, and then she helped me to haul my pack out into the car.

As I pulled down the driveway, I watched through the rearview as my mother waved goodbye. *Be careful*, she mouthed. Through the living room window, I could see my grandmother, her hand raised in a motionless wave. I tooted my horn twice, but the sound didn't come out cheerful the way I'd hoped. As I turned onto the main road and peered through the hedge back toward the house, I saw that my mother still waved, and I drove up and over the hill, watching her wave and wave, until she was entirely out of sight.

At the memorial for the Disappeared, the sun shines. Halfway down the row of signs, I notice something in the distance, out in the water. It takes me another second or two to make out a drowning figure, arms raised. I stare at it long enough to confirm that it's a sculpture, a statue, not a survivor but merely a reminder of the actual lives this river disappeared.

I come to the center of the museum, a wall with thousands of names. Each name has its own little stone, one stone for everyone who lost their life to the dictatorships in Argentina. I peer in: *Welay, Carlos Miguel, 28 años. Welares, Hector Antoni, 42 años. Wuzzese, Julio Cesar, 33 años. Wornoz, Maria Cristina, 26 años.* Plastic flowers tucked between the stones brighten the names. *When Maria Cristina Wornoz was my age, I* think, *she was dead.*

When I began my journey, I anticipated danger at every turn. Ours is the era of WebMD, helicopter parents, and amber alters. We fear the danger and poverty of the developing world, the disease and bad water and the prospect of witnessing defecation in the streets. Travelers are told it will be much worse over there than it is here at home, and so they dress in canvas cargo pants, wide brimmed sun hats, and all-weather leather boots, none of which has ever been worn back home where it's safe and the streets are clean. We fear being deviceless, without our social media and list of contacts. We fear unfilled free time. We fear being alone with ourselves, and most of all, we fear the unknown.

Meanwhile, when my Finnish grandmother was my age—twenty-six—she worked on a chicken farm, starting her days at four a.m. She didn't speak English yet, couldn't read the words on the newspapers placed on stands outside the grocery store, knew only a handful of Finns who lived nearby and had immigrated on the same boat she'd been on.

And by the time my mother was my age, she had already worked in a syringe factory, an airport-meal factory, and a car-parts factory. She worked nights because it paid better. She went off to nursing school, but before she did, she saved up her money and spent a summer in Europe. She still talks about it sometimes, dreamily, the way she'd ditched her friends and wandered the streets of Barcelona and Paris alone.

As a woman setting off, I was told many times to beware of sketchy men, empty dark streets, and venturing out at night—advice anyone, in any place and of any gender, might be wise to take. The Latin American people would be especially appalled at the sight of me, manless and backpack clad. *Where is your husband?* they'd inquire fretfully, all the way from Xela to Bariloche. I'd channel my grandmother then, imagining her onboard a ship bound for a place she'd never seen. I'd remember her half-smile, her crooked teeth, her darting, amused eyes. *I made it this far,* I'd think to myself, imagining I was sending the message to her.

How little I knew about the world before I left for Latin America. How little I understood about what it meant to be a white American woman in the twenty-first century and how much, in my lifetime, I've been spared. How many gifts I've been given. How naïve I was as I fumbled through Latin America; how stupid I was at times, and how lucky. How much I underestimated the power of the road, which turned out to be a mostly welcoming, often beautiful place, a place that both challenged and healed.

Be careful, everyone in the States told me, just before they kissed me goodbye. It was more a warning than advice. *Good luck*, I would have preferred, for I have come to believe that travel is necessary, and if we're going to do it, we'll need all the luck we can get. Be it taking a walk or hopping on a plane, it is in feasting on the unknown that we come to know ourselves.

In the end, only my mother said it right: "This year will change your life."

WINTER

It was a morning of paralyzing frost, the perfect day to leave for South America.

—Paul Theroux, *The Old Patagonian Express*

GUATEMALA CITY, GUATEMALA

I make a list in my mind, as I wait for the plane, of the things I am leaving behind.

There is the cat, off to live with my parents in their rambling old house in upstate New York. There is the Cambridge apartment, that miracle I stumbled into three winters ago on a day when new snow occupied most of the street parking. There are my mother and father, my brother, my grandmothers, who seem years older each time I see them, who seem to recognize me less and less. There is my lover: butter skin, an amber voice. A year is a very long time.

A woman stands with a little boy at the edge of the customs line. They are holding hands and both of them weep and wipe away tears. They're not talking to each other, not looking at anything, just standing and sniffling and blinking their eyes. I watch them and want to give them something, buy them coffee and donuts, maybe. The view through the airport windows reveals only the brightly lit drop-off and pick-up zone, a place that looks the same summer and winter both, covered as it is with five stories of parking garage.

There's the Cambridge apartment, not mine anymore, on the corner of a quiet street and a noisy one, the first place I ever lived all alone. There is the job I left behind—a good, sturdy job, but the office windows never opened, and the elevator shuffled and creaked. The four of us, just out of college and paying the bills, and our boss, who flew fighter planes in Vietnam and never forgot.

They've stopped weeping now, the boy and his mother, and she is giving him juice from a carton. The cabs slow past, and then speed away. Now, the airport wind shifts; the people who were waiting are standing and gathering their children, their purses and breakfasts; there's a woman at the counter unhooking the latch on the retractable gate. We remove our coats; there are no seasons, there is no time. I have a United States passport in my hand—the ultimate ticket, I remind myself, as I watch the freezing morning through sliding panes of glass.

I picture my mother and grandmother in the kitchen together, the too-bright bulb buzzing above them, the yellow Finnish runner stretched evenly over the wooden dining table. I can taste their coffee: strong, rich with a slip of cream from the pitcher. I think of the rush of water that sprang from my grandmother's kitchen sink, which overlooks her clothesline and the river in the ravine. *Of all the funny things,* I say to myself, *the water in the sink on my mind.*

Last, I imagine my lover. E— is speeding away from the airport; she makes her way down Storrow Drive, the river still lit up for nighttime, and crosses the bridge from Boston into Cambridge. Now she's driving down Mass Ave, through Central Square, past our favorite Chez Poupin and past the Middle East and The Plough and Stars, bars smelling of spilled beer and sweat. Past an eerie, lamplit park. Now she's turning, slowing, parking. Here is the bed, and it is just barely still warm.

The sheets still smell of me, but in the days to come, she'll wash them, and I'll be gone.

In Guatemala City, I recognize Lorena's car from the description she sent in an e-mail: a beat-up black station wagon with crooked bumper stickers. She gets out of the car and comes to me, speaking jolty English, insisting on hurtling my pack into the trunk for me. We lurch away from the airport, and now I am moving over land I've never seen.

On the plane, I took a crash course on Guatemala, the first of many crash courses my *Lonely Planet* would provide. Guatemala, as far as most North Americans can tell, is still reeling from the civil wars of the seventies, eighties, and nineties, civil wars that rocked Latin America from Argentina to Mexico. Had the United States left well enough alone in the forties and fifties, Guatemala might not have the war-torn reputation that it does. As in so many Latin American countries, I'll come to learn, North American intervention did more harm than good. In Guatemala's case, it mostly started with 1950's president Colonel Jacobo Arbenz Guzmàn, who tried to break up enormous colonial estates so he could redistribute land to native people. The country's poor were inching upwards in economic status, and hope glimmered. With land redistribution, a certain level of equality would have been regained, equality that had been cut off at the time of the Encounter—in Guatemala's case, Cortez's arrival in the sixteenth century.

But the United States intervened, conducting an invasion in 1954 with the help of exiled Guatemalan militia. That was, in effect, the end of land reform—and Indian rights—and by the time the 1970's came around, upwards of 70,000 people had died in classist, racist violence. Most of the dead were the rural, indigenous poor. Now, Guatemala is mostly peaceful, though in the years after I leave, more tumult will ensue. I've come to Guatemala at a lucky time, a time of peace and general goodwill towards tourists, though I don't know it yet.

Lorena drives fast, chatting and humming along to the radio. *This is how easy it can be to escape*, I think to myself, watching out the window at the palm trees that line the road. We won't be going into the city, Lorena tells me; the hotel is in a gated complex, and we drive only five minutes. An armed guard unlocks the metal door and swings it open slowly, tipping his hat. Lorena's hotel is the last house on a one-way street that, at lunchtime, is silent. The sun sits exactly in the center of the sky, but inside, after

Lorena punches in the alarm's code, the rooms are dark and cool. Strains of Christmas carols play from the kitchen radio. I pay Lorena then: the price of the bed, the airport pickup, and a bus ticket for the morning is twenty US dollars. Lorena shows me to a small room with two narrow beds and a light on the table between them. The single window looks out through steel bars into one of the hotel's three gardens.

After I've paid for my room, Lorena closes the door behind me and leaves me to rest, and I wish to tell E— about the flowers, the faint hint of lilies riding the air, the sun that beats the pavement gray. I store all of it away to give to her later, when she comes home from work and I call her through a connection on my computer. Yet I already understand that even one second's delay is enough to ebb the moment. This is how the time will pass from now on: the freshness of the day will have dried by the evening, and there are things I will have forgotten. The drops of the morning will have staled. This is the way we have chosen—the way *I* have chosen.

Today, on this early afternoon in December, rhododendrons are blooming alongside bromeliads, wild roses, and tall grass, but this morning, snow crunched beneath my feet. I kissed a lover goodbye, and then she drove back home through the darkness. Here, the earth is buzzing, and the tears from the morning have long dried.

A Chihuahua and a golden retriever live next door, and I discover them on my first-ever walk in Central America. The two of them sit on their lawn without barking.

"Hi there," I tell them, softly so as not to attract anyone's attention, and they sniff the air. The neighborhood is silent. Keeping in mind the warnings I've heard of this city's dangers, I tiptoe down the street, away from the good dogs. I pass no one but flowers, shuttered houses, wrought-iron gates hot to the touch; there are dogs who laze in yards behind steel walls. Once, a pickup rumbles past and startles me with a honk. Its windows are tinted dark—illegal in New York—and I feel a surge of fear. The hot sun turns cold, and I look for a place I might hide. Every yard has a gate. My mind sharpens the afternoon as if with a blade, turning the sweet-smelling yards ominous. I am thinking of all the warnings I received before I left. How silly I'll feel when, later, I learn that every passing car honks, not to scare me but to warn me not to step into the street. Honks are a courtesy; tinted windows keep the bright sun out. I hurry back to Lorena's house, reciting to myself the code to her gate, and then punching it in with trembling hands.

Guatemala is just one hour behind Boston, and yet I know I'm much farther away than that. In four hours' time, I was transported: I'm in the tropics now, and everything seems different—the language, the pace, the smell of the air, the way the wind feels on my skin.

When E— and I talk through my computer, we have both just finished our dinners.

"It's warm here," I say, describing the flowers and the way the wind smells faintly of jasmine. I don't tell her I was afraid.

"It's cold here!" E— protests, and then I tell her that I love her. "Sleep well," she replies, and I hear her kiss blown through the line.

I lie awake in my Guatemala bed and listen to the wind through the open window. I imagine that this wind has come down from the storms in Canada to rough up this night, rough up the palm fronds, silence for a while the barking dogs.

This is the beginning, I say to myself. The windows don't fully shut in this room. Now come the voices of Lorena and her husband, and even as he goes on and on about Saint Nicholas, on and on about his pasta primavera, there comes that steady wind in the palms, rolling all over the city and washing my clean-sheeted night.

A man named Victor is waiting for me at the curb at five in the morning, and he looks as if he's been up for hours: he's freshly shaven and his eyes are bright. He shakes my hand and takes my pack. His cab is clean and warm, and we drive through a morning electric with wind. On the way, Victor looks up at the sky, which tumbles with low, heavy clouds.

"Tiempo loco," he says.

"Tiempo loco," I whisper, thinking how closely the words match the tone of the lusty wind.

The streets close to Lorena's hotel are sleepy, reminding me of San Francisco's avenues, split by parks. But then the route winds and tightens and now we are passing close cement buildings with thick bars over the windows and narrow sidewalks, wet where women have poured water to clean them. Although it's still dark, people are out walking purposefully along. They wear dark clothing and carry American-made backpacks. The men have cowboy hats perched on their heads. Women crush oranges on corners to make juice, or slap together sandwiches, filling slices of white bread with ham and cheese and mayonnaise. As we drive, the buildings are increasingly layered in years of grime, and the trees disappear. The traffic thickens.

In the end, Guatemala City is not so terrible as everyone warned. It isn't even as bad as the guidebook made it out to be. I am safe, and Victor is kind. The sun is up, and no fights erupt. No one pries open the car door and brandishes a knife.

This city, it turns out, is just another place. It is a poor place, grimy and dirty, but it is a place with a morning like everywhere else. There are oranges to be crushed, coffees to drink down, a bus station to wait in until I leave for Xela, where, after Victor hands me my ticket, shakes my hand, and leaves me sitting on a plastic chair, no one even glances at me, except to tell me that the bathroom is occupied and that I'll have to wait.

The driver stows my bag in the dirty belly of the bus, then makes a rapid announcement through a microphone. I understand nothing, his words like gritty cacklings, briefly muted when the microphone faults.

My heart beats, I can hear it, but the other passengers just lean back in their seats, wipe the steam from their windows with their sleeves, and look out at the roil of people outside, who wait with their own beat-up suitcases and sleepy children. The woman in the seat beside me smiles at me once and then tilts her seat back and goes to sleep. No one else looks over; no one asks me any questions.

We roll out of the city, past signs I cannot read, past lives behind graffitied walls I cannot see. Then Guatemala City ends abruptly; the suburbs vanish, and it's just countryside now. The bus climbs up, up, through miles and miles of jungle and then into the farmed-out hills, where the land has been cleared in patchwork: corn, lettuce, coffee, plots for pigs to root around. Women march along the roadside, bales of sticks tied to their backs. Little kids are waving, and men stand between the dried-out lines of corn. Stands have sodas and oranges for sale; then come more swaths of corn, more flats of tomatoes. The bus is cold at first but gets hot fast as the sun rises, and Latin music videos, decades-old, flicker on the tiny television screens. Eventually, a violent Hollywood action movie dubbed with angry Spanish voices replaces the music.

At lunchtime, we park at a rest stop. A row of stands—jewelry, candy, magnets for sale—is set up by the entrance. There are racks of woven purses, woven bracelets, and little wooden keychains carved into the shape of quetzals, Guatemala's national bird. This lunch place is built of unpainted wooden beams that smell of pine, and it serves coffee and slices of pie and plates of beans and eggs. I fumble through my English-Spanish pocket dictionary to decipher the words on the menu tacked above the counter. *Manzana*, I search for, and *calabaza*. I buy coffee and a slice of pumpkin pie, which tastes nothing like the moist, dark pie of the Thanksgivings I have known. It is sweet, very pale, and crumbly in my mouth. *Manzana*, I practice saying in my head, and then think for one instant of my mother—her dense pies, her face bright at the table, eyes shining after one glass of wine. *Manzana, calabaza*, I say to myself. A year is a very long time.

The land grows dry with cornfields, which seem to bristle and crack in the heat, flashes of gold in the husks: acres that seem ready to burn any second. Hours pass. Occasionally, a volcano slides into view. The mountains are stripped bare by centuries of the wrong kind of farming—monoculture, without concern for the soil's long-term fertility—and so everything here is the same shade of brown, everything but the blue arc of sky.

XELA, GUATEMALA

Xela, short for the Mayan *Quetzaltenango*, perches at 7500 feet above sea level. It's a hilly city of winding streets and low, pastel-colored houses, and from certain vantage points, the Volcan de Santa María is visible. Xela, whose economy was boosted by the coffee production in the nineteenth century, remains thriving today: the city is famous for its Spanish schools, which lure tourists year round, and for its proximity to volcanoes, rivers, and the numerous surrounding Mayan towns. Once largely Mayan itself, Xela's population of 100,000 is now made up largely of mestizos and fair-skinned expats.

The bus bumps over cobblestones, rolling slowly past views between buildings of the surrounding mountains, green to the south, where the river runs, and brown to the east toward Guatemala City. The woman beside me rouses herself, touches her white hair lightly, and smiles at me, folding her papery hands. I climb off last and find my pack, a little scuffed but still snapped closed, and then I stand on the flattened cobblestones of this sun-baked city and take a deep breath, and then another.

In the cab, the driver drags on a bent cigarette and flicks it into the street. I reach back in my mind for the Spanish phrases I learned at the adult ed center six months ago, but I can only recall that the lilacs were still in bloom then. I draw up freshman-year French. The driver is kind and tries to understand as he drives me to the Spanish school. I wish to be back in the warm bus with its sticky, safe seats and scratched windows, my destination still imagined.

"I don't speak English," Norma tells me in English. She's very short, maybe five feet, but she's sturdy-looking, with thick black hair and smooth skin. It's impossible for me to gauge her age—somewhere between twenty and forty. She has come to the Spanish school to fetch me, and she hoists my pack as if it weighs nothing. I rush to stop her, miming a person collapsing beneath immeasurable weight. She pauses a moment, then laughs, but her smile is uneasy. *Manzana*, I think. *Calabaza*.

Norma is my host mother, assigned many months before through a sequence of e-mails from the Spanish school. I follow her outside, where a very old man sits in his car, waiting. He's left the engine on, and when he sees us he opens the door, puts his cigarette out on the ground with his shoe and unlocks the trunk. He shakes our hands. Inside, I see that the front seats are covered with stretched-out old t-shirts, and a bell on a fraying ribbon hangs from the rearview.

Up front, Norma chats with the old man and rests her arm against the sealed-up window. The plane ride took six hours, the bus four more. *This is what's been south of us, all this time.* There is broken glass in the road, and everywhere ancient cars are parked. A dog pees against a wall. There is a cloudless blue sky, the occasional cream-colored house, the mottled terracotta of the curving roofs. We stop halfway down a narrow street where the blocky concrete houses sit edge to edge.

It's so dim in Norma's house that my eyes pinch for a moment, adjusting from the bright sidewalk sun. I make out a table, which occupies more than half the room, and many mismatched chairs. A Christmas tree, decorated with tiny, blinking lights, takes up the remainder of the space, and, between the table and the tree, three small human shapes stand in a line. It is as if they have been waiting for us. I wait for my eyes to discern their dark hair and round cheeks. *The Simpsons*, dubbed in Spanish, hoots at us from a vivid TV screen.

Norma introduces her children: Carlos is short and chubby, seven years old maybe, and Alejandra is a little bit taller, with a heart-shaped face and braids clipped with red barrettes. Sergio's the oldest—fifteen, sixteen—and he wears thickly framed glasses and gel in his hair. Half-grinning, he holds out his hand to shake mine. We all follow Norma through a little cement hallway beyond the main room, past a low stone sink called a *pila*, past a tiny, dark kitchen with clean pots and pans resting on the stovetop. At last we enter a bright courtyard where, at the corner, one stubby tree drops its dried-up leaves. A fat white rabbit nibbles grass.

Norma unlocks a door on the other side of the courtyard; inside, there are two double beds, a white plastic table, a wooden chair, and three mirrors tacked to the walls. The room is cold and big. Alejandra steps forward and fingers the bedpost, touches the windowsill, takes the room in as if she's never seen it before, as if it's both hers and not hers. Then Norma shuttles everyone out, tells me something I can't quite understand, and shuts the door behind her, lightly. Through the window I watch them amble back across the courtyard, then disappear into their house's dark interior, where the Christmas tree and shrieking Simpsons wait.

So this, I think, the sudden silence a cloak around me, *this*.

Much later, I will wake in the dark, confused. My heart will still be beating hard from a dream I've already forgotten, and I will search the room for a few long moments before I remember where I am.

Just before dawn, a cracking pop outside snaps me upright. My heart pounds even before my clumsy, bleary brain says, instinctively, *Gun*. I lie tense, waiting for a knock at my door, a fear-singed scream, the howl of a witness cat, but nothing comes, not until minutes later when the same sound shatters me awake once more. This time, though, I can see colors through the window, falling pieces of red and yellow in the sky. Fireworks. Gradually, the sounds escalate, the glittering shards fill the sky, until all around me, it seems, colors crack and explode through the window and on the walls, and there come no other human sounds.

* * *

Linda's glossy hair gleams, smelling of shampoo, and during our second Spanish lesson she admits that she colors it to give it the reddish tint I can only see in the sunlight. She has big, dark eyes, and she does her makeup differently each day, shimmery eye shadow to match her clothes, rosy blush to accent her cheekbones. Twenty-four year old Linda, life-long resident of Xela, is my Spanish teacher, and we will meet at this table five days a week, five hours a day, for the next five weeks.

Men here prefer curvier women, Linda tells me. They're more fertile, that's what the men think. She enunciates the word: *furr-tell, furtyle*. This is how she speaks to me: half English, half Spanish, her mouth savoring the words in both languages. Her gestures make up for the vocabulary I lack. "Fertile," she says once more, and I look down at my own body, which is narrow and straight.

Linda asks me if I'm single. "Don't you have a boyfriend?" she asks, standing with her hands on her hips. I'd been with men before E—, men whose skin felt so fluid under my hands, whose voices in their depth contrasted so much with my own, men who treated my body like a sacred place. Still, I want to tell Linda, there was never anyone else like E—, no one else who tugged at me like she did, no one else I'd wait up for through the night and into the morning, no one else I'd stay on the phone with so long, no one else I'd touch the way I touch her.

"What's his name?" Linda prods.

"Eliot," I finally lie.

"Eliot," she says, rolling the name in her mouth like she did with *fertile*, like she will with *butter* and *waterfall* and *leaf*. I describe him as I would describe her: dark-haired, dark-skinned, beautiful inside and out. Truths coat the lie, and I never tell E—.

Instead, I describe the school to her, mentioning first the flowers: fresh flowers each morning, calla lilies out of a painting, an occasional blood-red rose. For my lessons, Linda sits on the couch, and I sit at the desk. She twirls her hair, checks her makeup in a pocket mirror, and turns her cell phone off. She pokes around in her pencil case for the dry-erase markers, picks lint off her sweater, and makes small talk, half-Spanish, half-English. In the five years Linda has taught, she has received five marriage proposals from students, mostly men aged fifty and up. Each one she's turned down, she says, because these *gringos* are not what she has in mind for a husband, even if they do have money and a car and a house. Even if they can whisk her out of Guatemala and up to some warm United State, or to far-off Germany, where the men are tall and clever (but not funny, she admits) and wear designer glasses. She wants to marry for love, at least right now she does, but ask her again in five or ten years and maybe she'll take one of those buttoned-up, pale-skinned men after all.

Linda has taught Japanese, Chinese, and Thai students. She's taught Russians, Swedes, Finns, Italians, Americans, and the French. She's taught Indians, Australians, and Kiwis. You can tell, too, because underneath all the hair combing and gossip, she excels. She knows the curriculum without ever having to consult her lesson guide—a thick, spiral-bound volume she created herself while earning her degree at the local university. She knows which words are past participles, which tense is the future perfect; she knows that *mine* and *yours* are possessive pronouns. "Dudas?" Linda asks at the end of each lesson before sweeping her eraser over her markered words. "Preguntas?"

All through Latin America, I'll encounter women like Linda: young professionals eking it out in a world that doesn't make it easy. So many times, for so many years, I took my privilege for granted: a college degree and then a master's; emotionally and financially supportive parents; access to good health care and birth control. Now, I admire Linda, who lives with a dozen family members in a house five miles from the school. She rides three buses to get here, riding in the darkness of morning and again after the sun sets. Her life has been a scramble, and her level of education is still, in Guatemala, somewhat of a miracle: she isn't married yet, she doesn't have children, and she wasn't so bound to her house— by her siblings, her parents, her grandparents—that she couldn't go out and study. I marvel at her enthusiasm and the way she masks her fatigue; in addition to teaching, she cares for a couple of young nieces and nephews. I discover that her staunch singledom is a feminist gesture, far more significant here than in the United States. Here, being single at age twenty-four means turning away from tradition and cultural expectation—with little help from anyone but yourself.

* * *

I will tell E— about all of this, starting with the way the minibus rattles up to us without stopping completely, and the driver's helper, the *ayudante*, stands in the doorway, holding open the sliding door. He ushers us onto the cracked plastic bench seats and then leans out again, one hand clutching the roof and the other outstretched, poised to grab whoever else needs a ride.

I am with Sergio, Norma's 16-year-old son, and I will tell E— about our flight on wheels through Xela. The *ayudante* swings through the van's low-ceilinged cabin, taking our bills and counting out change. The ride costs two quetzals. At first, we're the only passengers, but more climb on at every street corner, and by the time we reach the Mercado, there must be twenty-five of us in the ten-seater. There are young mothers with smooth skin and fine features whose babies lie strapped to their backs, wrapped close and tight, their heads covered. The babies don't cry; the mothers sit quietly as if they too once rode strapped and swaddled. As the packed microbus bumps along, I wonder how those babies can breathe, let alone sleep. The mothers, with strong-looking hands and unlined faces, keep their eyes on the road ahead.

"San Martin!" cries the *ayudante*, squeezed in between two old women with gray braids. "San Martin Chile Verde," he shouts again, as if he might persuade some passersby, motivated by the passion in his call, to take an impromptu journey to San Martin. Even as the van packs, crams, he shouts out the name of his destination, and I learn how to make space, tightening my body until I occupy far less of myself than I'm used to. Men climb up onto the roof; I can hear them moving around above me, laughing, pounding when they're ready to jump down.

We pass roadside stands of oranges and bananas and grapes, handmade bracelets and scarves and inexpensive tubes of toothpaste, racks of neon shoes, and bright key-chains that glow in the dark. I take note of things we pass: the botanical gardens, the rows of brand-new condominiums, and the huge supermarkets and industrial gas stations and electronics stores. I want to store everything away, and give it to E—. We exit the city and drive along curving jungle roads bordered by farm fields and villages and a cemetery built in the traditional Guatemalan way, with tombs of azure blue and brilliant orange, pink-red and marigold, all stacked upon each other and marching, vivid, up the hillside.

In the scooped-out valley of San Martin Chile Verde, Sergio turns to me and grins. We don't know each other well, but it doesn't matter. He knows a place; he will show it to me today. Norma packed us a lunch and sent us off. Sun beats onto the dirt roads of San Martin, and red dust swirls up onto our skin and into our mouths and noses. Out of the van, we unbutton our long-sleeved shirts and open our collars; I slather on sunscreen. The buzzing of jungle comes from all around. There's a rickety bridge and below it a sign instructing that only one person cross at a time. The bridge, built long ago of boards and rope, careens drunkenly left and right. Men working in the river, gathering stones and water, watch me as I cross the bridge, smiles playing over their lips.

"Hola," they call up to me. I can hear them splashing below, the water wetting their hot skin.

The road meanders through hamlets, where corn dries on ribbed tin roofs. Maize is sacred to the Maya, and no part is wasted, Sergio explains. Walls and furniture are built of corn. Fermented maize becomes *chicha*, and in the market you can buy hot corn soup, which arrives, nutty and steaming, in Styrofoam coffee cups without spoons. Maize is ground to make tortillas, the staple of every meal, or else *masa*—unsweetened corn—makes tamales.

The houses begin to disappear, their roofs of corn replaced by fields of lettuce and cabbage. We pass little boys who trek down the hill with huge bales of sticks strapped to their backs. The oldest is maybe thirteen, the youngest five or six. They call out *hola*, averting their eyes politely as they trundle down the hill, which grows steeper and steeper. We hike up in our sturdy shoes and backpacks. Sergio is snapping photos with my camera. Each of the boys greets us and hurries past.

Gradually the fields disappear altogether and turn to jungle. Trees stretch a hundred feet up, vines hanging off them, and then we can see flowers that flourish in the volcanic soil of this crater peak. Their pinks and reds and yellows dot the jungle and everything smells so good, like old leaves and grass in the sun and distant rain; drifts of jasmine and honeysuckle; noisy birds unseen.

And then we're pushing through a thicket of trees with ash-colored trunks, high grass, the whole forest buzzing. This, I imagine, is the lip of the crater.

The lake is a near-perfect circle. A thin strip of white beach surrounds the water, which is the color of an emerald, backlit in blue. No one, Sergio tells me, knows the exact depth of this holy lake. Others are lunching nearby, and we overhear a man say to his friends that two *gringas* died while swimming here some years ago. The lake's surface looks so still, so tempting to our overheated bodies, but because of the stories, we're afraid even to go near.

On a spring day six months ago, I took E— to a wedding venue. I knew of the place because I'd catered there. An Irish couple owned the catering company, and they had business every day of the week, especially in summer. Then, if I wanted, I could work as many doubles as I could stand. They weren't afraid of paying overtime.

The work was hot and hard and the hours were long, but the venues were fabulous. This one in Concord, the one I showed to E—, was my favorite. It had a wide lawn that scooped down into an orchard, a white columned house, and a perennial white tent. An old farmhouse on the hill had rooms inside that the bride and her attendants could use to prepare.

The best part of the venue was a secret, though, and this I showed to E—. That spring day, we parked at the edge of the lawn where the forest began. We got out of the car, and the humid buzz of the country swallowed us up. We inhaled flowers and water and grass. I took her hand and led her into the woods, down a little trail lined with stones, through a hedge, and into a clearing. There was a little pool of clear green water, a couple of opening lilies, and the sound of a bird splashing in a stone bath. A dark balsam hedge surrounded the clearing. This was the secret place: cool and silent, like a spot out of a fairy-tale. All the wedding ceremonies took place here, and the guests would stream out of the forest afterwards, dabbing their eyes and looking dazed. Then, we caterers would enter the clearing, fold up the chairs, and load them back into the van, and when we did that work we never spoke. There was always something holy about the clearing.

The day E— and I visited, the grass was trodden from a recent ceremony, and birds splashed water against stone. We closed our eyes together and inhaled.

Back in the car, she turned the engine on and rolled the windows down, then turned the engine off again. She put her hand on my leg, fingertips brushing the skin beneath my skirt. I remember not being able to breathe, the scent of green water still fresh on our skin, as if we'd swum and not simply stood before it and listened. Her lips met mine, and she moved her hand up.

Sergio and I watch as clouds descend onto the lake. White wisps seem to rise from the cloud forest, then sink to the water. The clouds are shapely ghosts: they could be the wings of birds, the leaves of trees, the bodies of two women who slid into the water to swim and never emerged. From across the lake, smoke curls from a campfire. The only sounds are the cries of birds.

Water, I think to myself, and remember her.

On the way home, Sergio and I catch a ride in the bed of a farmer's pickup. The driver, his young son beside him in the cab, speeds past fields and patches of jungle. Grit from the hot road blows into our mouths and eyes and down the collars of our shirts. I can't remember having ever felt so free, so utterly flung, as on this late afternoon, the sun-warmed wind whipping at our hair. My mouth is gritty and dry; my eyes sting. It doesn't matter; I wish for the ride in the back of the truck to last forever. I feel something rattle loose, some knot deep inside that I hadn't known existed. I have to remind myself where I am; the foothills of Guatemala, in the back of a pickup truck.

When we reach the city center, I try to give the man some money, but he won't take it. We give him two granola bars instead, and the man and his son shake our hands.

* * *

One morning, Lizzie, the neighbor's four-year-old, comes to ask me a question. I shrug and blush, not understanding, and I hate myself for how faltering my voice sounds. Here, I am a woman with less to say. I have very few words at my disposal, and I've never understood how that might feel until now. Without a solid grasp on words, I have very little power or control.

In class, Linda assures me that kids are the hardest. "They mumble," she says, and squeezes my arm. I watch *The Simpsons* with Norma's kids and understand nothing. I confuse Spanish with my high-school French. *Reconstruir, encontrar, recordar,* I remind myself. *Contar, desvestir, beber.* Each day, more words enter, but so few of them seem to stay. These lessons are a gift, I remind myself, and at night I try to silence my mind completely.

Linda teaches me the verb *esperar,* which means both to wait and to hope. When you wait, Linda explains, you are hoping for something: that the bus will arrive, that the winter will break, that your broken heart will heal, that the words you say when you fight will eventually disintegrate. I write down the verb, go home, and study my verb list in bed. I make hundreds of flashcards, and I keep my ears open on the street, in the school, and in Norma's bright kitchen. I wait and I hope.

* * *

We wait. Sergio and I sit in the grumbling bus while the driver buys a coffee at the gas station, then smokes a cigarette and calls to people on the street to see if they, too, want to go to Zunil. Finally, we are off, sitting right behind the driver so we're sure not to miss our stop, and the chicken bus begins chugging up the hill.

But it doesn't climb for long. Here are some Mayan women who want to get on. They are dressed beautifully and carry baskets balanced on their heads; beaded earrings dangle to their shoulders. They chatter as they board, ignoring us. The bus starts again, then stops almost immediately for more women and a few men. This is how we make it up the hill: starting and stopping, starting and stopping. Each person seems to have something to report to the driver, and they do this while leaning over him, gripping the rail, holding up the line. The placard above the driver's head reads, "Manufactured in Iowa City, 1995."

We've come to Zunil to see San Simone, a decorated deity for which the town is famous. Each year, a different household hosts the shrine, and people come from Xela and even from Guatemala City to admire it. We wander up and down the unpaved streets; the town is built at the base of steep hills, and so we climb and climb until we come to the place. This house looks over the green valley, the wide river, the noisy highway. We pay five quetzals to a woman who is sitting in a rocker, knitting. "If you want to take pictures," she says, "it costs ten."

In the dimly lit room, we find that San Simone is a mannequin dressed in a collared shirt and tie, a black robe, a cowboy hat, and dark sunglasses. An unlit cigarette has been tucked between his plastic lips, and empty liquor bottles cluster the floor around him. Beneath his seat is a bucket. Only candles light the room. San Simone is a combination of Western cowboy and Mayan god: there is the woven robe, the bolo tie, the packs of cigarettes leaned against his chair. Petals drop from drying flowers onto the floor, and candles spatter wax. We look into the eyes of San Simone, but there's only blackness. Chilled, we stumble back out into the street.

On the way home, the bus is held up behind a funeral procession hundreds of men long, who walk slowly behind a hearse. The trunk is open to the casket inside, which is wreathed in flowers we can smell through the open windows of the bus. The women walk last, their faces streaked with tears. I have to remind myself again where I am: at the end of a funeral procession in a remote Guatemalan town. I watch the women's tears run down and feel a streak of guilt, for how free I've been feeling these days, and how far away from home I am right now. To me, this line of bereaved is a marvel. It is not my right to observe their sadness, but I take it from them nevertheless, tucking the image—so foreign, so mournful, so eerily lovely—away.

* * *

In every place I visit I find a market, and Xela's comes first. Here, the city flocks to eat and to gossip, to buy, to sell, to feast the senses. By the time I've seen a few more cities, I will have discovered that the thing to find when you first arrive is the market. In Xela's case, a quiet street spills suddenly open to the hum of voices and the gyration of machines. Passing between the cars and stands, looking and looking, I am propelled by the crowd as if atop a curving river, and along this river's banks are a hundred different foods: pyramid-shaped cones of grains, stacks of raisins and enormous dates, baskets spilling over with oranges. *Chicha*, the fermented corn drink, is sold at periodic intervals, bubbling from cauldrons and doled out by wizened, deeply wrinkled, white-haired old women.

There are three types of apples and fat, wine-colored grapes; mountains of big, brown avocadoes; piles of bulbous white shallots. All who sell produce are women. They wear the *huipil*, the embroidered shirt of the Maya, and the wraparound skirt—the *corte*—which hangs to their flip-flops. They hold thick cardigans closed over their bodies, and they call out about stacks of plantains and bunches of scrubbed carrots. They sit nursing their babies or checking their cell phones or slicing open their avocadoes for passersby to sample. I buy a bag of dates from a young girl who takes my money and carefully weighs the generous bag of dates on an old-fashioned scale. The dates shine mahogany in their plastic sack; she watches while I suck the first pit clean.

Teenage boys sell scarves and woven bracelets at the edges of the market. Old men crouch on little stools and repair watches, and here are the bearded, light-eyed men with their silver. Now come stacks of toothpaste and soap and shampoo, and here, in the market's very last stall, is bright pottery for sale. I wish to buy some, but I can only take what I can carry, and so I don't let myself imagine those indigo plates and marigold bowls on the maple kitchen table I once owned.

And then the Mercado spits me out. It ends. I find myself a little dazed on a sleepy sidewalk, where the only person around is a man passed out drunk. The shops here are all closed, the barred doors drawn down. A cool wind passes through, and I can see the mountains from here. Two old men shuffle by, unsteadily eyeing me, giving me a little whistle, telling me I am a sexy baby, but in the end they stumble harmlessly across the street toward the church. The setting sun turns everything golden: the cobblestones, the paint on the walls of the buildings, the leaves on the dry old trees. In this sudden afternoon silence, the city shimmers.

* * *

In an Internet café, I video chat with E—. She looks exactly the same and yet unfamiliar somehow, though I don't tell her so. I couldn't name the difference anyway. "It's cold here," she says with a tiny wince, and I get the distinct feeling she is working too hard and sleeping too little. She's at work, and the walls of her office are bare. The bright lights wash out her skin. I imagine the way my hands might feel on her arms. I ask her if she's eating.

"I miss you a lot," she replies, and I am so guilty, suddenly, to feel the sun falling in through the window and to hear the buzzing market. Rhododendrons are blooming in a bucket on the corner. My days here are shaped around reading and writing, walking and speaking with Linda. I've been exploring; my mind and senses, at the end of each day, are left reeling. I can't put it into words: the way I have loosened somehow. I don't worry at night the way I did back in Boston. I live simply now, plain food and no indulgences, and yet it's hard to remember when I last felt so rich.

"I miss you a lot," E— says again, and her words are like a key rattling a lock. She told me to come here. She said I couldn't pass the journey up. *I miss your hands*, I want to tell her, but that wouldn't be enough. I feel badly for feeling such guileless joy, and I don't let her know how happy I've been.

Later, I wonder what work the months will do on the two of us.

* * *

Javier, one of the teachers at the Spanish school, warns me as we refill our cups of coffee that Christmas in Guatemala can be dangerous. He has kind, serious eyes and thick, dark hair. His square-framed glasses are like Sergio's. Both of them have a softness to their gaze, and the glasses sharpen that, adding years. I assume that's the intention. Javier wears sweaters with thick stripes, and he has a patient way of talking that reveals his time as a language teacher.

There is more alcohol on Christmas, Javier explains, than on any other day. People roam the streets all night, drunk, setting off fireworks, burning their hair and eyelashes right off.

"But it's beautiful, too," he hastens to add. People parade the streets with lanterns, he says, and they are singing. The midnight masses glow with candles.

In Guatemala, Christmas Eve is the party, and the next day is for cleaning up the mess. On December 25th, you sweep firework remains from your front step, wash your tablecloths, take the trash of banana leaves and empty bottles and Styrofoam containers out into the street to be collected. By Christmas Eve, nearly everyone has strung lights from their patios and balconies and windows, lights that hum and flash and blink, so that walking along, you never feel alone.

I take my classes in the morning instead of in the afternoon. Linda gives me a knitted scarf as a gift, neatly wrapped in paper and tied with a bow. I give her a card with a turtle on the front, sixty US dollars as a tip, and a bar of gourmet chocolate.

"You'll need gifts," my mother had said as we'd eyed the chocolate in the grocery store in the week before I left. She was voicing the hope we both had: that I would be looked after. And my dad had been the one to slip me the twenties, because it doesn't ever hurt to have some dollars, he had said.

Norma has hired a woman to come help her clean the house today, a girl younger than I. The three of us sweep and wash the linens and hang them to dry in the courtyard. I ask Norma what she'll need for the dinner, imagining she'll request pineapple or cinnamon for the rum punch. Norma pauses, broom in hand, and purses her lips.

"Chips," she says, after much deliberation. "Chips and rum." She nods matter-of-factly and beats her broom against the stair.

I squeeze through the frenzied Mercado. Hands fly between jackets, sweaters, books, dishware, electronics; snap decisions are being made. There is an aggression to this crowd, a bite I've not felt in this market before. An abandon to the reaching, inspecting, counting. There is no consulting. Fathers, brothers, moms, tiny babies in pouches, sisters holding hands, elderly grandmothers poring over the women's clothing; everyone is here, and everyone needs something. Everyone has a little bit of panic in his eyes, yet there is a glee to the wildness. One particularly narrow section lifts me off my feet, so tightly I am squeezed. But no one shouts, and no fights erupt. Everyone just pushes forward, keeping a tight hold on their purses, their baskets of groceries, their children's hands.

I load sacks of potato chips carefully into my pack and become lost on my way to the liquor store, wandering into the Mercado de los Flores, a market I've never seen before, with its own fruit vendors and flower stands and butchers, whose huge cuts of beef hang from hooks in the ceiling. Everything is different tonight; ordinarily quiet street corners clamor now. Wooden shutters are propped open, and open doorways spill light. Though lost, I am not afraid, for I am surrounded, and laughter rings all around.

I finally locate the liquor store, which is as crammed as the Mercado. Thirty or forty people wait in a hectic line, pressing forward with armfuls of liter sodas and bottles of Gallo beer. There is a wildness here like the wildness I felt in the back of the pickup truck, grit flying into my mouth, and again on the way out of Zunil, when the grieving women wailed. In the liquor store, the men behind the counter are whizzing around as if in flight, filling orders, catching money, tossing back change with seemingly reckless abandon. One man buys a dozen big bottles of rum and loads them into his car, which waits, still running, in the street.

So this is what it means, I think as I have so many times already. This is what it means to travel this way: I become a part of my hosts' lives, as close as they can get me. Beyond a certain point, though, I can't go with them. This is their Christmas: Carlos and Alejandra skip around the few gifts beneath the tree, and we lean in plastic chairs with plastic cups. It's warm, and delicious things are cooking; we are infected with the night, which runs too quickly over itself, as it did when I was a child. There is the wild market up the hill, and the men at the liquor store, whirling with money in their hands. Fireworks pop in the street and boom in the distance.

There's beer, more rum, and the hours turn over each other. Stars blink awake. Norma and Alejandra make the rice, slow-cooked into stickiness. Alejandra drops raisins into the pot, along with dates and chunks of chicken and pinches of cinnamon. Norma folds everything into banana-leaf packets, then sets those to cook, low and long.

Because no one eats until late on Christmas Day, Norma takes pity on us and makes ham sandwiches on white bread while the tamales cook. It becomes obvious that we won't be attending church tonight; only Alejandra, who retreats to the bedroom to watch Christmas movies with Carlos, seems disappointed. Norma lures them out eventually, telling them it's present time, and then they tear the wrapping open and examine their plastic toys. Sergio does not receive a present, but watches his siblings, his eyes glowing, waiting for them to see what he and Norma went and bought. I set out the rest of the chocolate. Carlos kisses Norma's knee, then Sergio's, and then, after a flash of hesitation, mine. He tugs his sister into the bedroom, where we can hear their murmuring, the click of plastic tapping against the stone floor.

Just before midnight, we take our chairs out onto the step and sit in the night. A silence, eerie after the hours and days of cracks and booms, has settled over the city. We wait, the darkness hanging over us, and Norma makes another round of drinks. Thousands of miles away, my mother and father and brother sit with my grandmother in her house in Connecticut. She immigrated from Finland when she was twenty-one, and she cooks enormous meals: moist turkeys, sweet potatoes, apple pies with soft New England apples nested in shell-white crusts. Outside, the air will be still and cold, and when my family ventures out for an after-dinner walk, they'll be able to see their breath. The stars will flicker.

The first flashes are silent, erupting from a distance. But the sound begins to build, moving closer and closer, snaps coming faster, until the erupting cracks of fire become a steady ripple. Our chairs begin to vibrate. To the left, whizzing shoots of red and green from the houses on the hillsides soar over us. To the right, a series of deep booms erupts from somewhere down in the valley, and a second later the sky is filled with shattered bombs of glitter. Down the street, the neighbors' kids shoot off crackers, making far more sound than light, and now Carlos has his own and is tossing them off his front step. Up and down, the road is smoking, the sky above us is smoking, and the whole city is exploding into light.

Fireworks crack all night and through the early hours of the morning, and when we go outside the next day we will see that the street is trashed, littered with the shells of fireworks, which blow into piles in the corners of doorsteps and windowsills and the cracks in the cobblestone roads. The air will still be smoky.

On the day after Christmas, Sergio and I take our last walk. We don't speak. I don't bring my camera. His presence has become like that of an old friend's, and our silences are easy, warm water and sun. I will miss him, I think to myself, but I don't say it aloud. I don't want him to feel embarrassed.

We pass a crowded church, where women serve food on plastic plates to a lively crowd of men and children and white-haired people in chairs. The women have woven ribbons and flowers into their glossy braids, and the men wear dark suits and ties and cowboy hats and polished black shoes. The little girls are dressed in brilliant Mayan skirts and *huipil* blouses, looping gold earrings brushing their cheekbones. Huge letters mounted on the roof of the church read "Christo Viene," or "Christ comes." People flow through the dinner line, standing and eating, talking, laughing, the women's jewelry making a tinny, jingling sound.

We walk up and up, away from the bustling church at lunchtime and into the hills, and then we come to a wall that divides an angled meadow. Sergio says that a rich Portuguese man owns the land beyond the wall, but he works in the city now. We take turns hoisting our bodies up to peer over the wall at the stands of piñón that break up the rich man's property, and then we keep walking, past little fields of dry corn, wild bougainvillea, farmers walking with machetes. The sight of those long, curved knives has become, like the children with fireworks, a sight that has ceased to startle me.

Today, Sergio has brought along the stub of a joint wrapped in tinfoil. When I ask him where he got it, he says, "In the streets." He lights the joint with the swift strike of a match, and we sit and watch the corncobs drying on the roofs. His weed smells like old flowers and pine. If he asked, I would tell him about E—. But he'll never ask.

We find an empty hut painted green. A few wide beams hold up open-air walls, and beyond scoops a gulley with a dried-out river at its throat.

"This is the place," Sergio tells me, and I think that right now, we're the same age, he and I. We are sixteen, we are twenty-six, we are five. We look down into the green of the gulley, and the shouting from the soccer game below disappears. The wind ceases temporarily. The heat swells, but I am cool. Clouds pass fast overhead, dunking us in sunshine and then shade.

At the base of the valley, there's another open-air hut, but this one is lined with little statues of men with circular heads and squat legs, round bellies and long noses. There are dozens of them; all wear petrified rivers of melted candles, which run down from the crowns of their heads. Inside the hut, white flowers litter the ground, their petals scattered. Two candles still burn in an altar carved into the front wall of the room.

"It's a Mayan place," Sergio says, and points up into the hills. "They live there; they pray here," he says.

A mile south, the Catholics are celebrating, praying for Christ to hurry up and come, but this holy place is but a sieve for the wind. The earthen floor holds statues of clay and petals, squeezed and scattered, the years measured by each season's subtle turns.

"I'll miss you," I tell Sergio in English. I say the words without thinking and am embarrassed, but from the way he smiles blankly, I can tell he doesn't understand.

Or maybe he does.

* * *

On one of my last Xela nights, there's a lunar eclipse.

"The moon will look red," my dad writes in an email. "There's a volcano in Indonesia, so the moon will look red." He urges me to go outside and watch the eclipse, which will happen tonight, very late.

For as long as I can remember, my father took us out to watch the sky. We would stand with our hands on our hips, gazing up until we grew dizzy. The snow squeaked beneath our boots and I'd shiver, my flannel pajamas the only thing between my skin and the coat, and I'd follow my gaze to where his finger pointed.

"Venus," he would say, then point out Polaris.

I set my alarm for two-thirty, but in the end, I don't need it; after a few hours of sleep between ten and midnight, I am awake and listening to the roosters crowing and dogs barking. Fireworks crack and pop from the north and from the east, but tonight there aren't any shaking booms. Sergio drank some bad water over the weekend, and I can hear him stumbling back and forth to the bathroom, or clattering dishes in the kitchen for tea. His light goes on and off. He's caught a cold as well, and so I also hear him coughing, such long and ragged sounds that my own throat begins to hurt.

The alarm finally screeches, and I silence it and slip outside. I imagine my father getting up and going out, no sound jolting his sleep, his body alone telling him when to wake. He pulls on big boots, a puffy jacket, and a hat with flaps, then tromps out into the cold to peer at the sky. I imagine his breath visible in the night air, as mine is. Here we both stand, beneath the muted stars, their brightness blotted by the moon's round face.

The cement ground glows ice blue in the moonlight. There is the Big Dipper, there is Cassiopeia, there is the section of the Milky Way that Guatemala sees, different than the one my father watches. And there is the moon.

It's gone red, just like my father said it would. It's hazy and small. I wonder whether my father has a clearer view, whether he's woken my mother, too. There is the glimmering white outline, a thin and perfect sphere, and the center is the color of blood. I think of my father in his boots, his crooked hat, his hand in mine. The light through the kitchen window is a warm square, and my mother is heating milk. My father stands in his boots.

How far away I am from home, I think another time, but tonight, I'm not sad. I don't feel like a stranger, a foreigner, a tourist. For weeks, I've felt something shifting inside me, a leaning—or maybe a straightening. I've been sleeping so deeply, lately. I've been eating such simple food, and yet everything tastes so good, hearty and homemade. The avocadoes are cheap and delicious and I devour several a day. I've grown used to wearing the same t-shirt over and over. I walk for miles up roads I've never explored; I ride buses to crater lakes and Mayan towns. I practice a new language; every day, I learn a hundred words. I've missed my parents, I realize, and yet I know that they're happy for me, thrilled—and I'm more grateful for that now, sitting beneath this red moon on this Guatemalan night, than I've been so far.

I hear the door to the main house creak open; it's Alejandra in her pajamas and socks and jacket with the faux-fur lining. She meets my eyes and puts a finger to her lips; I suspect her mother didn't give her permission to sneak out into the cold. Not with Sergio so sick already.

She tiptoes over and, as quietly as we can, we drag two chairs from my room out into the courtyard. We blow on our hands to warm them. I imagine my father is stomping his feet in the cold as we gaze at the same blood moon. When Alejandra and I have had enough of the winking sky, of craning our necks, we whisper goodnight. She gives me a hug and a wink; we now have a secret. And then we slip back into our beds, the sheets still warm from our bodies, and we close our eyes to the insistent moonlight.

ANTIGUA, GUATEMALA

Antigua smells like trash and bananas, blooming flowers and water. *Antigua*, I say to myself. No one stares as I pick my way down the street.

I find a hostel at the end of an alley and rent a room from a stooped-over man in suspenders. He smiles kindly at me and charges me seven dollars, including breakfast. He tells me that if I stay more than a week, he'll strike up a deal. The room is tiny, more a cleaned-out broom closet. There's just one tiny, high-up window, but it's clean. I can't smell mice or mold. He shows me the shared toilet and explains, apologetically, that the water in the shower runs with good pressure but never gets hot. He tells me things slowly, checking my face to make sure I understand. I do. *I do*, I say to myself, *I understand*, and I tuck the realization away to share later with E—.

When I reach into my purse to find money to pay the man, he shakes his head, snaps his suspenders, and hands me the key.

"Tomorrow," he says. "Now, you relax."

So I put down my pack and climb to the whitewashed roof, where sheets flap on the line. The volcano rises cone-shaped up out of the horizon. Nothing calls to me here. There is no place to be, and there are hours before the sun sets. The journey to this city drained me of my sense of obligation. Later, I will open the pages of my journal and write. I will find someone and we will talk. I will find some food and I will eat. I will call my mother. I will call my lover. "I have come to another place,"

I will say, doing my best to describe the roof deck, its view of the volcano, the hazy air around me, the sounds of barking dogs and honking horns muted in the jammy afternoon.

Antigua is an earthquake place, a city defined by constant, near-predictable shudders in the earth. The sliding plates deep below Antigua's sidewalks, below even its crypts, represent the rifts that occur above ground—the tumult of civilizations rising and falling, before and after the first Europeans set foot on this lava-rich earth. Here in Antigua, earthquakes are part of the psyche.

Last year alone, the hostel owner says, he felt twenty earthquakes. He bends down to light a candle, then goes into the downstairs bathroom and replaces the toilet paper roll, folding the square at the edge so it resembles a lotus. He isn't afraid, though, not for his life at least, because most of those tremors were horizontal quakes, which slide the ground back and forth. The up-and-down quakes cause the damage.

In the early 16th century, when Antigua was founded, the Spanish built their buildings the way they made them in cities like Seville, with two floors and high ceilings. They didn't know that Central America straddles a fault line, where two plates have ground up against each other for millennia. The earthquakes of 1717 and then 1773 rocked Antigua, so the inhabitants boarded up their houses and took everything away with them: their dishes, their furniture, their artwork, even the doors to their houses. Three thousand buildings lay crumbled, and Antigua was abandoned for decades.

Antigua is known for its eternal summer, and today tourists stroll the streets, which are made friendly to them: travel agencies with open doors, coffee shops with croissants and yogurt, manicured parks with ticketed entries and lawns and gardens to explore. I imagine that beneath the ruins of this city, seen so many times through a camera lens, the old colonists lying in wait, for they have seen the quakes that sent their people running. I imagine the cobwebbed gloom, the smell of dust and death, the ancients stirring in their unexcavated crypts.

Antigua abounds with Spanish schools for tourists, and the crumbling streets are jammed with students: Japanese in wiry glasses, Scandinavians in linen, jostling Americans. Maria, my teacher, is petite and serious and often looks tired, the skin around her eyes smokily thin. She drinks cup after cup of instant coffee and makes me talk far more than she does. She is the opposite of Linda. I sit with Maria four hours a day, except for Sunday. A week passes and then another; I can't tell whether I'm improving. My days become a stream of sunny afternoons, of a volcano in fog and of the market in the morning, which smells of fruit and corn. Some students, Maria tells me once, study with teachers ten hours a day. "The Japanese," she adds, her voice a whisper.

She says to me one day, "I don't know why you all call yourselves Americans." She turns her pen in her hands, but doesn't write anything down. "You're *estadounidenses*," she says, "but we're all Americans." A note of anger creeps into her voice. If I hadn't been sitting with her four hours a day, I wouldn't have detected it at all. She glances down, and I can see the stormy blue powder she's brushed over her eyelids.

"We're all Americans," she says again, "you, me, someone from Ecuador."

"You're right," I say. "You're absolutely right." I feel my face turn red, though I'm not quite sure why.

Later, I give it more thought. If I could, I would call Americans *estadounidenses*, and I will from now on. Except *estadounidense* translates literally as 'United Statesean,' just as you might call someone from Uruguay 'Uruguayan,' or someone from Hawaii 'Hawaiian.' Those from the United States we call "Americans," and Maria illuminates the injustice in that. All the people of the Americas are American, and it's hoggish, if you think about it, to go around claiming it—at least as we *estadounidenses* do. American, plain and simple, is a title I've inherited but which Maria also deserves.

The next day, I tell her I won't say 'American' anymore, but ask how I'll get around it in English. I explain the conundrum: 'United Statesean' sounds weird, and no one says it.

"So?" she says, shrugging, looking down into her mug of instant coffee as if she's dropped something precious in there. Suddenly, I feel like what she really wants to say is, *Your English is not my problem*. She looks up and meets my eyes, and I get the distinct impression she doesn't want to be there at all. *She's at work*, I remind myself. *She'd rather not be.*

I continue on with Maria; for all her sullen glances, she gets me talking. Unlike Linda, Maria would rather listen than contribute, and with every error, she corrects me. It gets annoying, until I realize that what's important is that I say things right, not that I provide interesting anecdotes or make curious reflections about the world. Maria loosens me, and my Spanish improves. She doesn't care about the stories I tell; she's there to help me talk. I ramble on about my parents, my old job, my day in the market, and she listens and fixes my mistakes. She sips her coffee and files her nails and yawns, discreetly, into her hand. I decide to tell her about E— one day, just to see what she'll do, and am a little disappointed at her reaction, which is nothing. I say *novia*, the Spanish word for girlfriend, a couple more times deliberately, but she makes no corrections about that.

"Maybe she is one herself," E— suggests, but I know I'll never ask, and she'll never tell.

On one of our last classes, Maria invites me to visit a farm—*finca*—just outside of Antigua, where coffee is grown. We will do this instead of the lesson, she explains, a fragment of hesitation lodged in her voice, like skipping class for a *finca* visit might not be allowed. "Of course," I say in Spanish. Just the day before we worked on the pronunciation for 'of course': *por supuesto, por supuesto.* Maria's smile is relieved, and for a second I'm surprised she's so worried. Back home, this would be seen as a field trip, a learning adventure. Only later will I realize that for her, like so many other language teachers I'll hire, this job means much more than she lets on.

On the day of our field trip—a term I teach Maria—there are a couple of tall German guys headed to the *finca*, too. Both wear glasses with thick frames and floppy canvas hats with round brims and metal-rimmed holes for ventilation. One has skin so pale it's nearly translucent, and sitting behind him in the van we share, I can make out the fine veins at his neck and beneath his ear. Their teachers—a middle-aged woman with her long hair knotted into a bun, and a young guy my brother's age—take the front seat and first bench, respectively. The young teacher banters in easy Spanish with the Germans while we rumble over the cobblestones and out of town. The buildings, which sit in even rows, all one-story, are cream and white-blue, coral and gray—muted Mediterranean. They dwindle and then disappear. Tall eucalyptus trees with patchy bark like an artist's palette rise up along the road, and then we enter the *finca's* silence, passing through tall wrought-iron gates onto a drive lined with bougainvillea.

The crimson bushes are heavy with flowers, and then come fenced-in fields of grazing horses. Though we'll learn that most of the pickers live with their families on this property, all we see now, riding up the paved, tree-lined avenue that leads to the welcome center, is the lush grass and white horses grazing in fields. This is a pinup *finca*, I realize, one that must earn as much on tourists as it does on selling coffee.

Nevertheless, I watch out the van windows, waiting for some trace of that poverty described to me by fair-trade campaigns advertised at trendy coffee shops back home, or by activist groups on my college campus selling buttons and canvas grocery bags to raise awareness.

But there comes just more bougainvillea and fields of gentle horses, the promised curve of the prosperous field. The sky above is blue and washed with thin clouds, which the wind pushes fast over our heads. When we climb out of the van, the air smells of coffee and wet grass.

We're led inside; the cost for each student is forty quetzals. The teachers don't pay. "We're teachers," Maria explains, and the Germans nod, understanding. A half-dozen French students, high-school aged, are milling around, and there's a tan, dark-haired couple who speak Spanish with a lisp and tie red raincoats around their waists. The students from France whisper and tease, snapping noisy pictures, while a blonde girl steps away from her friends and asks frequent questions in recently learned Spanish. Paulo, our guide, is small and soft-spoken in a smart polo shirt, the *finca's* coffee-bean logo stitched on the breast pocket. He explains things in slow, easy-to-understand Spanish: the many roasts of coffee, and the process of the harvest. The French yawn without covering their mouths, and a girl with a bony face and braids sketches into a fat spiral-bound notepad. I wish I could justify feeling out of place, but I blend right in with the fair-skinned group, and so I stand in the back and try to listen.

Paulo directs our attention to a blown-up photo of a woman picking red beans from a coffee plant. She is wearing the *huipil* and *corte*, and when Paulo explains that all of the coffee labor in Guatemala is still done by hand, the tour group nods and murmurs their approval.

In *Open Veins of Latin America*, Eduardo Galeano described the way, throughout the nineteenth and twentieth centuries, poor Guatemalan farmers from the highlands were shipped like cattle to the *fincas* at the coast, working for slave wages or conned into payment in booze. Paulo does not mention what Galeano documented: that even after the Industrial Revolution, even if they could afford it, owners keep labor unmechanized because it's far cheaper to just hire the Guatemalan poor to do the work. *A man is cheaper than a mule.* The mountains of Quiché, to the north, hold only rocky, fickle soil, and people lived off the most basic foods: tortillas, salt, lime. When the brittle land gave out altogether, or the spring rains made harvesting impossible, working the *fincas* became the only alternative to starvation.

Indigenous farm families came to the hot, humid Guatemalan *costa* twice a year, and although those *finca* owners needed all the workers they could get, the workers needed even more desperately the money they could earn. The laborers paid for the red, ripe beans they accidentally spilled on the ground under the overseer's watchful eye.

In the museum, the tour group nods and murmurs their approval. "Handmade," Paulo had said. Galeano explains that land ownership as we know it—plots of land owned by individuals, carefully mapped and easily defined—did not exist before the Encounter, when the Europeans reached the Americas. Land was collectively used—people staked claims over certain crops, certain gardens, their homes—but communities owned the land, not families. No documentation of these arrangements has been found. The land was pulled right out from under those who for so many years had tended to it, and the bushels of red beans funneled into the homes of the colonists in Quito and Cartagena and Antigua, and onto barges that would cross the sea to Europe. Before coffee there were mines and lumber, indigo dyes; coffee is just the current mode of exploitation.

Paulo doesn't mention the migrations or the cattle-car journeys. He doesn't tell us that in the 1960s, the coffee bubble burst; like ink, coffee could be produced cheaper elsewhere, namely in Asia and Africa. The coffee money drained fast out of Guatemala, crossing the sea, and the Guatemalan *finca* owners found themselves with massive loans and nowhere to send their coffee. Many burned their inventory; a flood of suicides ensued.

As for the laborers—the hands of all that coffee—many moved to Guatemala City to inhabit growing slums under the city's massive bridges. Linda told me this, on a day when it was raining and we sat in the kitchen, drinking instant coffee loaded with sugar.

You can still see those slums today, she had said, the ones that formed when everything else fell, as you drive to and from the airport. You'll see that only a trickle of water runs in at the bases of those deep gorges, but there are thousands of shacks, flimsily erected on either wall of the steep ravines, constructed of cardboard, of cheap tin, of plastic tarps. Beneath the longest bridge in the city, a coffee refuge sprawls, cycling between destruction by natural disasters, government crack-downs, and redevelopment. But when the police aren't around, this bridge-city functions under a kind of self-made government, with its own police comprised of the oldest, strongest families, and its own laws, its courthouse of loans, favors, and grudges. Meanwhile, most workers had gone their whole lives having never tasted a real cup.

I remember then the chocolate I gave out as gifts—fine chocolate I bought from a North American supermarket. I feel a twinge, a shaft of heat rise from my neck to my cheeks to my ears. Perhaps my gift of chocolate had always actually been theirs.

Paulo takes us outside, where we immediately smell the fermenta-tion—the process that loosens the beans' shells. We pass piles of little red skins to stand before the fields, spread with bare beans, bone white and baking in the sun. The workers, good-natured about allowing us tourists to wield their rakes, instruct two Canadian girls on how to push the beans back and forth. They do this so the beans will turn and dry, Paulo explains, laughing as the first blonde girl struggles, shaping the beans in an uneven line.

Outside the storeroom, clouds are moving fast across the sky, dark-ening and lightening the beans on the ground, and looking into the jun-gled hills surrounding the *finca*, I can make out individual trees. For a moment I'm seduced. So remote, this *finca* seems, so quiet except for the sounds of the wind and the rake across the white beans. Paulo says that coffee drains the earth, and on one plot of land, the crop should only be harvested once every three years. In between those, the *finca* grows black beans instead. The tour comes to a close, and now it's time to taste a little cup of coffee, but the liquid tastes too mild for me. I realize I have not tasted real coffee in months, and have grown accustomed to the instant.

I think about the way Maria corrects me snappily. I remember the times I imagined she was being sullen. I think about Americans and North Americans and *estadounidenses,* and all the while I can almost taste the coffee my grandmother served just before I left the States. Her coffee is eternally strong and very smooth. I can conjure the smell of it now, the way the steam felt against my skin as I brought the cup to my lips, the way my grandmother and mother sounded, bantering together in loud Finnish. Here in Guatemala, everyone drinks instant coffee; the only café in Xela with drip coffee is priced for tourists. How very many things I never questioned.

At the very edge of the property, just before we come to the main road, I see three little children walking barefoot, the boys without shirts on and the little girl holding a baby on her hip. As we pass, the girl pushes her hair out of her eyes and watches us. Her gaze looks both at and right through us. *Will I go home and drink it again?* I think. *Sugar and cream and the thick, rich brew? With each sip, there in my other life, will I forget a bit more?*

* * *

My father and I traveled to India a year ago, and we met two English travelers there, a married couple from just outside of London. We were all trekking a five-day route that inches and winds along the border of India and Nepal. My father and I were hiking, at least. The English couple had hired horses. We thought that was so funny, that they would ride horses, because in the evening, at one of the guesthouses, they had boasted of the hikes they'd completed in the Annapurna, how many days they had spent in the mountains, how many freezing nights in tents, how close they had come to Mount Everest.

They'd spent a year in Thailand training as Thai boxers; they told us, as we sipped tea together in the evening, that they preferred Thai boxing to any other type of boxing because of the wildness, the lawlessness. You could use your elbows and knees, and you could hit above the neck. Thai boxing is the dirtiest kind, and the English couple liked that, especially the woman, who told us she'd trained eight hours a day, back in Thailand. You could kick her in the shin with a boot and she'd never bruise, never even feel pain. She ate more than her husband did, slurping down bowl after bowl of noodle soup, endless tin mugs filled with chai.

The couple had been everywhere. They'd driven all over Africa and straight through Europe to Afghanistan. They'd been in Russia, China, South America. They'd been to Guatemala. They told us about a trip they'd taken once to the South Pacific island of Borneo, where they'd slogged through the jungle on a week-long trek. The Englishman told me with relish that by the end of those seven days, they had grown used to peeling dozens of fat leeches off their legs in the evenings. They'd stayed up all night once with a tribesman there, who poured homemade rice liquor down their throats until all three of them threw up, passed out, and then resumed drinking until the light of morning broke.

On our last night of that five-day trek in Northern India, my father and I stayed at a little guesthouse built beside a river. The rivers up there are wide and shallow, very rocky, and on the day we arrived at this guesthouse it began to rain. Long into the night it poured, the rain on the roof meshing with the sound of the river so that all you could hear was water running. It drained out our voices and formed a calming, uniform sound for us to sleep to. The showers ran cold with rainwater. The English couple stayed there, too, and the four of us sat and ate our dinners that night by candlelight, speaking little, while the rain poured down, filling the river. In the morning men went out onto the wide, flat rocks at the riverbank to catch big fish in nets. Steam from the rain rose from the jungle up into the sky. The English couple left a little bit earlier than we did that morning, and we watched them go, seated on their horses, until they crossed the rickety bridge and disappeared into the trees.

On an Antigua street corner, I poke my head into a bookshop. There are mostly Spanish titles, a few English, and I browse for a moment. When I go back out into the street, a couple is just passing by, holding hands, the wiry man in a loose t-shirt and cargo shorts, the woman strong and sturdy-looking. Both wear dark glasses and wide-brimmed hats and hiking boots. I recognize them immediately: the slightly ratty quality of the man's face and the strength in the woman's gait. I stop them. I ask them if they remember.

"We met in India," I say.

And then, for a few long moments, all we can do is laugh and look at each other with round, astonished eyes. After they returned to England, they tell me, they'd decided to spend three months in Central America. They'd booked a trek; it left tomorrow. They'd go to El Salvador, Nicaragua, Panama. They are envious that I have more than three months to travel; they are thirsty for more adventure, they say.

Later, I will think of their time in Thailand, and of the leeches they endured in Borneo. I will compare their experience to my own: shuttles taking all of us to the most far-flung places in the world—places of worship, or bustling markets, or picturesque coffee *fincas* that smell of soil and rain.

I will think again of the English couple's rugged boots, their sturdy hats and zippered clothes, the way they walk so sure and fast down the streets of every city in the world. *What are they after?* I will ask myself, suddenly homesick.

What am I after? I'll wonder, and I'll feel so idly adrift. *Why am I here?*

And then the feeling will pass, and I'll do my best to keep my ears and eyes open, learning and tasting. I'll spend my dollars, and I'll get better at the language. I'll learn to focus my energies on projects and tasks, adventures, all the while reminding myself that this year is a gift, and if it wishes to change my life, I must let it.

On the sidewalk outside of the bookstore, I remind the couple of the leeches in Borneo. We laugh about that, and then they look at the sky, at their watches, and we part ways without shaking hands. I still don't know their names.

MONTERRICO, GUATEMALA

On a squeaky-bright morning in January, I kiss Antigua goodbye. It's so early only a few tourists are out, bleary-eyed and searching for coffee. I tell them where to go. I'm headed to the bus station; in two or three hours, I figure, I'll be in Monterrico, the black-beach town.

How easy it was, after almost a whole month in Antigua, to pack my bag and vanish. There weren't any goodbyes to say. For Maria, I left a forty-dollar tip tucked in a plain notecard along with my email address, which I knew she'd never use. To the owner of my hostel, I left a twenty-dollar bill on the bedside table: he had been kind, charging me, in the end, five dollars a night for a bed and breakfast in the morning and use of the tiny kitchen.

How easy it is for me, I realize. Of course the prices seem so cheap. I come from a wealthy country; I am, I realize, the one percent, if you're looking at the whole world. How free I felt, paying the hotel owner with cash and then boarding another bus, riding across the country beneath the morning sun. How rich I am, though I've never realized it so acutely before. It's a difficult place to inhabit, I've realized; this belonging and yet not belonging. We are desired for the money we bring, the services we request, the food we consume. Yet we are resented for having what most can never have. As much as we wish to see the *real* places—the "real" Guatemala, in my case—we will never be a part, we tourists, and we will never, ever truly understand.

* * *

The bus drops me by a cheap hotel with bamboo walls; thin, graying mattresses; and a café that looks right out onto the ocean. The waves roil in the afternoon. The sun beats onto the black sand, streaking it silver, and dogs bark in the surf. That night, I eat fish tacos and drink beer, lime juice sticky on my hands. There is no Internet connection here, no telephone. I don't think of the howling wind through Cambridge streets, or the eyes of my lover, weary after a long week at work. I feel no guilt. My bed costs three dollars, my dinner two. The Internet café is closed for the weekend. A voice, as if calling to me from far away, is telling me that I'm being selfish; I should find a way to contact my lover. I shouldn't feel so free when she feels so stifled. That voice tugs a little, and then like a tide recedes.

I ask the bartender about swimming, and he warns me not to go out too far. He's tall and muscular, fair-haired and shirtless. "The surf will pull you under," he says, and turns to his girlfriend, who works beside him.

You can tell by the way she runs the tips of her fingers lightly along his bare lower back that she loves him. She touches him there absent-mindedly, and his eyes close for just a second. Sara, she is called. She moves around him, her fingers occasionally reaching for him as if to make sure he's there. Her long, sun-streaked brown hair clings to her shoulders. They are French-Canadian, she from Quebec City and he from a small mountain town north of Montreal. While he asks me questions, she wipes down the bar, rinses the glasses, squeezes lemons into pitchers, slices mint. They work together here at the Blue Piranha Beach Resort each season, he tells me, flying down before Canada freezes, then leaving just as the Guatemalan monsoon begins.

The Blue Piranha is a long building split by a breezy open hallway, with doors that unlock twenty or so small rooms, which contain only beds with cement frames and mosquito nets fixed to dried, thatched-palm roofs. But the hotel boasts a small pool surrounded by big old mango trees and tables with umbrellas. In the night, I can hear most everything through those thin palm roofs: conversations in other rooms; someone playing a guitar in one of the hammocks strung over the sand; the thumping, rhythmic beat of the music at the beach club next door. People go around in bikinis and salt-stained shorts, except on Sunday night, my second at the hotel, when all of the tourists leave. Then, the employees throw faded tank tops on over their bodies, their hair wet, as it always is, from being in the sea. On the walk into town, no one wears shoes except me.

Juan, the young owner of the Blue Pirhana, has invited me to join him and the staff for their weekly dinner out. He is short but handsome, and he speaks perfect English. He married a girl from the States, he explains, who came for vacation and stayed at the Blue Pirhana, and never left. The two were married in Alabama two years ago. Now, she's finishing a master's in tourism in Texas, and then she'll return, and they'll work together. Juan inherited the Blue Pirhana from his father.

For such a small town, there are many restaurants, mostly stands with open, dirt-floor kitchens and big vats of stew and plastic baskets of ceviche. The restaurant Juan chooses, though, is built of thick, dark boards and has cool tiled floors and bright oil paintings of fish on the walls. Sara and her boyfriend walk a little behind everyone else, passing a cigarette between them, their heads bent so that we can barely hear them murmuring to each other.

Last Halloween, I went out with E— to a party in a Somerville house. We stood in the backyard around a bonfire and drank beer. Someone passed around a joint, and there were flasks of whiskey and vodka. I got drunk, leaning on E— while we walked unsteadily home.

That night, I lay with my head in her lap. The room spun; I couldn't close my eyes. E— made tea with honey, blowing into the mug to cool it for me. "I love you so much," she had said. She'd slept sitting up; I woke, my head in her lap, her hands in my hair, sun through the windows on the floor and sheets and walls.

On this night in Monterrico, we order gnocchi for the table. It arrives plump and grill-charred, a rich vodka sauce spooned on top. Platters of vegetable curry are placed in the center of the table, with fried bananas and tart pineapple salsa on the side, and to drink we have white wine, the bottles cold and glistening in their buckets. Everything tastes so rich, right down to the bread and the olive tapenade that keep coming and coming—small dishes of olive oil spotted with pepper. And for dessert, hot slices of thin banana flan, drizzled with chocolate. It is the most expensive meal I've had in weeks; each of us pays eight dollars. When we leave the restaurant, the sky is dark, and the stars are blinking awake. We walk down the dirt road, our footsteps crunching the shards of shells, the waves an even crush against the shore.

On my way to the café the next morning, I pass the room Sara shares with the bartender, and I see that they have left the door open. There are the rumpled sheets on the bed, their clothes strewn around, and a single, stubby candle on the bedside. His guitar leans against the wall, propped on the sandy floorboards. Bamboo walls and an open roof, so that all night long they might hear the waves. It seems that they need so little. Things move in accordance with the waves and sun here, the swing of the weekend and the ebb of Sunday. Here, love may be found and sustained.

The next evening, a crowd gathers on the beach. It's mostly children and teenagers, but there's one old man, his white hair brilliant against his skin, his shorts tattered and salt-stained: a beach man. His bare feet leave only very faint prints in the sand. He brings around a bucket of baby turtles, and one by one, we reach in.

My turtle's shell is still soft and jet-black, and its eyes are beady and bright, but its neck is withered already. It's a leatherback, and it will be released today with thirty or forty of its brothers and sisters. It cost almost five dollars, a price only tourists can afford. As such, most of the baby turtles still scrabble in the bucket, which the man has set down on the sand.

"The turtles need encouragement," the old man calls to us. "A proper goodbye! All the money goes to raise more turtles!" With a stick, he draws a line in the sand.

We come from all over—Canada, the States, Guatemala, Costa Rica. Chile, Sweden, France, the Netherlands. The Americans are the loudest; a group of teenage boys noisily name their turtles.

"Mine's Myrtle!" one shouts.

"Mine's Yertle!" echoes another.

The few Guatemalans stand at the edges of the line, posing for pictures away from the group. They're dressed the finest of anyone on the beach, the women in pretty blouses and makeup and platform sandals, and the men with jeans on and gel in their hair. The lady next to me wears a long white dress and designer sunglasses, which sit perched on her head, restraining her thick hair. The noisy Americans wear bright shirts open at the collar, no shoes, and torn shorts. Only tourists are allowed to dress like children, I once heard. The woman in white kisses her turtle and smiles at me.

"Okay!" the man shouts over the banter, and suddenly, even those American boys get quiet. Now it is time. I crouch and place my turtle on the ground, just behind the line.

The turtles are not afraid of the violent surf pounding down onto the beach and roiling the sand. The water is a gritty black, this shore a relic of volcanic eruptions eons old. The turtles scrabble across the shell-studded sand, determined, knowing.

My turtle veers a little too far to the right; I pick him up and reset him, straightening his course. When a little wave washes over his shell, flipping him onto his back, I lean way over the line, setting him right-side up. The white-haired man sees and says, "Let him do the rest."

It takes a long time. Five feet to the water means a lot of resting, a lot of low, fast waves that scoop the little turtles up and move them farther back up the beach, flipping them onto their backs so that their flippers wave helplessly while their comrades inch forward. The white-haired man takes the bucket and dumps the unclaimed turtles onto the sand. Though they don't have benefactors, they scrabble like the rest did, and even if they aren't turned right-side up when the waves flip them, the white-haired man with the bucket knows that the sea will swallow them all eventually. After a while, even the American boys stop cheering for their turtles to win the race to the sea. We stand, our toes still behind the line, watching the sea take the turtles in.

In a sandy hammock strung to the beams of the bar, I sip beer from a sweating bottle and watch the phosphorescence at the crests of the waves. The sea is sunken at low tide. The other person in the bar is a man in blue board shorts and a white linen shirt that's only half-buttoned. His hair and skin are wet from swimming, and he has large, dark eyes. He asks me, in Spanish, for a cigarette. I shake my head, and he leans back against the salty couch cushions and grins at me with large white teeth.

"No worries," he says in English. There is only the trace of an accent. He's very tan, and at his neck he wears a necklace of waxy black thread with a stone, or maybe a bone, tucked into the place where his collarbones meet. "I'm Michel," he says, pronouncing it the French way, and he reaches over to shake my hand.

"You are from the States?" he asks. His words come quickly despite the lazy way he grins and leans into the couch. Gesturing back toward the hotel's entrance, Michel tells me that he lives across the street. I try to picture what's there: a run-down hostel with one window made of bottles; a soup shack where a lady stirs a pot all day long and calls out, "Lunch special, dinner special," each time I exit the hostel. There's an old parking lot, long overgrown and inhabited by dogs. He has lived in Monterrico eight years, Michel tells me, flicking his wet hair from his eyes.

"You have to want to live simply to live here," he says. He fiddles with the bracelet on his right wrist, then scratches the tattoo on his forearm. It's a Mayan design, a mask with roundly outlined features. The black lines are clear and even, the work of someone skilled.

"If you want glamour," Michel continues, purring the r, "you can go somewhere else." He pauses, smiles to let me know he is teasing. His eyes move around the room: to the couple behind the bar, to the gray-haired man and his blonde teenaged daughter, to the girls with dreadlocks in the hammocks next to me.

"Just a second," he tells me, and goes over to the dreadlocked girls. They arrived at lunchtime, speaking French and sprinting toward the sea in triangle bikinis. Now, I watch Michel squat to talk to them, playfully pushing one of the hammocks to rocking. I think of how easy it has been to fall into the life of this beach: open doors, floors strewn with sand, bare feet, salt wind. I wonder how long I would last here, how quickly the sweet, lazy days would sour and my mind would start jumping again. Maybe this is what travel is: a search for imprints, for a chance to see places fleetingly, to take them with you and keep them forever without having to live them each day. To turn beach towns like stones over in your mind, remembering the warm sand on days when freezing wind blows.

When Michel returns, he's got a lit cigarette between his first finger and thumb. He takes a deep drag and closes his eyes.

"You have to let go of something, too," he says, the conversation unbroken, eyes still closed. "You have to *not* have..." he trails off, thinking. He takes another long drag and looks out onto the ocean. I realize I am leaning forward, my elbows on my knees. There's something hypnotic about his voice. He's not a beautiful man, but he's interesting-looking, jagged. The chunks of black hair. The gold tooth. The dark eyes that move fast.

"Ambition," he says finally. "That's the word." He's drawn out the middle syllable—ambeetion. He finishes his cigarette and then stands up, shaking his wet hair from his eyes once more. This is a gesture he's practiced. "So nice to meet you," he says, and I notice a narrow gap between his top two front teeth. I have this gap too. I've been told those who have it are liars. I watch him amble out toward the water.

The night thickens around me, and against the sound of the surf, I think of E—. The beer has loosened me, and now I wish for her to be sitting beside me, finishing the glass of beer, breathing salted wind. Once, on a day in late summer, she took ice from a glass and drew the cube over my skin: first my forearm, next my neck, finally down my back. She put the ice in her mouth and then sucked on my nipples. I can see her eyes, half-closed. I can feel the way she touched me: like it was about more than just desire. It has been many days, I realize, since I've craved her like this. I'm vaguely grateful it came to me so fully, this wanting her. I say her name to myself, then say it again.

I see Michel once more before I leave. He's standing, a cigarette between his fingers, talking to a very old man with a white baseball cap and only a couple of teeth. I have just eaten dinner—rice, plantains, and beans in a plastic bowl. It was delicious and inexpensive, and I am walking slowly, digesting.

Michel sees me and says my name. His teeth are bright white in the darkness. He says goodbye to the old man and offers to walk me home, and for a while we amble without speaking. I let him buy me a beer at the bar, and we walk a little ways out onto the sand. Music from the hostel nightclubs beats a rhythm, and above that we can hear voices, laughter, occasional shrieks. Dancers from next door stumble out onto the sand for cigarettes, the colored lights from inside spilling after them. I think of E—, and a slight sickness bends deep in my belly. *Be careful,* a voice says, and I think that in this place I'm being tugged. Another latch has been lifted, another door swung open. This is a life I've never seen: the beach life. Easy, like a hammock swinging in the wind. There's an abandon to Monterrico that I wish to keep with me forever: the hard waves, our salty skin, the taste of beer and lime on our lips.

I ask Michel where he learned his English.

"America," he says, surprised. "Couldn't you tell?" He went there when he was just seventeen, with his father and cousin and some family friends.

"We ran over, you know?" he says, and I nod, though at first I don't get it.

"You mean over the border?" I say.

Michel makes a show of shushing me. "It's a secret!" he says, grinning, then takes a long pull from his beer.

"We went at night, you know?" he whispers. "From Mexico. Before they built that wall. It took us eight days to get from Guatemala City to Houston, Texas, and we only went at night."

"So what did you do when you got there?" I ask.

"What did I do when I got there," he repeats, turning it into a statement, not a question. He's the type to stare into your eyes until you get embarrassed and turn your head.

"Well, I went to California," he finally says. "To San Diego. And I got a job at the port, you know? And those jobs pay real well. Back then I didn't have any problems getting my papers. And then I worked there. I worked there one year, and after that I bought a car." He leans back, satisfied with himself, and draws on the bottle of beer.

"A car?" I ask.

"A van." He nods. "I didn't do too bad working at the port." He pushes the base of his beer into the sand and takes a cigarette from his pocket.

"I have seen your country," he says after a while. He smiles at me, but this time he doesn't show his teeth. "I've been to the South, to the North-east, through the Midwest twice." He takes a drag of his cigarette, exhales.

He tells me that, seeing my country, he was pulled over many times by police wary of a young Latino man with a braid. "Sometimes," he says, "they just made me lie down on the floor while they checked my papers on their computers." He coughs, puts his fist to his mouth. "Sometimes they made me get out and walk, you know? Like maybe I was drunk? But they never brought me in."

He finishes his cigarette and stubs it out on the ground. He had his working papers, after all. "Sometimes they would talk to me," he says, "asking me how I bought the van, how I made so much money, how I got here from Guatemala. Sometimes, I think they were jealous, those cops. I was young, and I was free. I got to your country with nothing, but I saw everything."

He tells me he moved to Germany after his years in the States. He met a man who built wooden furniture, and he got the man to hire him as an apprentice. "I learned German, and I learned wood," he says. For the first time I notice his hands. His nails are long, longer than mine, and his fingers are sliced with scars, silvery remnants of nicks. He catches me looking; he winks, stretching his palms open wide before me. There are scars there, too, fine white lines running over the skin.

Once I met a man who read palms. He took your hand and stretched it open, rubbed his fingers on your palm to bring out the lines, then peered closely. He affirmed that I was a writer, and said I would see more of the world.

"Anything bad?" I'd asked.

There were bad things about every palm, he'd replied, things you wouldn't tell a friend. He was like Michel: both smile with only half their mouths. There is the way they stare at you, right into your eyes. And there is the way they talk; both have these accents acquired from years shifting over the world.

That night, I dream about a man with dark eyes and a white linen shirt walking the streets of San Francisco. He is the first in his family to ever see the rock formations of the Grand Canyon and the quiet sidewalks of a New England town in fall. In my dream, he learns English in bars, in diners, on campsites. One night, he flies to another continent, and there he walks cobbled streets, learning German in bars, in diners, on campsites. He meets a man, an older man, a man who has worked with wood all his life. In my dream, the young man works for the old one, cutting his hands, watching the seasons pass. But one night, he awakes to someone shaking his shoulder, hard, and telling him to get out of bed. That night, he buys a ticket at a noisy bus terminal and goes away. He doesn't tell anyone where.

USPANTÁN, GUATEMALA

The bus terminal is rippling at six in the morning with men hawking tickets and women selling oranges. Businesspeople, showered and sprayed and perfumed, rush to catch their buses, which wear a sheen of dust the color of the big dirt lot, and beneath the dust they wear their painted murals, their hearts, their peace signs, their crosses. Brilliant flames, messages turning the mind toward God. Some bear painted representations of popular destinations: palm trees, deep crater lakes, markets. I climb onto the Chimaltenango bus, which depicts Christ, once on the cross and once alive, distributing fish. I take my seat, pressing myself up against the window, because even though the bus is empty now, they always fill.

Hilary, the sister of a friend from graduate school, lives in Uspantán. She's been there with the Peace Corps for a year now, with one more to go. We've met only once, at graduation, but when I told her I'd be in Guatemala, she urged me to come and visit her.

The bus to Chimaltenango halts for ladies who carry their babies strapped to their backs in blankets, young men in overalls on their way to construction jobs, teenagers with cell phones and knock-off designer bags from the market, businesspeople carrying along the scent of their baths. People come on, one by one, until I turn my head to look back and see that the bus is packed, and there are four people in my seat alone, four adults on a seat that was once designed, in some Midwestern factory, to carry three American schoolchildren. The people behind me have blank, tired expressions on their faces; they stare ahead, now and then glancing down at the children who hold their hands, or at their cell phones. New speakers have been piped into the bus, and the driver blasts the Guatemala City pop station. We hurtle along, stopping and starting, out of Antigua and up into the hills.

Traveling is like being flung. In the end, you have little say in the way the ride will go; you just have to hope that you'll reach the destination you had in mind. You don't know how your landing place will look, how it will sound, how it will feel to arrive.

In Chimaltenango, the streets are wet from the rain that came in the night. There are no signs in English, no calm, cream-colored lines of homes, just music and billboards, voices and rickshaws. I must find my next bus, the one that will take me to Quiché. I ask and ask, and finally a rickshaw driver pulls over and drives me to the side of another busy road farther down. All the buses come here, he tells me in Spanish, and he takes my ten quetzales and putters off, up the hill. Buses fly past, the *ayudantes* shouting the names of their destinations, and finally a man is calling out, "Quiché!" I step into the street; the bus barely slows to let me on. I stumble down the narrow aisles and fall into one of the seats. My heart is beating wildly, and I struggle to compose my breath. *Flung*, I think again, grateful that I've landed in this empty seat.

This is a longer, quieter ride, but even so, I learn why people crowd into the front seats of the bus, even when those in the back are empty. The frequent speed bumps shatter my system, smashing my jawbones together. On the way in, through and out of every town, we bang our heads on the overhead compartments and hold on. No one speaks as we drive over the speed bumps, anticipating the jarring. I'm careful to keep my tongue away from my teeth.

We leave the towns, eventually, passing through Achagua, San José, Chichicastenango, Santa Ana, and then the speed bumps disappear. Now we are in the highlands, where the roads wind around mountains, tracking up and down valleys, cutting through fields of corn, of banana, of lettuce that grows so thick and strong and green on hills like these. We are flying down and belching up, and if I turn my head I can see the black cloud of the bus' exhaust. It takes three hours to reach Santa Cruz, where I will make my final connection.

At the terminal, I have just enough time to shake hands with the man who helped me hoist my pack down from the overhead compartments, and to return his grin, which reveals numerous gold crowns, before another *ayudante* runs over, jumping out of his micro while it's still pulling up to the curb. It is as if he already knows my destination. "Uspantán?" he asks, the strap of my pack in his hand. He nods to the man with the gold crowns and ties my pack to the roof. There's no time to use the bathroom, to eat something, to drink something, to take a breath of fresh air. Hilary had said it would take three hours from here to get to Uspantán. I take a deep breath, wishing I'd slept better the night before, wishing I'd taken the time for a proper breakfast. I learn on this day to always bring food. The micro tears out of town, stopping short several times to pack in more people, and by the time we're out of Santa Cruz, I count twenty-six passengers in a fifteen-seater van.

Still, we pick up more and more people—babies, grandmas—and when room inside runs out we continue to collect workmen, who climb up onto the roof. It is in this way that we reach Uspantán, where through the wet fog we can see little villages set in the crooks of mountains. No one talks in the van. I can hear bumping above me as the workmen shift around. The little boy beside me gets sick in a bag. He sits on his father's lap, surrounded by people, and coughs quietly, the plastic bag pressed expertly to his face.

When I was a child, queasy in the backseat, my dad would pull his old Jeep over, waiting while I retched in the road, and then my mother would give up the front seat so I could get more air. The ride is smoother up here, she would say, her cool hand on my arm. Now, we throb over the cracks in this Guatemalan road, whipping around the sharp, blind curves, and while the little boy is sick, the rest of the passengers stare out the window, their minds miles from their bodies, their eyes on the shifting horizon.

Hilary sent directions to her host family's house, and eventually, after a few dazed moments in Uspantán's central park, I make my way there. In the doorway of a two-story white adobe house, Hilary looks thin and tanned in a long black skirt and a purple top. At the end of such a journey, in this place where I've been flung—dirt roads and a low, tarp-covered market—Hilary looks elegant. She is grinning, and though it has been many months since I've seen her, we fall into conversation as if picking up from the day before. Today is her birthday, and in the doorway of her host family's two-story house at the edge of town, I give her the gift that I've brought, purchased at the artisans' market in Antigua: earrings made of jade and shaped like slender diamonds. Chickens come over to scratch and cluck. As Hilary examines the earrings, cooing, and then puts them on, I think how grateful I am to have landed here. Arrival can be as merciful as the moment of travel. The hours on the *camionetas* melt from me, and the aching in my jaw dissolves. People are oases, I realize, and that is how travelers navigate and understand their routes: stewards of places become like island, and if I look carefully, I have discovered, I'll find them anywhere.

"Let's go inside," Hilary says, but I will not let her help me with my heavy pack. I tell her I'll need the bathroom before anything else, and she says, head cocked, holding the door open, "I think we can arrange that."

Hilary's host mother, Juanita, is a small, black-haired woman in a pink *huipil*. While we eat stew cooked from a chicken she killed herself just this morning, she moves about, in and out, hoisting a barrel of water to the counter, hurrying the dogs outside into the yard, shouting at the chickens in the yard to shut up. Everything she says, though, is kind, and her voice is much softer than her strength, which is evident in her wiry arms and sharp cheekbones. The stew, I tell her shyly in Spanish, is the best thing I've tasted in a very long time. It has a smooth, buttery flavor, rich and brown and salty, and I eat ravenously. Juanita grins, refilling my dish, pouring me more juice. Hilary shows me Juanita's weavings outside: long bolts of striped cloth made by kneeling and holding the loom, neck bent.

Hilary lived here for the first six months she served in the Peace Corps. After that, she moved into her own apartment, just up the hill. Before the Peace Corps, she lived in San Francisco, where she taught gymnastics, earned a master's, and worked for a handful of nonprofits.

On the day her brother and I graduated, I'd stood in the grass with Hilary. We sipped wine from plastic cups. She'd just been accepted into the Peace Corps. "I need a jolt," she had said that day. I wished her luck, and then the conversation had turned to other things—our lives in our respective cities, our respective jobs and lovers. I could never have known then that I'd be here with her now, eating fresh chicken in a two-story house in Uspantán. Funny, life.

After lunch, we go to her small, whitewashed house. It is surrounded by a tall chain-link fence, and has a deep *pila* in the yard, which, Hilary explains, must always stay full of water in case the town supply shuts off. "This happens on and off," she tells me casually. There are three rooms, cool and dark in the late afternoon, and a two-burner stovetop. We sit on Hilary's porch while her adopted cat, Suerte, swirls between our legs. The night falls quickly, thickly, and Hilary lends me a scarf.

"*Suerte* means luck," she says.

In the morning, Hilary explains, we will travel to La Gloria, a tiny town five hours by dirt road from Uspantán. Hilary is apologetic but firm—

though I have just arrived, there is no other time to go but this morning. In La Gloria, she wants to build a school, and the man who will help her is driving her there. "It's what I always thought the Peace Corps was about," Hilary says. "Building schools." I'm surprised to learn how free Hilary's time is here, how open. From the looks of it, she creates her own projects, comes up with her own initiatives, and in general directs herself. I didn't realize the Peace Corps allowed such independence.

Geoff, a former Corps volunteer, will drive us in his Jeep to La Gloria, Hilary adds, and sure enough, he arrives exactly on time early the next morning. It's still dark, and we pile into the Jeep without talking much— *Good morning, good morning*, and a casual welcome nod directed my way. Geoff is tall and blonde and dazed-looking, and he's built schools in Guatemala before, all made of plastic soda bottles stuffed with paper. We sip the instant coffee Hilary brought in a Thermos, and after a while we perk up. The sky brightens. Geoff describes, as we leave town and rise up into the hills, the way blocks of stuffed bottles are set around a frame to insulate the school's foundation. The bottles are wrapped in chain-link, plastered with adobe, and painted.

An American nonprofit funded both schools Geoff built. Five-thousand-dollar pledges from well-to-do *estadounidenses* cover the cost of the materials; then, the residents in need of a school are asked to help with building. More pledges have arrived, and Geoff assures Hilary he can bring the designs to La Gloria. The two of them chat in the front seat, their voices growing louder with the rising of the sun. Static invades the radio; no channels work now, and Geoff flicks the radio off. While the two of them talk, I watch out the window: an *estadounidense* myself riding off into the Guatemalan hills. Now the horizon is visible, lumpy low hills and the sun rising above them. The clouds are pink; the sky is bright blue. A slice of orange comes, and I am astonished once again at where I've found myself today.

As we drive, Hilary explains that up here in these hills, Guatemala's civil war hit hard. Through the 1980's, many indigenous people were slaughtered. The women were raped; the crops and homes were destroyed; the families were dispersed or else forced to live in rural, secluded poverty. The Mayans weren't citizens, though they'd always lived off the land. For many years they survived, isolated, in the hills. The only path connecting La Gloria to the outside world was blocked by soldiers. La Gloria has two hundred inhabitants, Geoff adds, and each lives with almost nothing.

Uspantán produced Rigoberta Menchú, whose memoir, *I, Rigoberta Menchú*, I completed just before leaving Antigua. I'm grateful now to have read the book, which cost fourteen dollars, more than two nights at a hostel. I bought it at a gift shop for tourists, the counters stacked neatly with woven hats and gloves. Scarves were draped artfully over the beams, and serene music played. The ironies compounded each other there; such beautiful products made by people so poor, sold by a woman so elegant in a store that felt so empty. It felt to be too neat, too clean and sweet-smelling, far too expensive. In Guatemala, a book is a luxury item, the price of which can feed a family of four for a week. I took that mindset to heart, and read *I, Rigoberta Menchú* more carefully than I'd read in a long time. I took the pages extra slowly, savoring every word rather than skimming occasionally, as is often my habit. In my country, I remember thinking, media—books and magazines, television and film—are meant to be devoured, for the consumer knows that there's an endless supply. Reading *I, Rigoberta Menchú*, I took tiny, penciled notes in the margins, and I made a book cover out of a crinkled paper bag.

Menchú, a now-famous humanitarian and diplomat, grew up not far from where we're driving now. She came of age with the civil war, where leagues of highland guerrillas fought the Guatemalan military while Jimmy Carter, then Ronald Reagan, looked on. Money and weapons were funneled from the US to Guatemala, and the mountains of Quiché, where Menchú was raised, ran with blood. A young woman by the time the fighting turned to genocide, she and her family were poor rural farmers who travelled seasonally to the coast for work. They were basically indentured servants, so indebted to their employers that they never actually took money home. The book tells of the living they eked out for themselves: limes and salt, tortillas and limes, salt and tortillas and brittle, broken earth.

When the war reached them, it ravaged everything: their homes, their towns, their farms. Menchú's family members, guerrilla fighters themselves by the end, were tortured or murdered. Only Menchú was able to escape, in the late 1970's, to Guatemala City, where she worked in wealthy homes until her exile to Mexico in 1980.

Her book, *I, Rigoberta Menchú*, is a testament to her level of education and her background: the language is simple and plain, the story brutal but spare. As we drive down red-clay roads, I think of Menchú, of the bloody hills, and of the ghosts that must lie in these fields we pass now.

Salt from the ocean still stains my shoes; my hands are tanned. The Monterrico beach was another Guatemala, and now I am here.

We stop two hours in at a tiny town where we buy warm, dusty bottles of Coke. The morning rolls open; the cab gets hot. We crank the windows down, and the air smells of wheat and brushfire and rain. Eventually, we cross a perilous bridge over a rocky, rushing river, and finally we begin to see signs of the little villages that precede La Gloria. Hilary has been here only once, but the people on the roadside remember her and wave. We play a game, seeing who gets the most waves. Men who wave are one point, women two, little boys three, and little girls five. Geoff wins the most points; the little girls almost always give him a wave, though they stare unsmiling at Hilary and I when we try. We cross a massive puddle in the road, pond-sized, and drive along a ridge. The view reveals a low, sprawling mountain range that goes, Geoff says, all the way to Mexico. The mountains fade from inky blue to pale violet, lightning flickering in the distance.

Finally, we reach the town, a dozen homes on either side of the red dirt road and nothing more. Banana palms wave their wet leaves in the humid wind. We drive to the house of Juan, a man Hilary knows from town meetings in Uspantán. He looks to be thirty, and his five children run about while he shows us our room. We'll sleep in hammocks beside sacks of flour, an old bicycle, and a weary, whimpering dog. "He hurt his leg," Juan explains, and reaches down to scratch the dog's head. This storeroom is divided from the living area by a half-wall, and all night we'll hear the sounds of people rustling, tossing on their mattresses, murmuring in their sleep.

Chickens scratch and cluck outside, and I set my small bundle down. There are many smells in this storeroom, pleasant smells of bread and dirt and tea. There's the faintness of mothballs, and after the five-hour ride, it's nice to stand in the darkness, alone. Geoff and Hilary have gone back outside and I can hear them talking to Juan. I am thinking of the ride: the little girls, stingy with their waves; the massive puddle in the road, like a pond; the wet forest alongside us the whole way; the rippling range that stretched to Mexico. I dig my journal out of my pack and scrawl a couple of notes: *little girls waving, puddle pond, dusty Coke*. It's for E—, I think to myself, hoping the notes make sense when I'm able to get to a computer. An email to her is long overdue, I realize guiltily.

There is no running water in La Gloria; the *pila* is filled by a hose that connects to the spring, which is everyone's property. The bathroom is an outhouse, the door a torn sheet of tarp. I listen to the crickets outside, the voices down below, and hold the tarp shut, hurrying. There is nowhere to wash my hands, just the *pila* at the house, thirty feet away and down a rocky trail I imagine winds even more steeply at night.

Geoff and Hilary speak to Juan about the bottle-school project, and I try to listen. Juan's youngest, a toddler in red shorts that reach to his ankles, comes over and sets his hand on my knee. He looks up at me, unafraid, and babbles something I don't understand.

"I know," I tell him in English. "It's very warm here, isn't it?" He blinks at me, coughs, and sits quickly down hard onto the cement. *Ouch,*

I think but do not say, and glance around, wait for his first scream, pre- pare to reach for him, offer comfort, calm his cries. But no one looks over, and the boy, unhurt, unused to being coddled, is content to play with the ants that march over his toes.

In the afternoon, we attend a town meeting arranged by Juan. The purpose of the meeting is to round up helpers, volunteers—really get the community involved. Geoff presents a movie on how bottle schools are built. It's in English, with U2 playing in the background and Spanish subtitles. The attendees include many, many children, as well as some mothers and a few old men. Cell phones go off during the meeting, and the calls are taken. Kids get up and run outside and come back in. The meeting is hectic, but in the end, it's decided: the bottle school will be built. Only one man is not in favor; he stands up, swaying slightly, and says that since he does not have children, he will not help build the school. Geoff shrugs. The man makes his way noisily outside. The rest of the audience applauds briefly for Geoff, and the meeting concludes.

And this, I realize, is how a school gets built—without the govern- ment's help at all.

My elementary school was a long building with gleaming floors of bright blue linoleum tiles. I can still picture perfectly the bathroom, four stalls and three sinks. Warm classrooms in winter while the snow fell outside, and kind teachers, mostly women, who gave us rewards in the form of stickers and cookies and extra-long recesses. We had a play- ground made of wood, the most beautiful playground anyone in our town had ever seen, with turrets and slides and tunnels and bridges, swings and seesaws and so many little hidey-holes. My parents helped to build that playground, I'm remembering now, along with other par- ents. It took a summer, and they'd drive down to the playground after work, I think, to hammer nails and sand wood and then have a beer, or maybe go to someone's house to share a meal. At least, that's how I remember it. I can see the parallels, the similarities and the distinctive contrasts, between La Gloria's newest project and that playground, built for the town's children so many years ago.

We have been invited to dinner at the town mayor's house. He's a small, gray-haired man, far stooped. His house is dark and small, with dirt floors and many people inside. The girl washing the dishes has her baby with her, playing at her feet, and when Hilary asks its name, he shrugs.

"Who cares," he mutters, and kicks at a bucket on the floor.

For dinner, the mayor's wife makes scrambled eggs flecked with soot from the stovetop. We drink instant coffee without sugar. The mayor's oldest son has brought his new wife to dinner. She barely eats anything and then dozes on her new husband's shoulder. They are young and thin. The son apologizes, explaining that his wife doesn't feel well, and she opens her eyes a little. When we stand to leave, she doesn't say goodbye.

In the night, across the street, the evangelical church blasts music, the banging of a piano's keys and the shriek of a high-pitched trumpet, until very early in the morning. The music swings, frantic and slightly out of tune. I wonder how the people stay fervent so late. In the morning, we wake before six and go outside to sit on the little porch beside the *pila*, watching smoke from the neighbors' breakfast fires merging with the morning mist. Behind the house, the jungle sings with insects and birds and water dropping off leaves to the ground. We eat bread and oranges and instant coffee, and then we shake hands with Juan and his wife and his oldest son, who showed up this morning and sat drinking coffee with his mother. I kiss Juan's littlest goodbye; the child watches me blankly, unrecognizing. His look makes perfect sense: I've come for a moment, a blundering stranger, and now I'll be gone, leaving La Gloria behind. I'll probably never come back. I remember the English travelers, the ones who'd been to Borneo and Thailand and everywhere else. *What am I after? I wonder again.*

Why am I here?

On the way home, we have a passenger in tow: the mayor's middle daughter. She had eaten quietly at the table the night before, then taken her plate to the sink and left the room. "She needs to get to the town halfway to Uspantán," the mayor had said while she waited beside him, her bag already packed, her belly huge in pregnancy. She held the hand of her son, a small boy with no shoes, while the mayor gave his final instructions. "Her aunt lives there," he told us, and then he shook Geoff's hand and went inside.

I look at the mayor's middle daughter beside me in the backseat. I guess at her age, not daring to ask, thinking that she's sixteen, maybe eighteen. She wears red barrettes in her hair and carries a neon-pink purse. Her little boy falls asleep, and for a while she rides without speaking, watching out the window at the evaporating mist.

"What's your name?" Geoff asks her after a few moments, and I realize that the mayor didn't say.

"Ana," she says.

"What's your little boy's name?" Geoff asks.

"José," she replies. "He's three," she adds, looking down at him.

"Did you go to school?" Hilary asks. Ana shakes her head. And then it's as if something opens in her, and she strokes her son's head and looks at Hilary. She begins to talk, slowly at first, then raising her voice a little higher.

"My father says I don't need school," she says. "He tells me I need to stay at home and have babies, little boys like José." She looks down at him, strokes his head. She says, "He drinks." At first I don't understand and look aghast at little José. But then I realize she's talking about the

mayor. She has said it as if it's not news, not gossip, but simply something everyone knows. Geoff told us, though, that alcohol is illegal in La
Gloria and must be smuggled in. I recall the swaying man at the meeting
and figure it can't be that difficult.

"He drinks so much," Ana says, "and then he falls." She giggles, covering her mouth with her hand.

At the little town halfway to Uspantán, a young girl recognizes Hilary. She
leans into the car window, peering back at José and Ana and I. She stands
on her tiptoes and says something to Hilary, who bursts out laughing.

"She asked if you're my children!" she tells us in English, and the
little girl at the car window grins, understanding perfectly, pushing her
body farther through the window, her face almost touching Hilary's.

* * *

Hilary is tireless, jumping from idea to idea, non-profit to non-profit,
trying her best to make her unstructured Peace Corps time meaningful.
For a fleeting afternoon, we rest in Uspantán, sipping beers and sun-
ning our legs on her porch, and then Hilary announces that the next
morning we'll start another project: she's volunteered both of us to be
translators for a Canadian nonprofit, where volunteers from Ontario
pay to travel to Guatemala and build stoves for those in need. When I
tell Hilary I can't translate, she laughs and reassures me.

"They just need someone who can say numbers and directions," she
says. While she talks on the phone to Geoff about the bottle-school's
next steps, I run through the numbers in my head, then take out Linda's
old list of prepositions.

At the first meeting of the stove-builders—a group of pale Canadians in hiking boots—I learn that much of the world uses stoves that
burn too much wood, that pollute the home, that don't circulate the air

and smoke properly. These stoves hurt those who use them every day. The stoves funded by the Canadian nonprofit are built of cement blocks and metal sheets and stand slightly larger than typical Guatemalan hearths. The rule is this: families pay thirty dollars for a stove that costs one hundred and fifty—to ensure that they'll really use it. Accountability, Hilary calls it, because people, after all, get attached to old ways, and stoves installed by do-gooders have gone unused in the past.

We all ride together, the twelve friendly Canadians and the two of us, into the hills, where the road turns from pavement to dirt to stone. These villages are not so remote as La Gloria, but the outhouses are the same: thin walls, torn tarps, no water. One woman with a strong-looking face, gray braids, and a red apron shakes her head when I ask to use the toilet. "We don't have one," she says, and looks past me to the mountains. "Go around the house," she says.

Over the course of seven days we build twenty-six stoves. I'm better at entertaining the children than translating between the Guatemalan families and the eager, curious Canadians, and so I color and ask questions and let everyone try on my sunglasses while the stoves go up. Afterwards, I help sweep the floors and distribute crayons equally between the children. I am good with the children, everyone says, and the praise pleases me. For the first time in a long time, I feel useful, and suddenly grateful to the Canadians, so kind, so earnest and pale. I'd mocked that about them to myself at first, their gear so brand-new, their faces smeared with too much sunscreen. Now, though, I smile at them, ask them questions, and teach them the Spanish numbers and the relevant prepositions.

After installing each stove, we say goodbye and hike to the next house. We are always offered food and boiled coffee, which we accept in small portions, *to be polite*, one young Canadian whispers to his dad. Half of the families getting new stoves are Mayan, the other half Christian. The Mayan families, I can't help but notice, are much larger, children and grandchildren and grandparents and dogs, all under one roof. The older Mayan women ask us the price of our jewelry, which, according to Hilary, means that they like it.

After each stove is built, we take a group picture. Many months later, holding the images in my hands, I will marvel at how little time we spent in each home. We walked all over the floor, looked around, ate food, shared crayons, and then we were gone. *What have I taken?* I'll wonder, seeing my face sunburned, my limbs so gangly and long. *What did I give?* And I'll hope that the stoves are still working, and that the women have to walk fewer miles, fewer times, to gather the wood that they need to keep their families alive. For months and years to come, I'll think about the stoves and the La Gloria school with affection and sorrow, and guilt. I'll remember the hopeless way I felt in La Gloria, and how good it was to work for a day building stoves. I'll imagine the rugged, raw beauty of those places, and the woman who had no toilet, and the little boy who looked at me when I'd said good-bye, both of us knowing I'd never return.

SANTA ANA, EL SALVADOR

The trip takes ten hours—six more than scheduled.
To start, the bus bound for Santa Ana leaves the terminal two hours late, and getting out of Guatemala City itself takes another hour, the bus crawling through the black market past tents shading stolen cell phones, knock-off watches, imposter designer bags, fried chicken stands. This city is unlike any other Guatemalan place I've seen so far, and I yearn for Monterrico's black sand, or even the hammock in Juan's dusty storeroom. In the center of clamoring Guatemala City, we wait onboard while the *ayudante* jumps off the bus to buy a DVD, an American action flick dubbed in Spanish and played, in all its noisy gore, for the first two hours of the journey.

The traffic sits at a standstill, and no one seems to mind. The men hop off the bus and reenter, zipping up their flies. A few women make their way to the back of the bus, yanking open the sticky bathroom door and slamming it closed behind them. Another gruesome movie begins. It takes two hours to cross the border; we all must line up at one window, then another, windows and little rooms where uniformed police behind bars stamp our passports, one after another. These windows will shuffle the landscape past, first Guatemala and then El Salvador.

Travel is like being flung.

I am going to Santa Ana because of Paul Theroux. The trains brought him there, and I follow him because he is my only guide. The pages of his book are leathery and the binding loose; the book is like a worn deck of cards. It occurs to me, as the bus idles for hours at a construction site near the border, that without him I wouldn't be here at all. How tenuous our connection feels, all of a sudden. I bite my nails and marvel at my audacity: I had thought that a man, a route in a book, could be a reason to go to Santa Ana.

I sip water and eat granola bars. I watch out the window. I wait. I hope. I remember that Paul Theroux also waited here, here in this city for a slow train to come. Then I remember that I don't know Paul Theroux at all. The night is not so far away, and I am afraid.

Meanwhile, the driver, his *ayudante*, and a few friends they've picked up along the way stand around outside the bus smoking and eating ice creams, *pupusas*, tortillas, sandwiches, and frozen fruit out of skinny plastic sacks. Our passports are stamped in Guatemala and again, a hundred yards later, in El Salvador. Two Canadian guys on the bus are having problems; the soldiers at border control scrutinize their passports while the rest of us wait, sweating, in the bus. Finally, beneath a sky settled into dusky gray, we enter El Salvador.

The bus makes frequent stops here, and women in ruffled aprons stream on with buckets of soda and bottled water, baskets of hot tortillas, tostadas, and plastic bags of sliced mangos. I look out the window to see whether anything's different. But El Salvador has the same rolling hills as Guatemala, the same expanses of scrub brush and sand that give way to the same dripping forests. People stand in their doorways watching us pass, and huge moths flutter at porch lights. The evening turns grainy, sultry. I notice that many men sit outside in wheelchairs, missing legs. One man stands on the roadside, waving with his only arm.

One of the driver's friends, a heavy guy the *ayudante* calls Gordo, hurtles down the aisle toward me. He says something in Spanish; I shake my head.

"Slower?" I ask, and he repeats the question with the same rapidity. The lights in the bus come on. Again, I shake my head. He repeats himself again. Finally, I get it; this bus won't go to Santa Ana after all. Now we are pulling off the road into a gas station parking lot lit by one sputtering streetlight.

There is nothing else around, just the dark expanse of fields and trees and the distant homes of the crippled soldiers. Just before I get off—the only one, it turns out, destined for Santa Ana—one of the Canadian guys comes up and asks if I'll be okay. I tell him yes, though we both know I can't be sure. In any case, there is nothing he can do. Gordo hails a taxi, pays the white-haired driver a few dollars, and loads my pack into the trunk. The Canadian waves through his window as the bus pulls away, and then I'm alone, standing outside the taxi, and the driver is shouting at me to get in. It occurs to me that the currency has shifted; I'll need the remaining US dollars tucked away in my wallet.

The driver seems only to know how to bark.

"Where are you going?" he cries, his voice sharp and gravelled. I shuffle through my guidebook and take a stab at pronouncing the first hotel listed.

"What?" the driver barks. "I can't understand you."

I repeat the name of the place—"The Faro," I shout back. "Faro!"

While he reaches around and takes my guidebook from me to peer at the tiny map of his city, I stare out at the sky lit by artificial light. I can smell factory smoke and car exhaust and stale cigarettes. "Faro," I say to the driver again, weakly now. I feel small and sick in the backseat, the adrenaline come and gone.

We drive for a few miles toward the city. When we pass a lone man on the sidewalk, the driver heaves the wheel to the right and reaches to open the passenger-side door. He calls to the man, who is young and has thick, dark hair he's grown long and tied back. After a brief exchange with the driver, the young man hops in and slams the door.

"Careful," the driver says, and steps on the gas.

For a moment I think of the turtles: their tiny black eyes, their black flippers, their little tails. The Monterrico beach at sunset, the lavender-salmon sky. The American boys in t-shirts and flip-flops and the woman in billowing white. The turtles again, scrabbling toward the waves, already understanding that water is home. E—'s hands, her eyes, the sound of her voice, the way it used to feel to sleep in the bed with her, or to sit at the kitchen table, light pouring in through the windows and onto that pale maple floor.

Over the radio, a woman is reading the news in a droning voice. The taxi's seats are worn but clean, and the air smells of cigarettes and bodies. The man in the passenger seat turns to talk to me in slow, kind Spanish.

"Where are you going?" he asks patiently. He is wearing a black t-shirt and a baseball cap.

"El Faro," I say for the third time, passing the guidebook to him, my finger pressed to a spot on the page.

He glances at the map.

"El Faro," he repeats to the driver, who nods, suddenly understanding everything.

"Faro," the driver says, glancing at me in the rearview. I am grateful for the man with kind eyes who spoke slowly. *I am safe,* I tell myself, to still my trembling hands. It is so dark outside.

Of Santa Ana, Theroux described a coffee-scented heat. He'd eaten fresh fish and slept deeply. He'd admired the colonial lines of the city and the mountains in the distance. He wrote, "The town only looked godforsaken; in fact, it was comfortable…In every respect, Santa Ana…was a perfect place."

Since Theroux visited Santa Ana in 1975, civil war has shredded the country. By now, I'm starting to see a pattern: the countries of Central America mostly enjoyed a few decades of independent sovereignty before the United States stepped in—usually by the mid-seventies. In the case of El Salvador, the United States' interference was merited, according to Jimmy Carter, in retaliation for the rape and murder of four American nuns; Carter suspended all United States aid.

By the time Reagan was in charge, though, money was flowing into El Salvador again in the form of military aid, which fueled the already vicious fire of civil war, military against civilians against the FMLN, El Salvador's guerrilla army that formed in the 1970s. Into the nineties El Salvador fought against itself, certain factions funded by my country's government. Finally, a peace accord was signed, but not after an estimated 80,000 had been killed over the course of ten years. A few years later, Hurricane Mitch raged through and left around 75,000 people homeless in El Salvador. Not long after, a magnitude 7.6 earthquake struck the country, displacing 100,000 and killing thousands more. The earthquake rocked Guatemala; tremors even reached southern Mexico.

The city finally appears, and at the crest of the hill Santa Ana sprawls. I crack my window and sniff for the coffee-scented heat Paul described, but there comes just woodsmoke and the smell of rotting fruit. "Close the window," the driver barks. I hurriedly comply.

While we speed into the city, the young guy in the front seat asks me if I know what Hot Topic is.

"What?" I say.

"Hot Topic," he says in English, lighting a cigarette for himself and one for the driver. Both crack their windows. He explains that Hot Topic is a punk-rock store in the States, and that he owns a store like that, not called Hot Topic but something else. He passes me a business card, and I see that his shop is called Punky Girl. He's thirty-one and has been once to the United States, to Cleveland, and he has a girlfriend who lives there still. Then, abruptly, the driver veers over, stops the car, and the guy jumps out.

"Good luck," he says as we rattle away, and then we're driving without speaking through the city.

It is ten minutes past midnight when the driver pulls over and turns.

"We're here," he says impatiently. A huge billboard above the Hotel Faro advertises the rate: five dollars for two hours. It takes me a second to figure it out: an hourly room, not a nightly one. An hourly room. I ask the driver to wait for a moment, and he grunts something at me. He pops the trunk but doesn't get out to help me with my pack, and before I've shouldered it, he's gone. Dust swirls up from the still-warm road. There is no one around; there will not be a choice. A buzz enters my head, as if I've just left a rock concert.

Through metal bars I speak to a young, unsmiling man with light skin and dark hair who takes my money—ten dollars for the night—and passes me a key on a chunky wooden keychain. "Upstairs," he says, and returns to the messages on his cell phone.

I creep up the stairs to find a blank, dingy room: one sheet on the bed, one folded towel, and a wrapped bar of soap on the chair. There's a big fan in the corner; I switch it on, hoping it will be loud enough to block out the sounds of those hourly rooms through paper-thin walls. There is the smell of floor cleaner and fungus. The faucet drips.

To Theroux, Santa Ana's whitewashed buildings at night shone luminous, and the coffee in the morning was crushed velvet with cream. Much has changed since those decadent years, and Santa Ana, at least, seems to have eroded significantly. But what do I know—I'm only passing through. I remind myself that in the morning, I'll be gone.

The moment of travel is merciful.

I shower in flip-flops and then eat a granola bar, bringing the day's total to five. I don't dare leave the hotel in search of food. I wonder how I will bear this thick night, and I wish for E—. Even her voice would do, but the cell phone doesn't recognize this country and blinks helplessly.

She must be so worried. All that's left to do is turn it off, climb into bed, and try to sleep, erasing as best I can the night.

I dream I am sleeping beside my mother at my grandmother's house. I feel her hand reach over to me to check that I am there. I hear the sound of my grandmother's light snores, and from the breezeway the dog's whimper. In my dream, the lace curtains whisper over the open window above me, and all the sounds combined become a lullaby. In the morning, I wake and lie in white sheets for a moment, unsure of where I am. I cling to the dream—the curtains, the snores—until I hear something slam against the wall I share with the next room over. A desk, a chair, a body—I can't know. I pack my things and creep from the hotel.

The fresh, early sun sweeps over green lawns, whitewashed two-story houses, hotels scattered everywhere offering competitive hourly rates. Women in tiny aprons and halters sell cigarettes and wash the sidewalks in front of their shops with brooms and buckets of soapy water. I walk to the plaza and crane my neck to the faded grandeur of the old theatre; the coral-colored government buildings; and the dusty, creaking palms. People stare at me. I give up on Santa Ana once and for all and ask at a bodega for the bus stop.

SAN SALVADOR, EL SALVADOR

I have read of San Salvador's crime and its gangs, and my heart beats in my throat as people climb aboard the bus, city-bound. I think of how E— must be worrying, yet there's nothing I can do, no phone on this bus and my cell dead in my purse. And so I put her from my mind and think of breathing. All around us, the earth is flat and dry, so hot that the women wear tank tops and short-shorts and children go barefoot. Gone are the traces of the indigenous that so defined Guatemala; now I see only cheap sweatshop clothes, plastic shoes, babies cradled in women's arms, not strapped to their backs.

"I never carry a purse in San Salvador," a woman in Guatemala City had said. "They'll steal it right off of your arm."

I wish to never reach San Salvador, for on this bus, at least, I am safe, and the sunshine tips in. A woman comes on with a flower in her hair.

Already, Guatemala feels distant, cold Xela nights replaced by beach replaced by sweating trees on an El Salvador street. I am flung; that is the point, I remind myself.

In the end, San Salvador's bus station is orderly. Each bus has its space, and the traffic is thin. A well-pressed cabbie approaches me right away and leads me to his yellow car, which is polished and clean. Still, I don't let my guard down. I am clutching the little paper with the name of a hotel written down, one the guidebook heartily recommended, and

I decide to forgive it the mistake of El Faro. Maybe there were two El Faros, I reason. The cabbie and I ride in silence, and I wish again that my Spanish were better and that I had the courage to open my mouth and try. I worry that he won't know the way. I wish he'd say something, even if I don't understand. I swallow, remembering to breathe.

The city is hot and white. I roll down my window a crack; the cabbie glances at me through the rearview but says nothing. After a moment, he cracks his window, too. It's been two days since I've eaten anything but granola bars. We pass KFC, Pizza Hut, Wendy's. McDonalds and Hertz Rent-a-Car. San Salvador has endured too many earthquakes to have any historical buildings. In my hand I clutch wilting dollar bills to pay the driver.

By the time we reach my hotel, safe and sound, and the driver shouts a loud *adiós* as he drives away, I realize that things might not be so bad. The hotel smells lightly of flowers. My room is spotless, sparsely decorated in white. My bed is soft, with generous pillows. The lady at the desk is nice. This place costs eighteen dollars a night, and it's worth every penny. Santa Ana feels comfortably far away, the hourly hotel already turning comic in my mind. Still, I wonder if, had I stayed, I would have discovered something beautiful.

Now, I breathe in, breathe out, turn on the fan, take a cool shower. I eat at the Italian restaurant next door, where the pasta tastes better than any I've had.

Though every shop and corner is guarded by a uniformed man with a gun, they each smile at me and tip their hats. The boy beside me on the bus headed downtown asks me questions in polite, stilted English, and then walks me to the place to wait for my connecting ride. I visit the Museum of Anthropology, meandering through panels displaying the history of this country, from the days of maize and dye, to the grave-mounds, to the Spanish colonization. Afterwards, the man at the desk helps me find the bus to get home. The lady at the coffee shop tells me to have a wonderful time in her country. I get used to the heat and to the whistles from the guys leaning against the *tiendas*. After a few hours, I even get used to the guns. I run the shower cold; I walk slowly. I go back to my rented room at the end of each day and I write San Salvador down. There's a little park beside my hotel, with swings and huge old trees, dust-pink petals of bougainvillea scattered on the sidewalk. In the evening, a haze comes and settles on the grass.

This is a city I like, I decide, even as I clutch my bag close to me, even as I carry my money, as advised, in its belt against my skin. You must rent the rooms in this hotel for the whole entire night, and I never thought that four clean walls could make me feel so rich. I am lucky, I remind myself, and remember my grandmother again: the ship that sailed for days; the foreign place; for so many years the foreign words. I remind myself that a pleasant few days in San Salvador is nothing, and that this year is a gift.

Outside, the street has grown quiet, the sky velvety as coffee, but it's still as hot as it was in the day, so I switch on the fan for another night in this country, another night beneath the press of this San Salvadorian heat.

THE ROAD

The journey to Managua takes all day, beginning at four in the morning, so early that the lights in my hotel are off, the street outside is dark, and I can hear the man in the room by the front door snoring. I slip out through the garage, sliding the bolt locked behind me, and I'm grateful for ordering a cab the night before. It idles now, the only source of light in the silent street. We drive through sleeping San Salvador; on one corner, the driver leans back and pushes the lock button on my door down.

"Just in case," he says.

In the bus, we ride with the windows open. The sky brightens as we cross El Salvador, which turns parched and treeless. The wind blows in, dust-laden. I am sweating; we're all sweating, and after a few hours my water is gone. We stop once to use the bathroom and buy lunch from a woman who doles out rice and plantains on plastic trays, and then again to cross the border into Honduras. The passengers fall into a listless quiet.

Managua, where I'm headed, is said to be the ugliest place in all of Nicaragua. Other travelers shuddered when they mentioned passing through. With a population of almost three million, more than twenty percent of Nicaraguans live there. Floods, earthquakes, and fire have ravaged Managua, whose sprawling network of streets and parks is built along the shore of Lake Managua. Furthermore, Nicaragua's seen its own share of civil war, alongside Guatemala and El Salvador. The 1979 civil war to overthrow US-backed dictator Somoza ravaged what artistic centers and bohemian avenues Managua had, and efforts to "recover" the city seem perpetually underway.

It's late afternoon by the time we enter Nicaragua, but there is no traffic at all. We have the empty landscape to ourselves, which resembles the American southwest: Prehistoric somehow, with oddly shaped peaks on the horizon and deep crater-like valleys along the roadside. The trees are sparse and spindly with delicate green leaves. We stop again for gas, but no one eats dinner. It's too hot. Instead, we buy bottles of warm juice and Gatorade. The sun has begun to set. That is how it is here, on this stretch that links South America to North—the sun sets at the same time each day, and then night falls, near-immediate. Beneath the sunset, this desert is coral and crimson, the horizon a line of burnished gold. Cactus in long shadow tumbles over the pebbled ground.

Two stringy-looking, light-skinned travelers get off where the highway intersects with a dirt road, shortly after we enter Nicaragua. They're wearing baggy pants, and dreadlocks hang to their hips in long, beaded knots. They exude the scents of lavender and smoke as they make their way off the bus, their pockets jangling with coins, their dreadlocks slapping the seats. We leave them standing with arms extended and thumbs raised, packs on the dusty ground beside them. For a moment I envy them their companionship, their daring at giving up the surety of the bus for an unknown vehicle, but soon enough I remember Theroux again, his map, the book I will make. I watch out the window and let the landscape swallow me up, crimson canyons and sculpted mountains in the distance, the red sun simmering to the west.

From San Salvador, I booked a night in a cheap Managua hotel, which sends a woman in pink shorts with a sign—*Katy*, my Spanish name—to meet me at the terminal. She says nothing, just nods when I go over to her and then guides me to the gated hotel one block away. I could have found it easily on my own. The evening simmers with cicadas. She unlocks a thick padlock and pushes open a creaking gate. A dog is barking somewhere, but otherwise the street is lazy in the setting sun. Because they have sent someone to meet me, I imagine the quiet to be eerie, and I follow the woman hurriedly inside.

I do not leave the hotel that night—not to buy dinner, not to visit the *tienda* with its strange new-country bars of chocolate and its new-country type of beer. I do not exchange any currency. Instead, I shower in the shared bathroom, a tiny, windowless room with a showerhead, a drain in the floor, and a toilet with a cracked seat. The shower doesn't run hot or cold, only lukewarm, the exact same temperature as the air. In a plastic chair outside of my room, the night beginning to buzz and sing, the traffic amplified in the darkness, I begin a translated version of *The Country Under My Skin*, the autobiography of Nicaraguan poet Gioconda Belli. I paid more for this book than for two nights at the San Salvador hotel, plus breakfast in the mornings.

But I am grateful now for the purchase. It feels the perfect time to read Belli's words, her descriptions of Managua's corruption and its literal collapse at the mercy of a string of earthquakes. She describes in detail her marriage and love affairs, her devotion to Nicaragua's independence and to freedom of speech. She published sensual poems that set the tongues of Managua's elite wagging. She used her own status to make her voice heard, hers and the people whose voices—in the campo and in the city barrios—had been silenced. Nicaragua's recent history resembles Guatemala's and El Salvador's, marked by dictators, natural disasters, and a US intervention—though in Nicaragua's case, the Sandinistas triumphed, the national group successfully overthrowing US-backed Somoza.

I remember a museum on a leafy street in San Salvador, old photographs of combatants hiding in jungle caves with radio transmitters. Black-and-white posters of the Disappeared, young people with bright eyes who paid for their cause with their lives. Belli's story describes the same kind of fear—a fear of talking on the phone, visiting a friend, or going to work.

Despite everything, Belli's love for her country emanates. She describes how Nicaragua feels this night, hot and pulsing with an energy that lies beneath the quiet streets and inside the shuttered homes. The branches of flowering trees brush over the hotel's high cement walls, blocking and unblocking the stars.

GRANADA, NICARAGUA

In a rented room in Granada, I sleep beneath a thin ceiling of long, slim bamboo poles. Between that and the actual roof of wooden beams and curved tiles, bats live. In the night I hear them scratching, chirping, screeching, and clicking, jabbering to each other in the darkness. These bats like the narrow spaces between buildings, dank and velvety places that humans can't access. At dusk, if I keep my eye on the eaves of any Granada house, I can watch the bats coming out for the night, swooping down toward the road and then up into the sky. From a distance, they are black butterflies, moving differently than birds, more aggressively yet somehow more gracefully, too. There are more bats in Granada than anywhere in Nicaragua, the woman at the coffee shop on the corner tells me. They like the church roofs, the narrow cracks that fill with wet wind off the lake. There are tiny lizards that skitter up the crumbly walls and then stop, suddenly motionless, and remain in that spot for hours.

"They're good," the coffee shop woman assures me. "They eat the bugs; they keep our houses clean. Bats and lizards—both are good." She pours me another cup as one of the green lizards skitters up the wall and out of sight.

Each Granada night is too warm for a sheet. These are Nicaragua's hottest months, just before the rain comes: February, March, and April. When I wash my clothes in the hostel's pale blue *pila* and hang them at the right time, the sun can dry them in less than an hour. My hair splits at the ends, and the sun bleaches long streaks. At night, I sizzle broccoli and plantains on the stovetop.

When the wind off the lake stills, the sun bakes everything, and the tiny gardens bear sweet mangoes, green plantains, and small, soft avocados. Tart *jocotes*, marble-sized and bright green, are sold in wheelbarrows and buckets on the sidewalks; the salesladies peel off the skin with sharp, tiny knives and then fill plastic bags with the sugared fruit. They let the peels fall like green half-moons onto the pavement; later, the dogs will sniff there, but only the gulls eat the peels. In almost every courtyard in the city, there comes the sound of water, moving through slim fountains and spattering onto stone. Through the bars of gates, there are banana trees, their floppy, torn leaves flourishing with abundant sun and little water.

Sometimes I will find plump avocados spread out on blankets or piled in baskets at the market. Always I can get cucumbers, tomatoes, and potatoes. There is no rain, and I marvel at the abundance of food, the artful presentation of fruits and vegetables. I buy dried beans, which simmer for hours over the little propane stove. I buy tortillas from a young girl in dusty plastic shoes; she keeps her pile of tortillas warm and soft in a cloth-covered basket and charges me five cents for each one. I buy cheese, wedges pried from huge blocks, salty and firm. This is the way the market smells: ripe pineapple, raw meat, and the slightly sour scent of those blocks of cheese. Hot corn on the cob, piles of narrow loaves of bread, flowers in buckets of tepid water. Urine stains the walls, and piles of horse manure steam, trampled, on the pavement. In the air I can smell burnt sugar and melon. The streets are jammed with people, but cars pull through anyway, almost brushing up against me, and the sun on my skin is a melting coat of paint. These are my days, and these are my nights: heat-soaked. The sky is a hard, firm blue, and though the clouds might come and hint at rain, it never falls.

I am lucky; my visit has coincided with the Nicaraguan Festival of Poets, to be held this year in Granada. In the plaza, the booksellers are still showcasing their collections on long tables under big white tents; people browse, holding the covers close to their faces, opening the creamy pages and whispering the lines. Plastic chairs are strewn all around beneath the mango trees, and people are sitting, chatting, reading, and smoking. They're drinking beer from cans and Fanta from plastic cups; they're feeding their babies or paging through the books they've purchased. One man plays his guitar and sings. Just as the bells of the churches are announcing five o'clock, the wind finally lifts off the water and filters through the streets, the trees, and onto the cobblestones. The clouds above me are moving again, and the colors of the paint on the buildings—salmon, butter, and ochre—are starting to deepen.

I run into a Chilean man I met at my hostel the evening before. He smiles at me, remembers my name, kisses my cheek. The rain begins lightly to fall. I watch it drop on his skin, on my skin, and I can feel the air growing cooler still. The Chilean tells me he's wandered all over the city today; he's seen churches, markets, beggars, and schools. He's gone in and out of galleries, and he went to see the water. He's fallen in love, he tells me, and I can see in his eyes that it's true. I can tell by the way he walks away from me afterwards that, if he could, he would wander these streets forever.

The scent of the rain is everywhere now: on the streets, in the walls of the rose and gold-colored buildings, in the leaves of the trees. It's a scent like earthworms, like the lake, like moss, and it's cooling my body down. I walk and walk, slowly, slowly, down one street and up another, past ladies sitting out in the street in rocking chairs, past kids playing soccer in the dirt, past horse-drawn carts, past baskets of bananas and sliced pineapple on sticks. I think that no one knows me here, not really—no one could name my hometown or my last name, and what freedom I suddenly, quietly know. An old man passes by, his cane tapping out his route against the stones.

It's as if I am in a dream, suddenly so far from my empty rented room. This is the gift travel offers: every moment gains the capacity to transform. The buildings crumble and peel while the sweet rain falls.

I round a corner and here is the Church of San Francisco with its massive façade which once was blue but has drained to a very pale gray. Water caresses stone, birds sing distant songs, and people in the plaza chat and laugh. The setting sun has made pink cracks in the clouds so that everything, this church included, seems to glow. The moment pours over me: the scent of the rain, the wet streets, the drops on my skin and in my hair. These churches, these poets, this pineapple juice on my fingers. I look up once more to the honey colored clouds and realize that I, too, have fallen in love.

Mitch, the dark-eyed guy from New Jersey who works the hostel's desk in the evening, becomes my first Granada friend. While he checks in backpackers and cracks open beers—ninety cents each—he talks and I listen. On my first night at the hostel, he asks me my name and buys me a beer.

"They're the best when it's hot, right?" he says, holding his sweating bottle against his forehead before taking a long pull. "Tastes like piss," he adds, setting the bottle onto the bar and looking thoughtfully at the label, then taking another long pull. "It's still the best thing," he decides aloud.

I perch on an unsteady three-legged barstool and listen to Mitch talk about his life in Nicaragua. He has fallen in love with the heat, the people, the streets, the unpaved roads, the massive lake on the edge of this city, and the farms on its outskirts. He has helped people here to build their own houses, asking them for only a fraction of the cost to build it and getting the rest through donations, mostly from the United States. He has taught farmers how to plant things that require less water, and how to grow vegetables alongside flowers and herbs, to naturally keep away pests. He says that the farmers knew these things once, Mitch says, but then they forgot. "I'm a Middle Eastern Jew," he admits, shrugging. "I like to help the disenfranchised save their money."

He talks as if he needs to fill the air around him. When he's not talking to me, he's giving advice to a sweaty couple straggling in. He offers them water; they buy beers and sit. He talks to himself when there's no one else, muttering at the list of songs on his open laptop. The sun goes down. The plants that grow in the courtyard's trodden grass close their leaves just slightly in the darkness.

Theroux skipped Nicaragua; it was too dangerous for North Americans then, in the late 1970s. Somoza's government was collapsing, and militants were everywhere. The place was in turmoil. Theroux flew over the country instead and landed in Costa Rica, where the cities were much safer, the whole country working in better tandem with the United States. And so I bury *The Old Patagonian Express* at the bottom of my pack, my passport and extra money tucked into its pages. It won't be the last time I leave him, but our paths will always cross in the end.

Granada's travelers are rugged. All they have to lose is what they can carry in the bulging pockets of their loose pants, the fabric heavy with weeks of dusty evenings: drawstrings sagging and knees patched over. Here, I no longer see sturdy zip-off pants that travelers buy before they visit the developing world, the ones they figure they'll need when they're tramping through fly-ridden streets or mosquito-infested jungles. The ones they wish they hadn't bought once they arrive, because when they do they see it immediately: these countries are just other places, with sidewalks and cafés and people who wake in the morning and put on the clothes they washed the night before and hung to dry. I brought those clothes, too: canvas pants that zipped, a heavy poncho, bug spray. In Antigua, I mailed them home, then shopped at the thrift store for a skirt and a tanktop, both of which I wear each day now, washing them in the sink and hanging them in the wind. With less stuff, I have discovered, I am more free.

Now, I walk up sidewalks tiled in red and white, pine and cream. I admire the pretty architecture: the detailed molding and bright, fresh paint on the pillars and sills. The massive Lake Nicaragua starts at the foot of Granada; in those waters freshwater sharks are rumored to live. The lake is dotted with three hundred and seventy islands, and in the rainy season a handful disappear. I can feel the wind off it now, faintly, easing up through the streets. I can smell the water in the air, droplets flung off the lake. The dappled wind and the lazy heat give the city an unperturbed, satisfied calm.

My hostel has a small, dark entryway and a large courtyard, four walls but no ceiling. There are hammocks tied unevenly to posts, and card tables, and people smoking and reading, and cups of instant coffee, the cream long curdled. One man whittles at a piece of wood with a knife; a long-haired girl sings while the boy beside her strums a guitar.

I think again that there is something raw to these travelers—their shaggy hair, their worn-out clothes, their piercings. There is bright-pink hair, and there are stiletto heels. There are arms inked in every color, stained with twisting naked women, Virgins de Guadalupe, roses, crosses, starry nights, and Nepali script. This crowd drains bottles of beer and counts their remaining cordobas, shelling out four or five dollars a night for the dorm-room bunks.

I begin to wonder whether the people here—the people who wake each morning to sell their fruit, to work in their *tiendas*, to go to their appointments, their universities, their families—roll their eyes when they see these tattooed tourists flitting through town, in and out, in and out. They have learned that some young tourists are rich people in disguise, parents or trust funds bankrolling their jaunt.

Or maybe they don't distinguish; to the locals, perhaps we're all the same. Deep down, part of me hopes that they snicker to each other while we drink our beers and take our pictures and make our quick assumptions, judging each other and comparing the bagginess of our pants. I hope they get a chuckle out of us, how naïve we travelers can be, as we bargain for the cheapest ride to the nearest beach, the nearest jungle—the next, best exhilarating place.

* * *

"Am I late?" Donna asks when she finally arrives, and she looks so concerned that I tell her no. She doesn't meet my eyes, not quite, but says that she cannot talk about one single thing until she has had her coffee, and so we sit quietly while we wait for it to come. She fidgets, looking around, touching her hair, the way a college professor of mine once had. Their thick white hair is the same—striking against unwrinkled skin, a dark mouth, black eyes. They share a scattered shyness, a way of talking in which stories spill out, disorganized, like they've long gone traveling and only today have returned.

Donna's been here since the nineties; the Peace Corps brought her to Central America. Our government brought her here, she says, and then left her. So much of her job in rural El Salvador was self-created: probing through neighborhoods and making fragile, tentative bonds with local families while looking for projects to take on. She built a cattle crossing, helped on a coffee farm, slowly wove herself into the fabric of the town in which she'd been assigned. She'd done what she could, and after two years, she went back to Pittsburgh, where she'd felt oddly homesick and perpetually chilled.

She's lived in this city going on twenty years. She knows nearly everything about its streets, its people, and its gossip. For example, she tells me that the café we're sitting in is owned by an old American man, a man who came here rich and then bought the café and got richer. He bought the most expensive property in town, a prime spot right across from the cathedral that tourists love to stroll past. This café has a long porch and a big dining room inside, and the waiters bustle around with pots of hot, thin coffee and plates of waffles.

"Granada is both dark and light," says Donna, draining her cup and then lifting it to signal for more. I can't be quite sure what she means.

Afterwards, we climb into Donna's beat-up truck and drive to the vet clinic she's opened. Two little boys run into the road.

"Little shits," Donna mutters, swerving to avoid them.

The clinic, from the outside, looks as rundown as this street's other houses, which crumble and crack into the dirt as we drive farther from the city's historic center. But on the inside, it's a clean place, where an old woman sits waiting, holding a small dog on her lap. There is no separate waiting room, and the doctor is examining a bigger dog on the table. Everyone greets Donna as if they've known her their whole life, as if she, too, was born and raised in this country. Donna shows me where the cats live, cats that once prowled the streets but were brought in, one by one, bleeding and bitten. Here, beneath the clinic's bright lights, they doze in their crates. They're clean and fat; bowls of food sit beside them. When we leave, the people in the clinic wave to both of us. It occurs to me that it's been so long since I saw pets, real pets and not just stray dogs and cats. Spending money on animals, I realize, is a one-percent hobby.

At the school, our next stop, the students range in age from three to fifteen; there are forty of them in total, divided into three groups. The school has three rooms, one of which has gone unused; the students are split between the large classroom inside and the patio. One teacher is a heavyset woman who smiles at us but cannot give her undivided attention, for her students are the littlest ones, and they fidget and knock things onto the floor the second she turns her head. There's a young male teacher who grins at us and then leans over the table where his students sit doing their math homework.

"You know a little Spanish, right?" Donna asks, and I nod. I hope she doesn't quiz me. "Then you can come by tomorrow," she says. "Nine o'clock." We leave the little school; Donna has to run. She has to bring a cat to the vet and another to her neighbor's, and then she has to pick up the boys. She doesn't take time to explain, but she shakes my hand and smiles encouragingly.

"You'll do great," she says, and leaves me in a cloud of dusty exhaust.

If the kids don't make it on time, the doors are locked and they're out of luck for the day. The students come to school in all manner of ways. Those who have taxi drivers for parents get rides with paying customers. Other parents perch their children on the backs of their motorbikes or on the handlebars of their bicycles. Kids come with their dogs in tow, or, sometimes, their cats. They arrive alone or with a trickle of siblings and friends. They show up with wet hair and clean clothes, except for a few who arrive in the same shirt each day, their skin and hair gray with dust.

One boy has the look of a vagrant: sun-bleached hair, torn clothes, a black eye, and no shoes. The teachers let him in with everyone else, and after classes I see him sitting on the steps of the crumbling cathedrals, begging. On those days, I try not to meet his eyes, until he sees me and waves, unembarrassed. Although he's older, he sits with the ten-year-olds, peering at his workbook. He is an earnest student, well-behaved if a little withdrawn.

I begin by working with the littlest kids. There is Orel, Ricardo, Stefanie, and Manuel. There is Angela and Jessica. And there is Carlos, who wears gel in his hair and shows up outside the school on his dad's motorcycle; neither of them wear helmets, and his young father smiles politely at me as we wait for the doors to be opened. Inside, I help Carlos form letters on the dotted notebook lines; we practice writing our names, this city's name, and our parents' names. We draw pictures of our pets and write what colors they are. I try, without much success, to understand the kids, who mumble and poke each other and tell me stories about their fathers, their pets, and the kids next to them. They don't seem to notice that I'm just nodding and smiling and pointing to their papers.

At the end of class, we usher the kids out and clean up the turned-over chairs, the scattered puzzle pieces, the forgotten notebooks.

There is a wall between the teachers and me, and I do my best to be respectful, to not overstep. Volunteering abroad is not work, I realize, it is school, and my journey is a lesson, not a project.

So each day, I ask the heavyset woman, Rosa, what she'd like me to do. I clean up messes and take kids to the bathroom. The teachers smile at me, thank me each day for coming, but after I leave, they stay, and before I arrive, they are there. I come, I go, and eventually, I will leave. All of us know this.

In the nights, I twist in my sheets in my rented room. Late at night and in the early morning is when I miss her most. She's saved up her money and she's taking a trip; we will meet in Managua in one month. The ache in her voice says she can hardly wait that long.

I turn over, listening to the sounds of the travelers outside my door: drinking and smoking, laughing and making music. I listen to the people in the private room next to mine. They're having sex, and their bed knocks against my walls, but otherwise they barely make a sound until the end.

On a hot Saturday morning in February, I follow Mitch out the hostel's front door and through town, where we change money from one of the men who stands with huge wads of cash outside the bank. It's a dangerous job, Donna told me. The men are called coyotes; some are young, with baggy pants and fake gold jewelry. These are coveted jobs, Donna said, inherited from grandfathers and great-grandfathers. One tall, dark-skinned man, always standing on the same corner, dresses in pressed pants and clean shirts. His hair is always combed, and his face is always freshly shaved. While the tall man counts our bills, an automatic door to the ATM slides open and closed. I pay Mitch five dollars, the cost of the tour, lunch included.

Mitch is riding his bike, keeping just ahead of me while I walk. We stop at another hostel to collect two Dutch women, who smile at me and carry one purse between them. They're dressed in bright tank tops, their bandanas indigo blue. Mitch is taking us to the Laguna de Apoyo, that deep crater lake north of the city. A woman is selling steaming coffee on the street, and I wonder how she'll make money today. I am sweating already, my sunblock running down my temples. The woman stoops to pour a cup for an old man leading a donkey. The man wears long sleeves and, like the neat-looking coyote on the corner and the women who sell blocks of cheese in the street, isn't sweating. None seem to ever perspire.

"You'll see the barrio," Mitch had said as a way of enticing us to take the tour. We meet our tour guides, Silvia and her niece, Margarita, at their home, which sits on a little mound on the side of a dirt road. Chickens with red heads scratch and cluck. Margarita wears jeweled studs in her ears and looks very young, with fine, long cheekbones, a bony nose, and thick black lashes. She is learning English in school, and practices with the Dutch girls, who speak the language impeccably. Silvia, in contrast, is short, with big, dark eyes, and she has dressed plainly. She's a mom of four, she tells me, speaking slowly so I understand.

We pass the graveyard—a stretch of low tombs, cement slabs, crosses, occasional flowers—and then we are flanked by dry fields of overgrown grass and shrubs and jaunty, munching cows. The buildings we pass have fold-up chairs in the front yards, broken cars, tiny gardens. We pass little *tiendas* that double as houses, whole families sitting outside in the shade of the awnings. One man is spraying a hose, washing his dog and his kid at the same time.

Eventually, Mitch turns his bike around and starts the ride back to Granada. He's done his job, and now he's going to go back to the hostel, back to sleep, because he didn't get to bed until five in the morning. He got lost in the party, he explained sleepily to us that morning, while dumping sugar into his coffee. Then we are descending again, steeper even than the walk up, and the path is a broken, overgrown cement road.

I ask Silvia about her four children, and she tells me about her three girls, the oldest twenty-one and married herself, with two children of her own. Silvia, who looks so young with her plain clothes and sweet smile, is a grandmother. Her husband joins us presently, coming up quietly from the jungle behind us. He walks behind Silvia, a huge machete in his hand. He doesn't speak at all, just crouches when we take breaks, his machete stuck point-first into the ground. Silvia tells me she is thirty-seven and her husband is four years older.

As we walk along a trail that once was a river, Silvia tells me that all of the houses on this road, including hers, just recently had running water installed. Before then, people hiked into Granada to buy bottles and hauled their wet laundry all the way back from the river in town. Now there is water every other day, and to prepare for the days when none runs, you save what you can in the *pila* or in barrels. Water costs seven dollars a month, much more than what a city worker here earns in a day. I remember the man washing his dog and kid. I think of the lake we're stumbling toward, a lake with water too salty to drink.

Silvia tells me that the lake is over two hundred meters deep. It's one of the cleanest lakes in Central America; through the water at the lake's edge, you can see how white the sand is, but then the floor drops off and all you see then is darkness. The Dutch girls pencil-dive down deep, and I watch their thin bodies disappear, white limbs into blackness. They rise, sputtering, and scream out that they couldn't touch bottom. Later, I will learn that the lake holds four species of fish found only here, and that boas and anteaters, howler monkeys and wild cats live in the surrounding forest. Silvia and Margarita don't swim, so the three of us sit in the sand and watch the water. It is cool here, and waves lap the shore.

"You're funny," Margarita says, watching the Dutch girls dive and resurface. She glances at the book I hold in my hands, the pile of cameras beside us, the backpacks and clothes tossed aside in the sand.

"I am funny?" I ask her.

"You all are," Margarita says, and she smiles before pulling the brim of her baseball cap down so I can't see her eyes. I want to ask her what she means, but can't find the Spanish words, or maybe I think that already I know. *You're funny,* she said. *You take off your clothes, wear bikinis of string; you have swum all your lives. You pay to do what we here do for free. You're surrounded by things, and you bask. You don't have a care.*

When I tell E—, she shudders.

"You shouldn't have gone that far out of town," she says.

* * *

My Spanish teacher, Ana, hints during classes that she could earn more if we worked together at my hostel instead of at the school. It is against the rules, but we begin to meet in the hostel's kitchen anyway, just outside my bedroom door. While tourists straggle in and out, the foreheads of recent arrivals beaded in sweat, I describe to Ana my day and my young students. She corrects my mistakes. She asks about my life before this. In return for each thing I divulge, she tells me something: she met her husband when she was seventeen, and he was her first. She believes that the tourists made this place better, but now they're making it worse. She gave birth to each of her three children in a room the size of this kitchen— she gestures at the hostel's walls, blackened with kitchen smoke—the size of this room but with forty other women, all screaming and begging for a doctor who rarely came around. There were no epidurals, and beside her, one woman died. Ana gave birth alone; no family was allowed in the ward. Now, she is six months pregnant and moves easily.

Ana is businesslike, never sentimental and even brusque sometimes when I don't understand. I overpay her, but she never says a word, just takes the bills without counting them and slips them into her purse. She told me once that of the five dollars per hour I was paying the school, she was earning one. Only in my last week of class does she tell me her age; she's twenty-three. And then we turn back to the lesson at hand: vocabulary of the environment. Leaves, grass, ocean, pond. Forest fire, recycling, global warming. Pollution, hurricane, drought.

My parents send an email one day in early March: the snow is falling onto the road and swirling in the woods, so deep their skis sink three feet.

"It's the best snow year we've had," my mom writes, and I try to imagine the quiet forest behind their home, the way light filters across the sparkling snow and through the branches of the bare maples and dark pines, the white birches with their cream-colored limbs. I imagine the hibernating daffodils, the sunken rocks and grass and lawn chairs, and deep snow over the place where we buried three pets. My father has been skiing for the last thirty consecutive days, making evenly-spaced tracks in the snow, and I know that as he goes he will pick up branches that the cold has broken from the spindliest birches. He will toss them to the side, out of the way. Snow will pile on the pine boughs, weighing them down but not snapping them. The air is so frigid at night that if you shut your eyes too long outside, you won't be able to open them, and when you breathe in deeply, you might hear your chest crack.

But in this heat it's so hard to remember the way a hard winter wind can feel, a wind that gains speed, funneling between buildings and rolling up the street, or racing across a snow-swept field, leaching right through your clothes into your bloodstream. Here, I'm sweating in the shade, my hair like a scarf against the skin of my neck. These trickling fountains, and the hot pavement beneath my feet. The distance from home seems to lengthen with each day I skip winter; each word I read, each time it rains, every moment thus converted to one more mile farther.

In her message, my mother gives the date that my grandmother is being moved to a nursing home. I think of the little river behind my grandmother's house, the Rose of Sharon that dropped magenta blooms onto the grass, and the way my grandmother's kitchen smelled, like bread and spring wind through the window. African violets on the sill. In the four months I've been gone, the house has gotten too big.

In less than a month, my mother writes, my brother and father will rent a truck and go to help. The plan is to move a few, familiar things—my grandmother's chair, some photographs, her dresser—into the room in the nursing home, so that she will be comforted. She is sad, my mother says. They'll bring some of her books, but there isn't room for all of them. The photographs of the grandchildren will go with her, but of course there will be no space for the canopy bed, the one that she's slept in for over half her life. There will be a new bed in the nursing home, one that sits up and folds down and comes with a button my grandmother can press when she needs help.

It's not so hard to see what my mother's not saying, which is that this will be the final move. The room in the nursing home, which gets such high ratings from the state and from my grandmother's doctor, will be the last home she knows. And when my parents pack her things into boxes, and wrap her framed photographs in newspaper, they will know that it will be the final time.

The sun is setting in Granada now, casting a copper-colored glaze over the cobblestone streets and the whitewashed walls of the colonial buildings. I pass my favorite Granada house: it's a two-story home without pillars or a gate with curving metalwork, but it's special because of its garden. If you're lucky and the owners have left their front door open, you can look in and see the plants they have: Bird-of-paradise, banana palm, and magenta bougainvillea creeping up the walls. I notice today that they've planted something else, some flower I don't recognize, with a tiny, furry orange bud. My grandmother would know it; she knew all the flowers. Primrose was her favorite.

As I turn from the house, it occurs to me that perhaps my grandmother is not so very far. Now, she resides in my mind, and if I stop and close my eyes, I can see her—not the way she is now, but the way she was years ago, moving about the garden. On the corner one block from my Nicaragua hostel, I close my eyes and go to her, and the dusty clamor of afternoon traffic falls away.

This is how, on the streets of a baking Granada, I find myself instead in a bread-smelling house, where outside the snow is falling. It is nighttime, but my grandmother's kitchen is warm. There are photographs of my family members on the walls, photographs older than the length of time my grandmother has been in this country. There is flowered wallpaper in the kitchen; there is baking soda in the bathroom for brushing your teeth. The African violets are still lined up over the kitchen sink, the leaves as soft as the strange little flower I saw in that Granada garden. And there is my grandmother, taking things from the kitchen cabinets and heating water on the stove.

Home, you are with me like a river. Long stretches pass when you come as a trickle, but without warning, you flood me sometimes. It takes but the tiniest thing—some smell in the wind, that color on the walls—to remind me you are here. You are my dreams, you are my eyes. You are my grandmother in the garden, so many years ago, and you are snowflakes that melt the instant they fall onto my hands.

LITTLE CORN ISLAND, NICARAGUA

A t four in the morning, the cab is waiting outside in the warm darkness, where stars still glimmer faintly in the sky. There is no one about, no street vendors this early, and the *pulperias* are all closed. We drive past the old, abandoned hospital with its long colonial pillars and its big empty windows that you can see right through. We pass the old train station, the immigration office, and then we're out on the unlit highway, where already people are standing by the side of the road. They're waiting with their baskets of vegetables, belts of tools, and sacks of grain for horse-drawn carts and micros, or pickups with guardrails and plastic-tarp roofs, to take them to their jobs in Masaya and Managua, jobs that might not end until the sky grows dark again.

In the night, I woke E— twice. I just couldn't believe she had come, that her work had brought her here. After so many months of aching, forgetting, ignoring, and aching again, I can't sleep. She is my lover, a part of my other life and now a part of this life, too. I couldn't let my eyes close, she so unfamiliar yet exactly the same. I traced her yucca tattoo. The dark hours passed. I couldn't stop touching her skin—it was like I had forgotten about touch, and now I was remembering it again. Everyone needs touch.

In the cab, I hold E—'s hand and let her doze on my shoulder.

"The driver won't notice," I whisper to her.

On the plane from Managua to Big Corn Island, I look down and can see that the landscape below us grows rapidly greener, less populated by homes and more clustered with wetlands, less marked by the prehistoric rises and falls in the terra-cotta land and more defined by the snaking river that widens beneath us and leads to the sea. We fly over Bluefields, over the long, even strip of coast, and then the Caribbean sea is beneath us.

From the small, windblown airport of Big Corn, a dreadlocked cabbie drives us along the coast, past tiny white beaches and gem-colored *pulperias* to the lazy dock. The ride costs us each one dollar. The boats docked here have misspelled English names painted in white on their sides: Sily Liza, Prinncess Lucia. They bob beneath the cloud-smeared sky, lobster boats strewn with wooden crates and rowboats rusted and anchored down. We eat eggs and *gallo pinto* and thick slices of white, flaky coconut bread in a seaside café. We sip from white mugs of instant coffee. We wait for the boat to come, and when it does we ride, bouncing, over the waves with twenty other tourists. We wear lifejackets, bulky orange things, but the boat driver's chest is bare and brown and his hair whips around his eyes. Little Corn comes into view, and then we spot the strip of beach, the coconut palms, the few bright boats that dapple red and sunflower gold onto the water.

We check into a little hotel by the docks and dump our packs out onto the knobby bedspread, selecting swimsuits and sunscreen. We take a little path that serves as the island's main road; there aren't any cars here. Little Corn has a population of only 700, but it seems like even less. We pass a handful of hotels and dive shops and a few beachside restaurants and that's it. That's the town. In the jungle, there are squat coconut palms and mangroves, grasses with sharp edges, and in this thicket the leaves squeeze the wind out and press the heat in. Patches of humidity steal our breath. We walk and walk, passing little huts with walls of scrap metal and an old abandoned well, and then the path turns to sand and we are on the other side of the island, on the beach. The white sand is littered with dried-out gray branches of palms and washed up strips of torn seaweed.

There's no one around, so I take her hand.

At night we share a fried fish, cooked as caught; we pull the flimsy skin up and suck the meat from the delicate skeleton, avoiding the fish's dead, open eyes. We draw ghost-thin bones from our mouths, and when we've drained our beers and paid our bill we go back to the hotel, lock the door, close the blinds, and take off our clothes. We notice that already the sun has drawn lines on our skin, and our shoulders and noses have grown red. I smooth lotion onto her back.

So many nights, I went to sleep craving her. Tonight we throw our clothes onto the floor; I kiss her mouth, her hands, her neck. I turn her head and kiss her ear. I let her bring my body to that place it can only go with her, and I think that I can feel her everywhere. I think, as I run my hands through her hair, as the rain begins to pound on the roof, as her body moves over mine, that I have never felt so full, so loved, as on this night.

The next day, we strap on rented goggles and fins and wade backwards into the sea. Sun glints onto the pale ocean floor, and tiny fish, gold and indigo, flicker in and out of the reeds. We spot a school of a dozen silver carp; they flicker past us like a wall, like a sheet, and then disappear into clouds of sand.

The sense of smell is the one most linked to memory. It is always the sense I imagined I would be most willing to lose, if I were ever forced to give up one of the five. But now, ever since E— left and went home to freezing Boston, I search for the scent of her in every gust of wind that comes my way. I close my eyes, inhale, try to conjure her along with that salty breeze off the sea, the musk of our beachside bed. The syrup they served with our breakfasts, and the fleeting, soaking rains. There weren't any cars on Corn Island, and I wonder who is in our hotel room now. I wonder if I will sleep through the night tonight, or if I will wake up and search my empty room for her.

In a tiny gallery on a Granada street, she said, "Let's get a place together when you come home. A two-bedroom, so you can have a studio." I squeezed her hand. I thought she meant: *I am going to wait for you.*

Days weave into weeks, and I call her at six every night. Her tan fades and her eyes look black against her skin on my grainy screen. I forget the exact texture of her skin. In my dreams, I long for the reassurance of coconut wind, or else those sprawling empty beaches strewn with palms.

SPRING

The bog-dark land smelled of mud and rain; the passengers slept or stood silently rocking in the aisle. The darkness was pure and serene. I thought: *I am alive.*

—Paul Theroux, *The Old Patagonian Express*

QUITO, ECUADOR

I n Quito, you must use a key to lock your room. You must use a key to unlock the front door, and you must slam it closed behind you, or else it won't shut. The people who run this volunteer house say these streets aren't safe at night, and so you must keep your key close to you. "Keep it in here," the woman says, the one who lives downstairs in the lavender room. She gestures to the space between her breasts.

You must not carry your camera, your laptop, or your backpack, which you never thought of as fancy. They call it *fancy* here. Instead, your Guatemalan *costal*, the one with the lettering long faded and the straps worn thin, is best for shopping and toting. You must carry your umbrella all the time, the umbrella you found at the drugstore on the corner, because this place will always be on the brink of rain, or else drizzling, or else, like it is now, pouring.

If you take a left out of the volunteer house, you'll come to a street with *tiendas* and bars and restaurants with pictures advertising grilled beef and tall glasses of beer. Gnarled trees grow out of the pavement, people shuffle past without looking at you, and homes with bars across the doors glare at you. These buildings are pink, they are red, they are orange, they are green; it's like this street is trying to preserve the little sunshine it receives in the colors of its walls. This street is narrow, busy, dirty. This street is beautiful.

If you walk and walk, you'll pass sprawling restaurants with tables set up outside, and everywhere the streetlamps will reflect the puddles of rain on the pavement. You'll pass whitewashed buildings, gates around gardens. You'll pass boutique hotels, lines of waiting buses, a post office, and a bookstore, door propped open so you can see the shelves within. There's a dancing school, door open again; the girl closest to it is a few steps behind everyone else. The music follows you down the street.

Gone is the Granada heat. Gone are those long, flat Nicaraguan roads and those wide, blank stretches of dry Central American plain. The burned-out grass, the broken trees, the long spells without rain, during which the sky grew swollen and puckered above your head, or else the clouds just split apart from each other, forming wispy trails before voiding the sky of water completely. How is it that just days ago I was sweating, dying for a breeze, begging for a drop? How is it that I thirsted so? Sounds ring off the mountains here, and it takes a few days to believe, to really know, that they're the Andes. How is it that the people look so different? How is it that one plane ride, an hour long, can take a person so far?

Ecuador, tucked against the coast between Colombia and Peru, boasts more ecodiversity than any other country. From Quito, a traveler could visit the Galapagos Islands, the snow-capped Andes, and the screeching jungle without ever leaving the country. "In Ecuador," Lonely Planet claims, "you can change your world as fast as you can change your mind." Ultimately, Ecuador will teach me that this statement is both true and false. The country is not the hop, skip, and jump the guidebook touts, though it's unlike any place I've seen on my journey so far.

Quito, to begin, feels more European than the Central American capitals. I still see rambling markets, slums under bridges, and pirated DVDs on every corner, but there are also colonial moldings on the street corners and curved roofs, skyscrapers and the Andes in the distance. And in 2002, the president at the time, Gustavo Noboa, officiated dollarization, so it's back to US dollars again for me. Strange, to pass over one dollar, two, to the cab driver, the grocer, and the baker. Here, I'll learn to save every penny, for a penny in Ecuador buys a piece of candy on the street. I learn to revere the Sacagawea coin, ubiquitous here but seldom seen in the States, where coins are more a hassle than a necessity. The dollar isn't such a comfort to the Ecuadoreans, who saw the prices of everything from taxi rides to gas to lunch skyrocket, everything suddenly rounded up. What once was cost sixty cents was now officially a dollar. It's been over ten years since the shift, and Ecuador to me feels settled, established, and enormous. Yet it's plagued by many problems, both fueled by and despite its environmental wonders, its natural riches, and its human diversity: the country's extreme poverty is impossible for gated neighborhoods and uniformed security guards to conceal from me for long.

Carlos, the Ecuadorian who lives in the room across from mine, knows all the places: where to buy boxes of wine for $2.50, where to hear the concerts in the mountains during the full moon, where to bargain for the nicest leather. He is kind to me on my first day at the volunteer house, looking up sympathetically from the kitchen table as I stumble from my room in the morning, unsure of where to find the bathroom. Wordlessly, he points, and when I emerge he has coffee ready, milk and sugar on the table. He passes me a spoon, a cup, and his eyes are dark and laughing. On this first morning, he tells me about himself. He is twenty-seven years old, a student of philosophy, not very good at English but interested in learning. He scrambles eggs, eight or ten of them, and flips bacon in the skillet. He slices thick pieces of cheese and sets plates before us. He eats ravenously, stopping only to close his eyes, kiss the air, and say *riquísimo*.

On Friday night, Quito's busiest, Carlos invites me to dinner. I hesitate. "It will be casual," he says, and I think of E—. I can still bring the coconuts to my mind, if I close my eyes and wish for them. I can still conjure her skin, can still hear her voice through the computer screen, but it is as if the miles I've flown have brought me much farther from her. It's cold here, but spring is breaking open in Boston now. Lately, people have invited her to have beers at outdoor cafés, and I imagine her in a chair on the sidewalk, smoking, sipping from a tall glass of red beer, the leaves on the trees just beginning to bud.

"It's just a short walk," Carlos says. "It just costs two-fifty." So I take coins from the top drawer in the bureau of my rented room. It's early, the sky still light, and I follow Carlos out the front door.

In the street, we hug our jackets to us, and Carlos wears a black wool cap. Though we can see our breath, everyone is out, smoking, strolling, or kissing. The girls wear impossibly high heels and short skirts and stockings. I've never seen the square so busy, people perching on their motos, passing bottles back and forth, dancing to the music that thumps from the clubs.

The streets of this district, the touristy Mariscal, are lined with restaurants: colorful, hip-looking places with menus outside in both English and Spanish. But we walk past those, and I follow Carlos through a little door into a crammed room. The restaurant has no sign. There's a fluorescent bulb hanging from the ceiling, plastic cloths on the tables, and barely enough room to enter. There's no music, just a low chatter and the sound of forks against plates.

"It's crowded because it's good," Carlos assures me. When I ask him later what the place is called, he tells me there's no name.

There aren't any free tables, but three guys in the corner make room at theirs, cramming onto one bench so we can take the other side. I think about long waits in restaurants at home, half an hour standing outside some busy place waiting to eat. Would I mind if sharing a table was a rule, not an exception? The three boys talk quietly together as they eat, and when they're done, they stack their plates and get up to leave and a couple immediately takes their place. These two have fair skin and light hair, and they're both wearing leather jackets. They look windblown, and they hold their moto helmets on their laps.

Carlos orders: pork, beans, plantains, juice. I ask for a Coke, but Carlos shakes his head. "The juice," he says again. A man strolls into the restaurant with a guitar; he makes his way up and down among the tables, weaving around the busy waiters, the bussers, and the people who are standing, waiting for seats to open up. Carlos sings along. An enormous black man sets before us huge plates spilling over with pinto beans in their own sauce; rice flavored with parsley and pepper; soft, yellow slices of plantain; and long cuts of pork. We eat without speaking. The juices arrive: flimsy plastic cups full of blended fruit, so fresh and lightly sweetened, perfect with the meat. I eat everything, and as soon as our plates are clean there are people nudging us off our bench to take our place.

We pay our bill—two-fifty, as Carlos promised—and then step back out into the crowded night. We crane our necks to look up into the sky, but we can no longer see the moon or the glinting stars. The city's lights seem brighter now that the clouds have moved in, and the street feels much warmer now.

Back at the volunteer house, I try calling E—, so I can tell her about the meal, about Carlos, about the bikers who sat next to us. She doesn't answer the call. I change into pajamas and climb into my chilly, empty bed, and I think about her: what she might have eaten for dinner, what she might be doing now. It's spring in Boston, and I know she's grateful for the long, warm days. I imagine her at an outdoor café, the sun long set, a glass of beer leaving a damp circle on the table. I imagine her hands on the glass and the beer in her mouth. I imagine Corn Island, her body wrapped around mine, sand in the sheets, and the ocean, so wild and close. I marvel that we were there together weeks ago; it already feels like so much time has passed.

* * *

I enroll in Spanish classes; the school also coordinates volunteer opportunities, and helped me to arrange my room in the volunteer house. My teacher, Patricia, is a long-faced woman who shakes her head when I tell her I've been placed in San Roque to volunteer. "Get in and get out," she advises. There is a sadness in her wide brown eyes and in her skin, which is tinged with blue. Her hair also looks bluish beneath the bright classroom lights, and her hands are bony, the fingers long and intelligent. I wonder whether the rain has made her this way; she watches it stream down the window as I recite verbs and repeat new words. "Get in and get out," she reminds me at the close of our lesson. "Be careful up there."

One of the teachers at the volunteer-school takes me to San Roque the first time, showing me how to use the bus, and introducing me to the principal, a heavy, bald man in a suit who checks his cell phone constantly and hesitates when I hold out my hand for him to shake. That night, I slip into loose, broken dreams, remembering the school's tall brick exterior, dirty walls and a smashed light bulb in the stairwell, glittering shards scattered on the floor. I dream of the children who touched my clothes, held each other's hands, and watched me, speaking so quickly and softly in Spanish. I understood nothing. The rain outside wakes me up, and for the rest of the night I don't sleep, my heart beating, my mind imagining, spinning, creating, worrying. This will be nothing like the Granada school, where I sauntered a few sunny blocks and then sat and colored. There's no need for my alarm when it sounds, and I silence it instantly, not wanting to wake the blonde-haired German man who sleeps next door and wakes each morning at eight, eats eggs and bread, and leaves to go work at an Internet startup in the center of town.

I board the bus off the rainy street and pay with exact change. There are many empty seats, but the bus soon fills, then crams, making its slow steamy way up and down the narrow streets, into the brand-new roundabout, where it sits in a long line of buses, waiting to merge. Meanwhile, women come on selling coffee, and men offer donuts in plastic bags for sale. A little boy comes on selling apples. The bus creeps onto the main artery and we enter a series of tunnels, each long and dripping. The passengers sit blinking in the darkness, and in this way, we finally reach San Roque. The market stretches far up the hill with its plantains in rows, its baskets of gum and cigarettes, its hawkers selling plastic sacks of thin, fried potatoes. At the school's front gate, an old man with a cooler of ice-cream pops stands just outside, his clothes faded and dirty, his back hunched. He passes the pops through the bars to the schoolchildren, who hand him coins in return.

The schoolyard is full of children playing at the swing set or standing in groups eating candy they buy from a woman with a little stand at one corner. The sky is thick and gray, and traffic clots the road. I remember where the principal told me to go: up the stairs, to the right, down the hall, where the littlest ones are. I go there now, while children in the halls step aside for me and giggle.

In a yellow room at the back of the building, two dozen little children sit at long, low tables waiting for their breakfast. I forget, all of a sudden, to feel scared, surrounded by all this strangeness and broken glass. They hold their hands out to touch me; they stare up at me with open faces. The women who work here wear aprons and hairnets and smile greetings at me. One tells me to go into the kitchen and help with the porridge, and I bring plastic bowls of it out to the children, who eat loudly and messily. After breakfast, my job includes herding the children to the bathrooms with their slippery stone floors. The stalls have no doors; the trough-sink is always gushing, the children's sleeves perpetually wet. We guide them into classrooms and I sit with the one-year-olds and a young pregnant woman, who shows me where they keep diapers and toys and extra sets of clothes. The children alternately wail, shriek, hit each other, and smile. Finally, we feed them their lunch and then take out mats and the children lie down, squirming and giggling but eventually sleeping. The pregnant woman thanks me and sends me home; I'm ravenous and exhausted.

I ride the bus home, staring out the window as we pass the long stretch of public gardens, the universities, the grocery stores, the other buses, the tourists. I look at my hands, smeared with paint, and my sleeves, which are still wet. I wonder why the tourists outside my window carry their cameras like that, looped around their necks like some kind of prize.

"You did it," E— says later, when I finally manage to catch her on the phone. She sounds breathy, like she just ran in. "You made it there and back," she says, and I can hear her smile, which arrives like a gift over the line.

I get to know the handsome man who works at the Sabe Rico *tienda* next door; most days, he is sitting behind the counter, his girlfriend on his lap. Both are texting on their cell phones. There are junkies leaning against the graffiti outside and smoking cigarettes. They wear puffy down jackets and have thin faces and stringy hair, and usually, they're either talking loudly or sleeping. There are hippies who lay their jewelry—macramé bracelets and silver cuffs set with stones they found in Nicaragua and Peru—on blankets on the sidewalk. The pale, dark-haired hippies sit, cross-legged and barefoot, weaving their threads, not glancing at passersby.

One afternoon, walking home from the park, two white-haired men in black suits stumble, a little drunk, in front of me. The taller one has his arm around his friend's shoulders, and as I pass them one says, "Buenas días, senorita." I walk past a little faster. "Buenas," I mumble, knowing that if they were younger, I wouldn't say a word. I hear one of them inhale sharply. "Que bonita," he murmurs, the words slow and clear. The other one cackles, and I want to laugh too. How smooth he managed to sound, and how young.

Couples stroll past, or women in suits on their lunch breaks, or groups of guys in skinny jeans and black t-shirts with gel in their hair. The man I saw this morning at the Café Amazonas is still sitting with the dark-haired woman, a large bottle of beer and glasses before them on the table, both of them in leather jackets. They are still smoking cigarettes from the pack of Marlboro Lights on the extra chair. They've gotten sunburned, even beneath the umbrella. They lean back in their chairs without speaking, their eyes concealed by sunglasses, their cigarettes balanced over the ashtray.

The woman by the Banco Central is still crouched against the building selling nail clippers and combs and tubes of lipstick and lollipops, cigarettes and gum and unrefrigerated bottles of water. She is here every day. She has laid all of these things out in even rows on a blanket. She wears a black wraparound skirt, a white blouse, a navy shawl, and a folded cloth on her head. Around her neck, she's looped dozens of strands of tiny fake gold beads, and she wears gold studs in her ears. Her wrinkles cut deep lines into her face, puckering her mouth and eyes. She doesn't glance up at me when I pass.

At the edge of the Patria Park, the shoe shiner is shining the newspaper vendor's shoes. They sit there in their respective seats, the shiner crouched and working efficiently, while they quarrel. A woman is selling sunglasses from a rack that must hold two hundred pairs. A man with slicked-back hair in a gray suit eyes me unkindly as we cross the street. We run a little to make plenty of room for the bus, which careens toward us with the names of its many destinations plastered to its windshield. As it passes, I watch the *ayudante*, who stands in the open doorway, clinging to the bar with one hand as he flies past, his blue tie flapping, his mouth open and ready to shout. In the grass, a man in a camouflaged army uniform sits with a young woman and a small child. The child stands, wobbles, sits back down, then stands again, and each time the man and woman laugh. Lovers tug at each other's hands, kiss in the grass or against one of the park's many sculptures, or shove and then embrace each other flirtatiously.

The artists aren't here today, the ones that line up their canvases on weekends and sunny days and then lean against their cars and smoke pipes and chat with each other, one eye always on their paintings. Most of the painters aren't that good, but a few, to me, are brilliant.

* * *

This is how the unraveling begins: a missed call here, an unanswered email there. Life is picking up for E— just as it seems to be slowing down for me: a quiet routine, early mornings and nights, the loneliness of a big city.

Meanwhile, E—'s schedule fills: a party, martinis after work, a weekend in Montauk at the vacation home of a well-to-do friend. I hear all about it afterwards: catering from a seafood joint down the road, and a long afternoon of rain, which everyone filled by drinking wine and playing cards. "I missed you there," E— says, but I don't hear longing in her voice, none of the honey that used to wash over the words she said to me. A storm begins outside, and rain begins to stream down the windowpanes of my rented room. These days, E— is always rushing off—to work, to dinner, to the gym. She goes to a fitness class now that she'd always refused to go to with me.

"Why?" I ask, but she says she doesn't know. "It's just easier without you there," she explains, and I know she doesn't mean to hurt me. Still, when the call ends, I weep, then blame my tears on loneliness, on the rain.

* * *

After a few weeks in Quito, the aching in my legs is gone, that pain that came from days and days of no rain, temperatures above ninety degrees, and long, hot nights with the fan whirring over me. Here, I close my curtains to the gloom in the night and sleep fully and long under blankets, just the way I did as a child growing up in a cold place. Seamlessly, I have exchanged my skirts and sandals of Central America for the clothes that are most familiar to me: heavy socks, long pants, fleece jackets, thermal underwear. The rain is still winter rain, cold and hard, falling for hours sometimes. I hide my money beneath my underwear in the drawer, and when I leave my room, I put my laptop there, too. "You never know," the woman downstairs warned me. In the streets, some nights, I hear the crack of a gun. Still, somewhere in this foreign place, within my foreign life, I've found a little bit of home.

And I've found a bit of every place I've ever been. Here, surrounded by the Andes, I am reminded of other mountain-cupped places I've seen: Hong Kong, Christchurch, and Montpelier, Vermont. But it isn't just here. There were the Costa Rican trails that were, somehow, just like the Adirondack trails I grew up with; the Nicaraguan beach could be a beach I found in India or Massachusetts. Once you visit a place, I have discovered, you will find it a thousand times again. If you keep it in your mind, you will recognize it in every place you visit: something about the buildings, the color of the mountains, or the music in the streets. You will feel it in the wind; you will hear it in the songs. I am alone in my rented room, and in the language in which I dream. My lover is pulling away, and there's no way to touch her from here. It's shocking how quickly things can change.

But every time I leave the house, I discover again: If I'm looking for something to recognize, I'll find it everywhere.

* * *

On my third morning at the daycare, a short, stocky woman called Elena hands me an apron and hairnet grudgingly, as if I'd proven myself by returning. The women have taught me not to let a child doze at mealtimes, but to stand him up on the table and let him wobble there, unsteadily, until he agrees to eat the remainder of his lunch. "Food is never to be wasted," Elena tells me, shaking her head sternly at a two-year-old boy whose brown eyes are filled with tears. His mouth is a rosebud. But the women have taught me not to coo over the children; instead, my job is to make certain they eat. Children who throw food on the floor must pick it up and eat it. Children who refuse to open their mouths for another bite are practically force-fed. Occasionally, children are permitted to share, but the older ones know to gobble down everything they're given. Only the youngest fuss and turn their heads, sealing their lips shut.

Even the babies are potty-trained. There's just one little girl who can't get to the toilet on time, and she spends much of the day huddled in a corner, sucking her thumb, sitting in her wet pants until someone notices. When I change her diaper, she keeps her eyes open, staring at me like she knows something I don't. Like I've never seen what she has. I forget about everything else at the daycare: my mom, my cat, my rented room, my fitful lover. I move this child's legs carefully, making sure the diaper's not too tight, making sure her clothes are tucked in right and her socks match.

This city is surrounded by hills, but the main roads run straight, north and south through the valley. I walk through the smoke of exhaust, then veer east, up the steep hills. The houses grow more elegant, their grassy yards and scented gardens protected with electric fences. I turn around to look down at the city, thinking that I'd like a house here.

Carlos said it was possible, that most houses, even the beautiful ones, were affordable for Americans.

"No one wants to live in Quito," he'd said with a laugh.

I wind through tiny barrios where women hang laundry and dogs bark lazily, until I come to the place where Ecuadorian painter Oswaldo Guayasamin made his home. I find my way by asking directions, then asking again, now from a young child with a dog yipping alongside him, now from an old woman who pours water out onto the street.

The house is surrounded by creaking eucalyptus trees. Orange cats slink along the property's outskirts, and the house itself has an abandoned quality, the garden tilled but unplanted, the tiled floors inside filmed in a fine layer of dust. Guayasamin's house is built of geometrical shapes, cones and eggs, rounded pillars, triangles accenting the windows. Only a few guards stand around, sipping coffee from paper cups; the tourists haven't yet arrived. A swimming pool, drained, overlooks the smogged city. There is an air of champagne-filled parties long past, of indulgence grown over by time and washed by rain. I am not allowed inside the house, but seeing the cool lines of the place is enough, and I am transported.

Before he died in 2002, Guayasamin built beside his house the Chapel of Man, a square monument of dark, thick brick, with massive rooms inside and reproductions of his paintings leaning against the walls in the courtyard. In the center of the monument, a fire always burns. Guayasamin painted the faces of revolutionaries, the weeping portraits of rape survivors and mothers who lost their children, the bleeding limbs of those killed in war, and the shadowed faces of the Disappeared. On this dark day, the paintings, with their gilded labels, evoke suffering from Guatemala to Argentina. I recognize Rigoberta Menchú's almond-shaped eyes, her accented cheekbones, the notes of crimson and azure in her skin and hair.

In the courtyard, there's a large diptych of linen posters. Guayasamin's words have been printed in Spanish, with an English translation in smaller font. I stand beneath the clouds, which are just now starting to ease out drops of rain, and I read his message:

> For the children that death took while playing, for the men that weaken while working, for the poor that fail while loving, I will paint with the gun scream.

* * *

Fanesca is Quito's Easter dish: a thick, creamy, yellow-brown soup bolstered by twelve different grains, dried fish, fried plantains, and various vegetables. It's a soup that fills you up after just one bowl, and it represents at once the twelve apostles, the plentiful fish that Jesus provided to the people when they were starving, and the absence of meat during Lent. Beginning on Monday, cafés tack "Hoy Fanesca" signs out front. Even the babies at the daycare smell of fish. Old women in the street peer at the curling, cracking fishtails and bargain in voices like crows', while the vendors, young men with cell phones tucked in back pockets, weigh out the choices.

There's no class on Good Friday, and when I wake, the street below is strangely silent. Carlos scrambles half a dozen eggs and eats them while I sip coffee and nibble on the farmer's cheese he manages to find; it is both sweeter and saltier than any cheese I can find in San Roque. He is hung over, he admits, but all he needs are a few eggs, and he will be ready. He drinks juice from the carton, smacks his lips, and reaches over for my cup of coffee and drains it.

"Better," he says, leaning back in his chair and closing his eyes.

We catch the trolley going downtown, and I notice again how subdued it feels, how orderly the traffic seems beneath the gray swath of sky. Carlos tells me that most people pack their weekend bags and head to the coast or their farms in the Oriente, Ecuador's jungled eastern region, for some time away from Quito's gray pavement and dark skies. Just as he says this, patches of sun begin to fall onto the empty sidewalks and against the bars of the closed *tiendas*. Carlos smiles with thin lips and draws a toothpick from his pocket.

The buildings get taller and narrower the closer you get to the center; they begin to show delicate molding, long French windows, colonial lines. The sidewalks get tighter, winding around corners and up hills, squeezed against the cobblestone roads. And the streets are beginning to fill; now there are women with long slices of plantain on grill carts, and a man with bunches of colored shoelaces looped around his neck and arms and open hands. Carlos and I get off at the Plaza Grande, and as soon as we turn off Diez de Agosto, toward the Iglesia San Francisco, we meet the crowds.

Carlos tells me that some people got here as early as two in the morning to get the best places. If I stand on my tiptoes I can see the people in their purple robes, the bare-chested men with crowns of thorns, the veiled Veronicas—all waiting to start their procession. Waiting to inch through the streets, slow like the buses in rain. Waiting to show Jesus how much they really love him and how much they remember of his life. Waiting and hoping he'll see them rejoicing there. We move along the crowded streets, searching for a vacant sliver of sidewalk. We wait with the other patient waiters, who buy gum and candy from the ladies who pass by, who fiddle with their umbrellas beneath the patchy sunshine, who take pictures of each other with their cell phone cameras, or who sit quietly, their hands in their laps. I think of E— and how she might love to see this street, this scene. I'll call her tonight, I vow, and then I allow myself to think of her hair, her hands. Maybe this whole thing, this strange distance I don't understand—maybe it's just a bump in the road. On such a warm and perfect day, it seems suddenly inconceivable, even a little bit laughable, that E— could have changed her mind about me.

A hush comes just then and settles upon the crowd like rain, and then a marching band's bright tune erupts, and now I can just make out the procession plodding toward us. For all the excitement, this is a solemn parade. No one shouts; no child shrieks; no hands clap. No one sings. First I see the tops of cone-shaped hats, enormous wooden crosses, and I realize finally that this Easter will not be like any I've ever seen. There are no white dresses, no Easter eggs, no brief church service followed by brunch. Beneath a gray-plumed sky, the men proceed first, not marching or even walking but dragging themselves beneath the weight of homemade crosses. Whole families pace solemnly alongside one cross, and while the father or oldest brother shoulders it at its crux, the mother and children help by lifting it a little, or by purchasing water from the women who sell bottles in coolers. The biggest crosses must weigh hundreds of pounds and extend three meters long; these require their bearers to shuffle quickly, then stop and rest, then hustle the cross a few more yards. Barefoot men with chains around their bare feet pass, shirtless, barbed wire twisted around their bellies so that you can see the blood where the sharp knots pierce. Thorny crowns, real tears of blood. People are weeping, an old man shuffling past is urinating, and the marching bands are playing. The women who stand pressed against us on the sidewalk clutch handfuls of rose petals, which they toss toward the walkers. Everywhere, there are colored posters of Christ, and gilt-framed portraits of the radiant Virgin, smiling demurely onto us all.

After the cross bearers come the Veronicas, women in purple veils and purple gowns who pass in lines, their heads bowed, their hair braided, their hands clasped. Behind them come the statues; first the baby Jesus, then the Virgin Mary, and finally—surrounded by dozens of police and an eerily quiet crowd of onlookers, followers and devotees—Jesus on the cross. Each statue, mounted on a covered cart that rolls solemnly past, is adorned with roses, bunches of red and pink ones for the Virgin, all-white ones for Christ. And then the official parade ends, the onlookers all fall in behind Jesus, and this new, informal procession swells like a river in rain. I hold on to the back of Carlos' jacket so I won't lose him in the crowd.

If you return to the old center the day after the procession, you'll find rose petals tucked in between the cobblestones and pressed up against the sidewalks, folded into the cracks between doors and walls and caught in the branches of trees. The streets will seem so empty without the sounds and the press of Quito's devout. You'll hear the wind as it tosses itself up and down the road, but all that remains of yesterday's procession are these rose petals on the ground: white and pink and crimson flecks, markers of that tragic and euphoric day.

* * *

The school principal in San Roque informs me on Monday that I'll be giving English lessons now to the fifth-, sixth-, and seventh-graders. He has come into the daycare, where the children stare at him wide-eyed, and he waits and taps at his cell phone while I hug them goodbye, then kiss Elena's cheek and thank her. The children are not sad to see me go, although they return my embraces and kiss me. *They are used to people coming and going*, I think, and when I turn to look back at them from the doorway, I see they're engaged in their breakfast again, Elena wiping up milk and scolding a boy who grins wickedly, the overturned cup rolling away from him and off the table.

In the classrooms, desks are arranged in orderly lines and the students wear uniforms, blue V-necked sweaters, and navy slacks for the boys, skirts with knee-length socks for the girls. About half of the students wear the complete uniform; many of the girls wear the sweater but have forgone the skirt and socks for sandals and long, plain-colored *cortes*. The principal introduces me to three groups of students in three chilly, high-ceilinged rooms; each time, when I say hello in English, they reply enthusiastically and in unison.

In the second classroom, I ask the kids how they are doing. "How are you doing?" they parrot. The third classroom consists of twenty seventh-graders; though they're just a year or two older than the others, they look like little adults. Almost all the girls wear the long *corte* in black, and most knit or sew as the principal introduces me in hasty Spanish. The seventh-grade teacher is a young, handsome man with light skin, very dark hair, and eyes that strike me instantly as warm and kind. He comes to the front of the room and shakes my hand. "I'm very happy you're here," he says in English, while the principal and the students blink at us, not understanding.

In the days that follow, I print out Googled lesson plans at the cyber-café on the corner, and I try to think back on what Linda first taught me. I decide how to teach basic verbs: to be, to go, to know. Mostly, though, for all my planning, only the seventh-graders sit quietly in their seats, taking notes and answering questions, presenting to me the lines of translation they've done for homework. The fifth-graders have the principal as their teacher, and he leaves the room as soon as I enter to go talk on his cell phone. He's already punching in numbers before he's even out the door. His students sit straight as ramrods until he leaves the room, and then as soon as the door clicks shut, they are bouncing, talking, laughing, whispering, passing notes, throwing things—spitballs, I discover, something I've only read about and never seen, not even in middle school myself.

On this first hectic day, paperclips whiz past my head and pencils roll toward me on the floor. A rubber band hits the board, and then another. I ask the kids their names; they shake their heads. I glance at my watch and will the time to pass faster, the children to pay attention, the principal to end his phone call and return to the classroom to restore order.

A spitball lands near my feet. *Enough*, I say to myself. I turn from where I write on the board—*I am, you are, he is, they are*—and I point to a spitball on the ground. I imagine my face turning red, or maybe it's gone white, but all of a sudden, the room is silent. The air thickens, and the kids blink at me, waiting to see what I'll do.

"No," I say simply, loudly. I can hear that I sound stern. My voice has an effect. I shake my head emphatically, my index finger still pointing to the spitball.

"No more," I say, slicing the air with my hands. "Okay?" I ask, but no one moves or makes a peep.

"Okay?" I ask again, for *okay* is the most universal of words. Finally, the children look at each other, then at me, and slowly nod their heads.

One of the bigger boys in the back leans toward his friend to whisper something, and the other boy cackles.

"Hey!" I shout at the two boys. "Enough!" I am saying the words in English, but the two boys sit quietly. The bigger one's ears redden. The other students bow their heads toward their papers, suddenly interested in taking notes.

But the two boys in back still mutter to each other, and I go back in my mind, moving through the teachers I've had like they're cards in a Rolodex. Mrs. Varney, I remember, was consistently the most frightening, but the others, even sweet Mrs. Kelly with her rose-colored sweaters and pale lipstick, could boil with anger. What did they do to scare us into behaving? I close my eyes briefly, sending myself to those classrooms, which smelled nearly identical to this one.

"What's your name?" I ask the big boy in back, the one who started it. The other students continue to copy what I've written on the board, keeping their heads down, but the big boy looks at me blankly, not understanding.

"I only speak Spanish," he says in Spanish.

"What's your name?" I say again, more slowly. "Cuál es tu nombre," a small boy whispers fast. "Raul," the big boy mutters, glancing at the small boy, who covers his paper with his hand.

Raul, I write on the board. "And what is your name?" I ask the boy beside him, and then write *Miguel* on the board below *Raul*. I look sternly at the two boys, point to their names, and then continue with the lesson. There aren't any problems after that.

The sixth-graders are a welcome sight, sitting comfortably in small groups while their teacher, a middle-aged woman in a silky lavender blouse, goes around checking on them. They all look up when I knock and then enter.

"Hello," I say, newly courageous after the fifth-graders, who have gone out to recess in the courtyard with the texting principal.

"Hello," they chirp, and the teacher goes to her desk, sits down, takes out a gradebook, and puts on her glasses. She glances at me, nods, and gets to work. I am grateful to see that she's staying. Rain drizzles down the dirty windows, and through them I can hear traffic. When it's time for their recess, one boy, Jaime, jumps up and comes over to me to shake my hand while his classmates giggle. He is small but already handsome, with rosy cheeks and walnut eyes, and a ready smile revealing tiny, even teeth.

There's broken glass on the floor; a window's been smashed. Outside, I can hear the market, the shouts and televisions, the bargains, the workers' children in class next door. The bathrooms used by students don't have doors; there's no paper, the floors are filthy, and the water runs freezing.

For the children that death took while playing, I remember.

* * *

Raphael moves in across the hall. He's French, with a broad, sun-burned face, bushy eyebrows, and a black beard. He sleeps late in the mornings, just waking by the time I arrive home from the school. He toasts white bread for the both of us and shares his *dulce de leche*, a gift from an Argentine friend. At night, he pops popcorn for everyone. Raphael's not sure what his plans are for Ecuador, but while he figures it out, he collects money in the morning and then prepares dinners for everyone, enormous stir-fries, spaghetti with red sauce, omelets and salad and cheese.

"I talked to my girlfriend today," I say to Raphael once.

"You mean your boyfriend?" he replies, thinking I've confused *novia* with *novio*.

"My girlfriend," I say again, and he raises his eyebrows, surprised, but says nothing.

Carlos' fingers twitch when he talks. His mouth turns up. His thin eyebrows rise and fall. He paces.

"Why a girlfriend?" he asks me sometimes, and then frowns when I shrug and tell him I love her.

"Such a waste," he says, shaking his head, but he resigns himself to it, bringing other women over. In the morning, they wear t-shirts of his and sit at the kitchen table while he makes eggs.

Raphael moves easily, slowly, and he is kind without seeming as if he wants something more. When I leave the door to my bedroom open and type, he knocks and then wordlessly enters with what he has made: bread with coconut in it, or cookies, or a sliced piece of tropical fruit drizzled with crème fraiche.

"My one indulgence," he says in English the first time he produces the plastic canister from the fridge. He's labeled it in permanent marker with his name, which surprises me, as he normally shares whatever he has with us all.

Two German women, both eighteen and about to start college, move in upstairs. They have matching ankle tattoos, which they got together in Thailand, and they wake before I do but arrive home in the evening much later, after I've gone to sleep. Their footsteps over my head break through my dreams until I grow used to their comings and goings and sleep through them. I see the two girls only at lunchtime, when they smoke cigarettes on the tiny second-story balcony. They paint their fingernails bright red and take salsa lessons across the street. They are always saying they're exhausted, yet they seem always to be laughing, moving, singing, cooking, smoking. On weekends, I stay up with the two of them. On those nights, Raphael and Carlos go to the shop on the corner and bring back boxes of red wine, which we mix with brown soda and then find, sticky and dried, on the floor in the morning.

Once, we go to the salsa club across the street, where the German girls know the owners and get discounts on drinks. While the two of them pair up and move to the music as if they were born understanding it, Raphael and I move clumsily to one corner of the dance floor and do our best beneath the beating lights. He dances as if he knows he is bad and doesn't care, his movements floppy but accompanied by a certain jauntiness. I don't know what time it is when we finally stumble outside, but people still wait outside to enter, smoking and touching up makeup, kissing. *I want him*, I think to myself, and then the drunken thought disappears into murk. We cross the street, Raphael unlocks the gate, and we trip up the stairs, exhausted in the sudden silence, barely able to mumble goodnight.

* * *

Meanwhile, there are other things I don't say to E—. Our conversations grow more tense, not less. She hates my faulty Internet connection, and when our calls are dropped, I swear to myself, knowing she'll be angry. I start to tiptoe, to step carefully around certain subjects. I speak sweetly to her, asking her about her day, her weekend plans. I'm grateful she doesn't ask me mine; some days, despite the bustle of the school and my housemates and the city in general, I feel deeply, achingly lonely.

And I sense that there are things she's not saying by the way she pauses sometimes, about to tell me something, and then changes her mind. "No, it's nothing," she repeats when I prod her. In turn, I don't mention Raphael, because she would misunderstand, and anyway, it feels good to have secrets, too. A month ago, the Corn Island breezes so sweet, it would have been inconceivable that I'd want to hold something from E—. Now, though, I cling to what I can. I envy her busy life: proposals for work, drinks in the evening, the gym on weekends.

Then, she goes to a friend's house in the country; I don't hear from her for four days.

"There was no service," she protests when she finally responds to my e-mails, four of them. I'm grateful she can't know how many more went unsent. I don't let myself think about the emails she didn't compose to me, the conversations she might have had with someone else instead.

"Don't freak out," E— writes when she gets back, calm and cool, as if she knows something I don't. I can't bring myself to write back. I go out into the Quito drizzle and walk and walk, not hungry, not thirsty, just sad.

And then days pass, and I wonder fitfully where she's gone. I write; she doesn't reply. I call; the phone rings unanswered, and the offer to leave a voice-mail never comes. Occasionally instant messages pop up on my screen, but they're rushed and thoughtless—*Too busy to chat now, try you tomorrow, have fun!*

I answer hastily, with anger: *How did it get to this?* I demand, but she doesn't reply. It's as if she feels she has nothing to lose. Maybe the beach was too much, I tell myself sometimes. The coconut wind washed my instincts away, and the sunset on her skin made me drunk. I wonder if I saw things that weren't really there.

Years later, a friend will say to me, "I knew what was going on." She'll be talking about E— and those final, unraveling days. She'll be talking about something she saw, some glance, maybe, or a touch. She was there, and I wasn't, and she'll look at me grimly, waiting for a response in my eyes. I'll try not to show one. I won't want the friend to know how stupid I was, or how little I allowed myself to see.

"I knew what was going on," the friend will say again, raising her eyebrows, "and I didn't like it."

* * *

Between rare days of sun, rain soaks the city. One Friday, I leave the house just before seven, and already it's pouring. I should have expected bumper-to-bumper traffic all the way from the top of the hill that looks over the parks, past the statues and the eucalyptus forest and through the tunnels. I should have known the second the sound of the rain woke me up, but I left the house at the usual time, didn't give myself those thirty extra minutes I'd end up needing in order to make it to the school on time.

The buses are always more crowded when it rains, here in Quito like everywhere else. Today, the bus smells faintly of sweat and soggy clothes, and you have to take care when you walk down the aisle, hurtling along as the bus starts and stops, slows and speeds, because the floor is slick with the drops that pour off umbrellas and ponchos and wet hair. The man next to me sits with his hands folded on his lap, umbrella between his feet, head down. I wonder if he's sleeping.

There's no chance I'll make it to work on time; I check my watch— five minutes to eight. We're still a mile away, stuck inside this dark and noisy tunnel that echoes with the horns of the buses and the pounding of the rain on the hill and the electric buzz of the fluorescent lights. I think about getting out and walking, then remember how hard the rain is coming down, how there are no sidewalks between the two tunnels, how walking in this darkness, alone with my light hair, might bring the sinister whispers I can hardly stand to hear, even in sunlight.

The man next to me is saying something. He cracks his knuckles and repeats it: *We'll never get there*, I think he is saying. Or maybe he is telling me, *We'll get there*. Either way, I nod my head and smile. He smiles back and then turns to look out the window at the black tunnel walls. I close my eyes.

I hear the man's voice again. This time, he is asking me where I am from. We start talking, me in jolty Spanish, he in a quiet, pebbled voice that runs his words together. He has a brother in Miami, he tells me. A musician. Another brother lives in Germany, but he, this man beside me, just lives on the other side of the city, up the eastern hillside.

"I've always wanted to visit my brother," he says. "The United States is a fine country." He adds hastily that he admires Obama.

I notice the faded cuffs of his black jacket, the fabric soaked, and I can see where holes have been mended. The pockets of the jacket are shiny from all the times he's slid his hands in. We wait together as the bus inches along, and his presence beside me somehow eases the darkness and the sharp lights of the bus's interior.

Just as we're making it through the final tunnel, the man reaches into his pocket and takes out a folded piece of paper.

"My number," he says, and hands it to me. "In case you ever need help." I shake his hand and stand and finally I'm out of the steamed interior and outside, where the rain feels cool and fresh with wind.

I forget about the paper until much later, when I find it one morning in the small pocket of my purse. This paper has been folded and folded, and the creases are gray with wear. I open it carefully so the brittle paper doesn't crumble. On one side of the page, in black pen, is the man's telephone number and first name: Jimmy.

I turn the paper over and find, in faded pencil, a list of sums: thirty-five cents, twenty-five cents, a dollar-fifty. Added together, the numbers equal four dollars and forty-five cents. The arithmetic is neat and painstakingly figured. I fold it again, the paper more like tattered cloth in my hands, and slide it into the back pocket of my wallet. My room is dark now, the light outside blotted out by rain, and the window is open a little. In the moments it's quiet here in this Mariscal boarding house, the quiet is eerie. I've grown use to the blare. We had waited together, Jimmy and I, in the rain, waiting and hoping and making conversation, as people on buses all over the world must have also done this morning. The paper was like fabric, kept warm in the same pocket for weeks, years maybe.

"In case you ever need help," Jimmy had said.

I make my last day of classes special. *What's up*, I teach them, and *hey man*, and *this rocks*, and *this sucks*. Their teacher, not understanding, doesn't glance up from his phone. The same two girls who sit in front ignore me, whispering to each other and doodling the way they have since I started teaching this class. *That's awesome!* I teach. *What's up, dude?* A few boys like the sound of that, the words vaguely familiar from movies and video games, and they stand up and swagger, *What's up, dude?* The last thing I teach is *I love you*, but they all know it already.

"I love you, teacher," one boy says, while the other students snicker and watch me expectantly.

"Thank you," I say, and hold open the door. Each shakes my hand, passing through.

I interrupt the seventh grade making cards. Their teacher glances up at me when I crack the door and nods me in. There's a record playing a tinny Spanish love song, and the students are humming as they cut and draw. The teacher often has them making crafts when I come in, wreaths of paper rings in the weeks preceding Easter, cards decorated with paper flowers for Mother's Day, posters describing the places the students come from. Most hail from Riobamba, a province to the south. Today, when they glance up and notice me, they hastily finish the cards, then put them out of sight.

I take from my purse my digital camera, which thrills the class, driving a ripple that surges through the room. There is shouting over who will take the first picture, who will take the second, and when I scroll through the photos later that evening, I'll find shots of the ceiling, of someone's blurred head, a close-up of the lines on someone's palm. In between, two girls are standing together in long *cortes*, unsmiling. Three boys have their arms around each other's shoulders and stand solemn-faced, trying to look mean, but not succeeding. In a group shot, the teacher is the only one smiling, leaning toward the group from the edge.

When the bell rings for recess I stand by the door once more, expecting the lineup of handshakes. Instead, the teacher goes to the closet and takes out a bag. The students have opened their desks and taken from them the cards, which they present to me. The teacher draws things from the bag: a small, hand-knit hat, a woven pink purse, a green pen with a feathery bird at the end, which I'd seen each of the students writing with at one point or another throughout the course of these months. Now, the handsome teacher presents the items to me, the students insisting that I try on the hat. I suspect it was one of the knitting projects the girls completed in between taking notes. It is much too small, and the students applaud enthusiastically, without the touch of mocking I might have expected in a North American classroom, where size and style are more important. The teacher ties the cards together with brown string, making a neat stack. "Read them later," he tells me in English. I hold the cards in my hands, along with the woven things and the community pen. Now it is mine. I feel the sudden sting of tears in my eyes, a bright sharpness beneath the fluorescent lights, and I blink my eyes in surprise. I had not expected sadness, but that's not exactly what this is. These gifts handed to me, such small handmade things, and again, the line of handshakes. The teacher covers the record player with a piece of cloth, shuts off the lights, and closes the door behind us.

And just like that, I walk through the schoolyard, waving and saying goodbye in Spanish and English both, shaking hands with students I never even met. I remember suddenly the hills of Uspantán, where we built stoves and tended to the children and then we hiked off, calling good-byes over our shoulders. I wonder about the bottle school in La Gloria, and all the little, dark-eyed, beautiful children there.

The principal unlocks the gate for me and thanks me for the first time. Then I am standing outside the gate beside the man who sells ice-cream bars and another who is hawking socks. He offers me a package of gray pairs with pink flowers printed on them. The students, I see through the bars, have forgotten my departure already and are chasing each other over puddles and splintered glass, both of which they've long grown accustomed to avoiding.

SANTA FE, NEW MEXICO

I've been to New Mexico once before, with her. We had just started dating. She took my hand in the airport, squeezed me to her, pulled me to the parked car. She drove us to her mother's empty house and led me to the small front bedroom. She took off my clothes, trying her best not to hurry, and afterwards we'd showered together in the tiny, sun-filled bathroom. I remember little of the plaza, the restaurants in summer, the aspen-lined trail we'd hiked up. What I always think of instead, when I think of New Mexico, is coffee in her kitchen, a goat in her neighbor's yard, a spiny aloe in a glazed blue pot, her rumpled bed. I fell in love that weekend, and she'd wept when I'd gone.

We had this trip all planned out: a chance to reunite, to rekindle the flame, to watch two friends marry in a Santa Fe field. Still, on the flight to Albuquerque, I force myself to face the possibility that she won't be at the airport waiting.

The man beside me on the flight to Albuquerque pretends he doesn't notice that I'm crying. A month ago, when I found a discounted flight at an agency in Quito, I had thought I could see E— and it would be the same as it had been on the beach, in the hut. Now I know better, but it is too late: the tickets are purchased, and the hotel room is rented. E— will pick me up in her father's car.

The man beside me on the plane offers chocolate chip cookies from a plastic box. When I decline, he looks at me with eyebrows raised. I turn from him and close my eyes, sending my mind back to Quito.

* * *

Two days before I left, Raphael made grilled cheese for lunch and then invited me to ride on his motorbike.

"There's a tram and a carnival," he told me. "We should go." He was looking at me in a way that said: *If you go, you will know something delicious.*

"No motorcycles," E— had said to me before I'd left, but she hadn't made me promise.

A bird hopped in through the open window, pecking unafraid at crumbs on the floor. I washed the plates in tepid, soapy water, scrubbing at the melted cheese that Raphael uses in abundance. He told me I'd need a jacket, something sturdy.

We went outside and looked at the motorbike, which he'd leaned against the gate. A wilted hibiscus blossom had fallen onto the seat, and Raphael stepped forward quickly to brush it off. He presented the bike as a magician might present his lovely assistant, one palm outstretched toward the creature in a gesture of restrained pride. Raphael was wearing a black jacket with embedded plastic geometric shapes.

"It is beautiful," I told him, knowing nothing of such things.

* * *

She isn't here, but I figure I knew that already. I walk through the terminal, past the expensive shops that sell turquoise and bright scarves, piñon coffee and tiny treasure boxes. I walk to the baggage claim and stand there, watching for my black pack that I had to check because inside is a black-and-white ceramic platter, the wedding gift. I look at the moving conveyor belt and try not to cry, try not to wish for Raphael, for the Quito streets that have grown familiar, for the buses that could take me out of there and to the jungle, or to the water. I can feel the dryness already, a cloying, smoke-scented dust that wafts in the revolving doors, entering our mouths and lungs and pores. I close my eyes again.

* * *

Raphael drove gingerly down our street and onto Diez de Agosto. I could hear little through my helmet's thick padding and so the ride felt surreal, the city moving bright and silent alongside us before fading finally into eucalyptus jungle swirled with mist.

It was cold and cloudy this high above the city, and we were the only ones waiting for the next tram, which came around the thick wires and paused, doors sliding open. Inside, we could feel but not hear the wind; we lurched as it picked up speed, and then we were staring down at the broadening hills and the smoggy expanse of the city, the rolls and dips encrusted with red-roofed buildings, the occasional dome and frail-looking steeple. The mountains were before us now, stretching beyond the city, now growing greener and empty save a few men herding goats. We rose up over one crest and then another, and when the tram deposited us at the top, our boots crunched on snow. I was grateful for my jacket, digging my hands into my pockets, envious of Raphael for bringing a cap. He caught my eye and offered it to me. I shook my head.

* * *

And then there's a rush of footsteps behind me, the smell of her, and now she's turned me around and is kissing me, just the way she did when I arrived in New Mexico the first time. I want to push her away, but my hands draw her closer instead.

"Sorry I'm late," she finally says, coming up for air. "You wouldn't believe the traffic."

In the car, I can't think of anything to say. I don't dare bring up the last few days, the longest we've gone without communicating since I left in December. It's been so many months. I watch her as she drives and see that she is a stranger now. Everything about her is different: her haircut, her new glasses, a striped shirt I don't recognize. Only her tattoos are the same, and the copper of her skin, and the hint of natural purple in her hair. I reach over to touch the tattoo on her arm, above her elbow, and she flinches, not anticipating the contact.

New Mexico is hazy now. There are fires in Arizona, E— tells me, and you can see the smoke every day. The air smells of burnt sugar and of incense and rotting fruit, as it did in India. We drive with the windows sealed shut, the AC blasting. The silence feels tight; E— checks her cell phone at the stoplights, punching out texts. I resist the urge to ask who she's messaging. Instead, I watch the casinos and banks and strip malls as we pass them, the structures lit up and freshly whitewashed despite the dusty heat.

We go to her mother's house again, and as soon as I put down my bag, she's kissing me. Again, I feel the urge to push her away, but it has been so long since I felt skin against me this way, and her mouth is something I remember. We make love as we did before, on the quilted bed in the front room. Afterwards, she weeps.

"It's just been so long," she says, but I know that's not it, and I choke back my own sob. This time will be the last, I think to myself. We shower together in the little bathroom off the kitchen; here is the same tiny, steamy window, and the same cracked bar of lavender soap on the ledge. We get dressed and go to lunch, where we sip margaritas and eat steaming green-chile enchiladas.

"Let's just enjoy the weekend," E— says once, and then I realize that she's thought this out already.

* * *

"Let's walk," I said to Raphael, and we marched together in the wind, and we failed, at first, to notice what lay around us.

For it took a moment to see: these were the Andes, stretching to the east and west. Now they were snow-capped, rugged and craggy. In the crook between two close peaks, we could see a dried-out, high-desert meadow where an old man with a stick prodded goats. The expanse stretched like water, silent and cold, after months in pumping Quito. We moved without speaking along the ridge, toward the meadow, and the wind smelled of ice and grass. It was as if this high-up place might whip the dust off of us and along with it the worry, our anxieties dissolving like sugar in water, or wisps of clouds off the surface of a deep emerald lake.

* * *

At a ranch dotted with adobe buildings ten miles from town, Bethany and Daniel grin toward us from where they're getting their pictures taken. Their faces are tired from smiling, I can tell; I can see it in their eyes, their mouths—a faint strain, like they've waited for this moment for so long and now they just want it to come, to rush through them and then leave them. They both come over and kiss me after the pictures are over, even though there really isn't time. That attention, those kisses from people I've known so long, makes her presence beside me fall away just a little. Suddenly, the long flight feels worth it.

Bethany's hair is coiled. Her sister adjusts her veil for her, and although her eyes jump, her hands are calm. Daniel described, in a poem he read aloud while we were still in graduate school, the way he was with Bethany on Christmas, so many years ago when she was just a little girl. He was there the day she cut her hand, and the night she wept for a dying friend. He'd never seen her, but he was there in the shadows, waiting, because somehow they could hear each other's voices, transmitted through the beating of their hearts.

At the end of the ceremony, a butterfly comes. It's a desert butterfly, with brown wings to match the color of the earth. It drifts light on the wind, and as he leans in to kiss her it rises lustily into the sky, looping toward the thumbnail moon.

Daniel reads aloud a poem afterwards, when we're all eating cake beneath the tent. *What waits within our cores?* asks the poem, pondering a future fused with another.

I turn to look at E—, who is watching the dance floor. She's still holding her phone. *We won't make love this night or any other*, I think to myself, *but now, at least I am free.*

I leave the tent to stand beneath the stars. It's hard to look straight up now, and I wobble a little and set my cup of wine onto the ground. There's a man with a blonde braid standing at the place where the light from the tent ends and the night begins.

"You have beautiful hair," I say to the man, because I am drunk. He's removed his tie but still wears a vest, rented, I imagine, for the occasion. He has pale eyes that rest on me steadily.

"You have beautiful everything," he says.

At first I do not hear him. He is watching me, and he stands so still that I wonder whether he is holding his breath. I want to move forward and take his hand. Afterwards, I won't remember if I did.

* * *

On the way down, instead of speaking, Raphael and I craned our necks to watch the last of the peaks dip from view. We went to the little carnival at the base of the tram, we the only people strolling in between the rides and games.

"Want to buy a ticket?" Raphael asked, but I shook my head. Darkness came so quickly. We found the bike where we left it, and when I climbed on after Raphael, I found my arms wrapping around him automatically. I considered how reflexive the gesture felt, the motion of my body toward his. Later, I would think about E—, the way she'd tried to make me promise not to ride a motorbike, the way we didn't speak for days and then our e-mails came short and curt, withholding and sad. Later, I would picture her face and feel guilty, but in that downhill wind, my arms around him, she never came.

THE ROAD

I arrive in the darkness, but I'm not afraid. After the stream of airports and planes, flight attendants and baggage claims and weary passengers—finally, in Quito's darkness, I'm alone. I missed it here. The cab driver barely speaks and keeps his radio on. The lights and signs, the buildings and long avenues and clots of motorbikes are all familiar to me, for I am returning. I check into a cheap hostel near Diez de Agosto and stay up late talking to the front-desk attendant, a young guy who cracks two beers for us and taps the ashes of his cigarette neatly into a small silver dish. In this smoky lobby, the journey to New Mexico already feels like a distant memory. Perhaps it never happened. He asks me about kids and a husband.

"I have none," I tell him, and he raises his eyebrows, disbelieving. He has two wives, he admits, and four kids.

"It's a little too much sometimes," he says, but he is grinning.

I stashed my pack here after checking out of the boarding house three days before. Three days, I marvel, as I sort my clothes and little bottles of shampoo. There's not much else: my Birkenstocks, the Neruda poem my friend penned onto the soles before I left nearly illegible now. I have two books: *The Lonely Planet* and *The Old Patagonian Express*. I have a water filter, a first-aid kit, a rain jacket. It's a relief to come back to so little and know that it's still more than enough.

A slip of paper falls out when I unzip the backpack's top pouch. A few scrawled words read:

If it doesn't work out with your girlfriend, think of me. Give me an opportunity! A chance! —Carlos

I slip the note into *Lonely Planet*, and I am smiling now. I will not go to him, of course not, but in the weeks and months to come we will e-mail and send Facebook messages. Not so many years later, he will post a picture of himself with his arm around a woman holding a baby, the two parents grinning and the baby's mouth open in a yawn, or a scream, it is difficult to tell. In another, he stands by a young boy, seven or eight years old. "Me and my son," the caption reads. I will remember Carlos and the note he left, and how it had lightened me that first morning, when I'd set out alone.

I say goodbye to the attendant, whose shirt and eyes are wrinkled after the night shift. I walk a few blocks to the bus terminal and book a ticket. There will be no calls to make today, no e-mails to check; I will write to my parents when I've reached the next place. They've grown accustomed to gaps in communication. It is a rare sunlit day in Quito, and people are meandering about, eating flavored ice and shucking their jackets. I do not let myself think of her, of New Mexico, of the flight or of Raphael. Instead, I look to Theroux's map: a tenuous partnership, but he's brought me this far. *I am free now*, I remind myself, watching Quito out the window for the last time.

OTAVALO, ECUADOR

Otavalo is a tidy, cheerful-seeming town, the elderly indigenous proud in their bright skirts and belts and shirts, the young people traveling in packs, both boys and girls in tight jeans. The girls have brushed glitter onto their eyelids, and they check their cell phones for text messages. The occasional white tourist, taller than the rest, hair inevitably mussed, saunters along, gazing into shop windows, pausing at a table beneath a tent to finger the fine embroidery on a shawl.

My hotel room overlooks the street, but although women cry out to each other and motorcycles backfire, I lie down and am able to sleep, deeply, for the first time in weeks. The sun eases downward as I sleep, dreaming not of E— or of the New Mexico desert, not of the coral-colored buildings in Otavalo or of the man who stayed up drinking beer, tapping his cigarette ashes into the silver dish, but of a place I've never seen, a smudged gray coastline stained by ocean salt. I hear the clamor of a busy dock, a line of people boarding a ship; I see my grandmother's hands, young and strong from drawing the milk into pails. I can feel her heart beating. There is no one to see her off. She'll endure the rocking without complaint for eleven days, and when she steps onto dry land again she'll be a stranger.

When I wake, the street noise is sharp, the room very black, my mouth very dry. For one long minute I lie there and think of her and drown, and then I dress and walk downstairs to find a restaurant. I let myself feel hungry, expectant for a meal. I can smell the salt of the sea for a while, but finally the dream falls from me, and I'm surrounded by Ecuador again.

In the morning, I follow the crowd through the center of town, over the bridge that crosses a lush gulley. We climb to the top of the hill, and although it's only seven, people are leaving already, packing the live chickens and guinea pigs into trucks or potato sacks and hauling them away. The vendors got here at five, and most had to wake by two or three to get to this trodden meadow overlooking the start of the Andes. From where I stand, I can see acres of treeless mountains, parcels of farmland, hazy clouds that cling to the tops of the peaks.

Otavalo sits in a floodplain grown lush by melted Andean snow, and the steep valleys offer panoramas of the red-roofed city and the knotty, steaming forest beyond. This market dates back to pre-Incan times, when the mountain inhabitants and the people of the jungle convened to buy and sell. Now, tourists comprise a good half of the market's visitors, and against the backdrop of the snow-capped ridges, blue-eyed guys with scruffy beards meander alongside tottering women in thickly embroidered blouses, their head cloths folded over salt-and-pepper braids. There are guinea pigs for sale in baskets, climbing atop one another, then suddenly, comically, falling asleep. I peer into buckets of tiny puppies, sleeping bunnies, and peeping chicks. One man holds two tiny kittens in his arms; he gazes at the crowd with no expression on his face as the kittens mew and scramble, trying to escape. A little girl stands with two goats on ropes. An old and very tiny man screams that his calf is for sale. Beyond all of us, the silent peaks are misted. In this light, the sun rising, they are glowing.

Here, some men wear their hair as long as the women, thick and silky and hanging in clean braids past their shoulder blades. Women stand around chatting in fedoras and long black skirts and white lace blouses embroidered with flowers, bright woven bands wrapped around the length of their braids. The older men, in spotless white pants and blue ponchos and wide-brimmed hats, gaze with dark eyes at the animals. Clouds pass over the sun, and the air grows colder, but the men with the braids just root their feet tighter to the earth, laughing with each other, admiring their beautiful women, their pulsing market, the rainbow their people have made beneath the slate sky.

The road away from the market turns to dirt and begins to crumble, thinning. Children run down, pausing to look back at me. Calla lilies seem to grow wild. One person has stuck an old door at the edge of their property, linking the gate. The door leans, its peels of blue paint flapping in the wind. Someone has tied a small, dirty pig to an old post, and it roots around happily in the muddy grass. Children in uniform walk home from school, silent as they pass me, only to erupt behind me in hoots. I have heard there is a lake here, and the road turns from sand back to gravel, then to broken pavement.

Before me, the way straightens and levels, and I can see green hills and reedy swamps. In the distance, a mountain stretches, her summit obscured by storm clouds. I pass a white church, jagged in its modern design, prickly bushes growing up black alongside it. I pass the center of this small town, where men barbecue beneath tents, prodding at meat with sticks. The park teems with children. Mothers shout at the scrawny dogs to quit lurking. The people look up and notice me and nod politely, watching curiously as I pass through before resuming their Saturday activities.

At the lake's grassy edges, I can see that the water is shallow for a long way out, the sand shimmering with mica through the little lapping waves. The mountains are deep blue, tinged with the violet and gray of the sky. A few flecks of rain fall. There is no one about.

Cattails stir in the wind, and just before I turn to walk back, a shuddering sound comes from the distant reeds. A heron lifts himself clumsily, splashing, but as soon as he's up, his movements become silent. He flaps once, twice. And then he is airborne, coasting, his wings the exact pewter shade of the sky. Still no one comes, no one but the heron and me. *You are alive*, a voice inside me says, and the words fill me as I make my way back down into the valley, back to my home for the night.

BAÑOS, ECUADOR

The Gothic-style church in the center of town gleams in the afternoon sun, and the peaks that surround the region are a hazy green. Clouds have already slid between the mountains, enshrouding the church steeple and blanketing the river. Mist winds down the streets. Baños, five hours south of Quito, is known for its pretty hills and deep river, but most of all for its mineral baths, the water heated by high-up volcanoes. In the streets, smoke from the line of grills set up outside the cathedral wafts into my second-floor hotel room, which shares a balcony with the adjacent rooms. As the sun sets, the church is illuminated by fluorescent blue lights, a beacon in the shifting dark.

In the morning, the man at the front desk assures me that all of the trails are safe. While he talks, he does a dozen other things: passes towels to waiting tourists, checks girls with huge backpacks out of their rooms, sips a cup of black coffee from a white mug. He wants me to get out of the way. I leave the hostel and walk down the one-lane streets until I come to the bridge, which crosses a deep gorge that divides the town from the eastern hills. The sky is brightening, the clouds are melting, and below me, hundreds of feet down, brown water in the river churns.

I let the walking calm me as it always does. In the night, I dreamt of cement-block walls painted yellow, of an unfamiliar body beside the body of my lover, of buses coming too close to the edge of the road—a gnarl of dreams that woke me many times. Maybe I've been trying too hard to forget. The bus rides make it easy; you let the road take your mind from you, you let the towns and forests you pass replace your thoughts. Now, I feel my blood shift inside me, my muscles warming, my breath deepening. I become aware of my body, letting my mind encompass the sensations within my arms and legs. Again, the path takes my thoughts from me, returning them to my body and to the sound of my footfalls upon this road.

As I climb, the road grows rough, turning into a rocky, bumpy path that pickups jolt down. In the back of each truck people stand, clinging to makeshift bars, watching me. I can hear dogs barking in the hills, above and below me, unseen. A copper-colored horse stands in the grass, gazing at me through long lashes, her blonde mane blowing in the breeze. Always there are dogs, sitting on the side of the road or trotting along as if they're on a mission, their noses raised and sniffing at the wind. They walk with me a while, then turn off.

Fewer cars are passing me now, and the breeze smells of eucalyptus, of juniper, of cut grass, of cow manure. I hear E—'s voice, then let it fall away. There comes a scent like jasmine, and the fleeting waft of lilies, which, as always, takes me to my cousin Liza's old apartment in Rome. The lilies she kept in wine bottles on her kitchen table would drop their petals and wither while we ate late lunches of pizza and I drank my first wine. Meanwhile, I pass pines and cows. I hear a rustle in the bush beside me; chickens are clucking, scratching, glaring at me. Water runs from a pipe on the hillside. I climb until I reach the top, and I can see over the town to the volcano beyond. The air is clean, and except for the wind, this place is silent. I listen to my breath, heavy at first then turning steady and quiet. I feel my feet on the ground and realize again that this hilltop is this moment only. Afterwards, the temperature of the wind on my shoulder will fade from my memory. There is no one to explain things to, now. This journey is mine now, mine alone. I shudder with the selfishness of the thought, the pure freedom inherent. There will be e-mails to my parents, and there will be my journal. The rest will be moments: conversations, colors suddenly illuminated, the scent of sugar and boiling butter—indescribable in their power, all. They are for me to have now, for one second only, but in that one second, they'll be mine.

Mine, I think on the way down. My feet upon this crumbled road, my eyes upon the family there, eating a meal at the base of extraordinary peaks. Their house is a wooden lean-to with a clear tarp for a roof, and it clings to the road, as if it might otherwise slide straight down into the valley. I wonder how many times the rain has taken it down; there is evidence everywhere of mudslides, the vertical washes of red streaking hillsides. The lunching family doesn't notice me; they sit on plastic chairs drinking soup while the mother fries plantains on a tiny grill. There are six of them sitting there, half-sheltered from the sputtering rain by their flapping roof.

There come steep stands of tree tomatoes, the fruit hanging like suspended red eggs. Tree tomatoes are both puckery and sweet, firm and a little bit crunchy, not at all like the juicy tomatoes my mother plucks from her garden and simmers for spaghetti sauce. On the hillside, I taste my mother's sauce, spicy with basil, for a fraction of a second. Then, the scent of eucalyptus comes in a wind and I'm here again, alongside an abandoned pickup, a donkey tied to a tree, a crooked wooden hut sprayed over with grafitti, and always these mountains, now shamrock, now sage, cut by waterfalls and herd paths or the track marks of rockslides.

I pass a woman who carries filled sacks in both hands.

"Buenas," I say to her, and she grunts and nods. I look back after a few steps; she has stopped and is staring at me, and when she catches me looking she glances away. The road cuts back and forth across the hill, and when I look up again, I see through the trees that she's watching me still. I hurry along, passing a parked red pickup whose engine is running. The bass exudes a steady thump.

"Buenas," I say to the man in the driver's seat. There's a child sitting next to him, fiddling with the rearview. "Come here," the driver says, but it isn't unkind. I step closer and wave to the little boy. Maybe they're lost, I think to myself.

"Where are you from?" the man asks me. I tell him.

"A beautiful country," he says. "Beautiful, like you." A sudden wave of cold comes up the road, and my skin pricks, the hairs on my arms rising. I turn to go, peeking quickly again at the little boy, who is now watching us. His expression doesn't change when I wave.

"And where is your husband?" the driver asks. I think to myself that there is no one around but the woman up the hill who stood watching me. I feel my heartbeat quicken just a fraction. I think of where I might run. He is waiting for an answer. I shake my head no.

The driver pulls out his cell phone and starts scrolling. "I have many nice friends," he tells me. "Would you like to meet them?"

I take a step from the car.

The little boy stretches his legs and arms and leans out his window, then breaks into laughter.

"What is it?" the man asks, but the little boy cannot talk. The man reaches over and tickles him, and the boy, hysterical, wriggles against him. The moment loosens and I allow myself to hear the distant rumble of other cars and trucks making their way down the mountain, the faint clanging of pots and pans as women in their houses, not so far away, wash up after lunch.

"Okay," the man finally says, and lets up on the tickling. He's forgotten to ask what was so funny.

"What was so funny?" I ask, but the boy just continues to giggle.

I leave them parked there in the shade, the bass still thumping, the sounds of people in their houses and cars, on foot. I walk until I can no longer hear the bass.

As I reach the bottom of the mountains, where the earth curves and flattens suddenly, giving way to the river, I hear someone running behind me. I turn around; it's a young boy in a blue t-shirt and jeans. He runs past without speaking, and I hardly hear his breath or footfalls. I watch as he makes his quick way down the last portion of the steep, rocky road. Just as he's about to turn the bend, he raises his arms up beside him and jumps, and for one moment I imagine that this mountain wind will suspend him, and he'll rise.

I leave my pack in the room in Baños I shared last night with two girls from England, the night before with a pair of dreadlocked French musicians, who stumbled in very late and slept in all their clothes. I've decided to forego the more expensive single rooms that, until now, have marked my nights. A room alone is too much now; there's too much time to think of her, to wake in the morning waiting for the sun to rise. I go to catch another bus, to visit another place; I am grateful for the certainty of it, the knowledge that a two-dollar ticket will take me hours from here, and I will see something I've never been before. Another imprint, another city written down. By now, I am greedy for it: the constant shift, the mystery every new place holds, the plunge again into anonymity.

On this day I showered early and drank one cup of instant coffee with a thin slip of watered-down milk. *Riobamba*, I remind myself as I make my way to the bus terminal. But, as it always is, the bus to Riobamba is easy to find; men are shouting the city's name, and they urge me over.

"When does the bus leave?" I ask them. They check chunky black watches on their wrists.

"Now," the shortest man says. I climb onto the waiting bus; we sit for another five minutes, and then the shortest man climbs into the driver's seat, starts the engine, and backs out of the parking lot.

Riobamba, the capital of its province—Chimborazo—sits in the Chambo River Valley, smack dab in the middle of Ecuador. People have lived in this region, both fertile and mountainous, since the fifteenth century. In the sixteenth century, Riobamba became an official part of the Spanish empire. Like so many cities I've passed through, Riobamba has withstood numerous, devastating earthquakes. At close to nine thousand feet, the city sits beneath the Chimborazo volcano, and has a near-uniform temperature all year. Chimborazo, whose summit reaches almost 21,000 feet, is Ecuador's highest peak.

The bus to Riobamba, two hours from Baños, is cramped but provides spectacular views. The tight mountains surrounding Baños flatten into hills patched with farmland. We stop frequently for more passengers, and a large, lanky man lumbers on and heaves himself down beside me. He sprawls in his seat and spits once on the floor, then shuffles a bit before taking his cell phone from his pocket and playing each of his cell phone ring-tones at the loudest possible volume. I make myself small as we drive alongside a river, where farmers wash carrots by the hundreds, letting them float in little pools before pushing them into huge sacks. In the dark water, the carrots look neon. Plots of land are divided by rows of tall, spindly pine trees and dirt roads, and the sky remains dark the whole ride. Finally, the man beside me grows tired of his cell phone and puts it in his pocket, then falls asleep. His snores rumble through the bus. I press myself up tight against the window, remembering what I learned so long ago at an ashram in northeast India: buses are the best places to meditate. "Send yourself away," the guru had said, "and your ride will fly past you like a dream."

In Riobamba, there are outskirts but not suburbs; these neighborhoods are made of tight, potholed streets lined with ugly cement buildings. Open doors reveal cracked floors, living rooms and bedrooms lit by television screens. There is graffiti on every exterior wall, barefoot kids in the streets, and piles of bruised plantains for sale on plastic tarps. I scan the diminutive skyline for signs of the colonial architecture that earned this city its nickname, but clouds have swathed the sky, threatening rain as the bus chugs into the lot.

Today is market day, but this isn't like Otavalo, that colorful and beating affair. Riombamba hosts the market for and by the poor, and it pulses in a different way, street after street packed with women selling vegetables and men hawking nail clippers and pirated DVDs, everything cheap and in great abundance. Meanwhile, there is the constant jangle of coins in practiced palms, and the rows of peppers and apples, perfect grand pyramids of limes.

There aren't any trees on the streets, and the mountains around are stripped bare to blackness. There's an incessant honking of horns. Once, I catch a glimpse of the volcano, massively close and covered with snow, but then the clouds suck the peak of it away, throwing the city once more into grayscale. I pass the cathedral, long ago erected of brick, back in the sultan days of Riobamba. Now, the sidewalk around the gigantic cathedral is lined with the homeless, who sleep on dirty blankets or beg, dented cups trembling in clutches of fingers. Across the street, in the cobblestoned plaza, indigenous belts are for sale, and blankets in every color, and buckets of individual black velvet slippers, piles that women pore through, searching for a match. Each stall sells the same items: picked-over piles of something and then, at the next stall, piles of the same thing, and between those there are many empty tables. The vendors watch me but say nothing, and I remember the practiced hawking of Otavalo, luring the tourists in with brilliant colors and negotiable prices. Here, nobody beckons, and I walk through empty market stalls, past grand old buildings crumbling down.

There is a woman sitting on the curb without shoes. Her feet are gnarled, her toenails black, and she has wrapped herself in a tattered blanket. In front of her, she's laid out a couple of bunches of bananas, a basket of overripe strawberries, and a pail of bruised peaches. She looks up as I pass, an empty look, and gestures, exhausted, toward the fruit. It is impossible to tell her age; she could be fifty, or she could be ninety. *She could be my grandmother's age*, I suddenly think, and it is then, imagining for a moment my grandmother crouched there instead of her, that I feel the urgent poverty of the place. It takes the wind out of me, and then I see it in everything: the gray of the sky, the way it chills the bone and hardens the skin, the body resigned to desperation.

It is the line of old ladies hunched over, polishing shoes. It is the little boy selling knives, and the twin girls hawking toilet paper. It is the old man with the battered hat and bare feet who has rope for sale, laid out on the ground. It is the wrinkled dollar that an old woman grasps so tightly, and it is the man dragging himself along the road with broken crutches. This isn't the poverty I saw in Quito, where at least there were signs of success in the shiny buildings and well-dressed businesspeople and uniformed students. It's not like remote La Gloria, that tiny community of old people and children, because there you can find rivers and trees, air cooled by fresh wind, growing things all around.

Yet Riobamba is a place, a place that wakes in the morning and sleeps at night, sells what it can, finds love where it can, makes families and reveals the rough mountains on days when the sky is clear. I have felt sorry for myself so many times, lonely in empty rented rooms, afraid in bus terminals, but in fact I was given choices so many times in my life. Again, I think: *I am the one percent.*

In the bus, the windows steamy, the road to Baños shrouded in fog, I remember a deep blue silk prom dress, a vacation to a grand old New Hampshire hotel, college classes in rooms sleek with markerboards and projector screens and windows looking out onto turning oaks. I came to Riobamba to solve another mystery, to see another place and gain an imprint. I came to take, and I was surprised when the city made me sad. In the end, I'm ashamed for confusing pity with shock, and for believing that my tears at the old woman with no shoes did not mean I was afraid.

Through the bus windows, I watch the rain fall onto green and supple fields. I watch schoolchildren hop off the bus and old women climb on; one family loads a bunch of live chickens, their legs tied together, into the luggage compartment of the bus. No one looks at me, and no one speaks to me. People recognize friends on the bus and chat, and men come on selling food. The day turns from afternoon into dusk; we hurtle along, the back windows open, air streaming in and us passengers sitting together contentedly.

Close to town, a young man comes on to sell gemstones. Any problems we have, he tells us, can be solved with the right stone. He's tall, which makes him seem distinctive in Ecuador and thus quietly handsome, his hair neatly trimmed and his face cleanly shaved. He is animated, but not jarring, not preachy. It's as if he doesn't even care if we buy. He quizzes us with riddles, and those who answer correctly win free gemstones. He's recited these riddles so many times, he doesn't even need to think. You can tell by the way he moves up and down the lurching bus without ever stumbling that he has done this before, many times. He reminds me of my brother, the way his voice pours over the passengers, turning their heads his way. He makes them laugh; he gets them to listen. Most of the bus-boarding salesmen go ignored, with their vitamins and teas, their miniature Bibles and stacks of colored pencils. Everyone, though, is watching the man with the gems.

After supper, I walk out of the town and up the road that leads to Ambato, a village that neighbors Baños. Now, the houses are spaced far apart, and in between there is green grass where cows graze. The stars and moon illuminate the mountains, and I can hear music playing from behind brick walls. One little boy walks by, a small girl slung upon his back, her pink shoes in his hands. He must stop every few moments to hitch her farther up his back, and every time he does this, she laughs.

The world is large, and there are all kinds of ways to live in it. I had not known this before, not really. I had not known that life can loosen, as it does here, and that a bus can calm your mind and put you at peace, make you a part of something larger somehow. A man passes; his arms full of things: a *costal* of oranges and a couple of framed paintings in a black plastic bag. He pauses, peering at me in the darkness.

"What is it, little daughter?" he asks. His voice is like torn velvet, both ragged and soft.

"I was just lost," I tell him. "Which way back to Baños?"

He smiles, sets down one of his bags, and points the way. I thank him. For a moment, we stand together beneath the stars, which here in Ecuador seem much closer, much brighter, the sky much fuller with those pinpricks of white and very pale gold. This night is a part of my journey, just as Riobamba was; it is all adding up to something, the moments building on each other. I don't know yet what it is, but something is being formed. This I suddenly know as I stand beside the man beneath a thicket of stars. He inhales deeply, closes his eyes, then picks up his bag and continues down the road.

"Don't forget to go to the baths," he calls over his shoulder. I watch his white shirt until it evaporates into the night.

A few days later, Raphael comes to Baños. He has begun a motorbike journey through northern Ecuador, and has already visited small towns all the way from Quito, towns that sold cheese and towns that sold guitars. In every town, on every night, there was a festival. His eyes are bloodshot, but his cheeks are ruddy, his hair a thick shock over his brow. He is sweaty and grinning. We meet in the central plaza, having arranged everything over e-mail the night before, both of us pecking away at keyboards in Internet cafés on street corners.

We eat lunch in the indoor market, a warehouse where a dozen women operate grills, stir pots of soup, and blend fruit to make smoothies. There are plastic tables and plastic tablecloths and little plastic stools. The menus are single sheets of laminated paper with pictures of the different plates; we choose piles of rice layered with beets and avocado salad and fried eggs, some slices of seasoned sausage on the side. We eat without speaking, and I pause, watching Raphael. For a moment I allow myself to remember the salsa club, the dark street, my hand on the knob at my bedroom door, his hand at my hip, his touch lighter than I might have expected, the cocktails doing their work. I remember the way I felt, wanting to pull him in, wanting to feel his mouth on mine. I remember it now. I'd forgotten all about her; he had made me forget.

"I'm glad you're here," I tell Raphael now, and he glances up from his lunch. There's a fleck of avocado at the corner of his mouth. You're not doing anything wrong, a voice reminds me. Raphael offers to pay, and I let him.

"A meal for a friend," he says. And I am grateful for him, the smell of sweat and bike grease, the fleck of avocado, and the easy way he smiles, like debt doesn't exist.

Raphael drives fast: fast out of Baños toward the southern mountains and the jungle, fast as he approaches the speed bumps, slowing down at the last second, then speeding up again. He drives fast past the trucks filled with cattle and past the little economy cars that haul families from Baños back to Quito. He pulls fast past a loaded tourist bus and through the tunnels, which are spooky, barely lit and dripping, the walls cave-like and earthen. Drops of water fall onto us. Raphael yells at me to lean into the curves, not resist them. I move my body with the bike, with the road, letting myself feel the wet, clear darkness of the tunnel and the glinting sunlight afterwards.

We're headed south, and on either side of us, the mountains rise up, foggy at the peaks and broken by rivers at the bases. We pass waterfalls a hundred meters high; for the tourists, there are cable cars and zip lines stretched across river valleys. We reach the Paila, where, we've heard, the falls form a deep, clear, pail-like pool before pushing the water on toward the jungle. The Paila is marked with a bright blue sign and a crooked white gate, and when we park the bike, a man who crouches with a hoe among pale blue hyacinths stands and brushes off his pants. He's dressed neatly, despite his garden work, with a pressed shirt and good leather shoes. For two dollars each, he shows us to the Paila, down a steep and narrow trail that cuts through bamboo and groves of mandarin trees.

The only sound, from our perch on a wooden platform that clings to the wall of the ravine, is the thundering sound of water crashing into the Paila. It is jungle here, creeping with curling vines and delicate flowers concealed in the green. Iridescent birds flap, visible for a second only, and the Paila is a deep bowl of blue and white. Afterwards, we tip our guide five dollars and take turns snapping photos with him by the gate.

By the time we drive home, the sun is setting. Again the tunnels are so dark, so dank with the water that drips from the walls, and when we break out into the evening light the clouds are glowing pink. I think, clutching Raphael's waist and feeling the soft wind on my skin, that I could ride this bike forever, perched behind Raphael through all of these Latin American countries. We drive to the baths, pay a few dollars to enter, change our clothes in wet dressing rooms, and store our things in plastic buckets. The pools smell of sulfur, and the water is soft and white and hot. There are cold pools, too, and we jump in and out between them while the Ecuadorians close their eyes and soak in the hot pools only. Lovers hold one another, and groups of old men with big bellies sip brown liquid from plastic cups and grunt at each other. The pools are open to the sky, and even through the lights of the city we can see the streak of the galaxy above us.

We eat dinner together that night, pizza and two glasses of cheap red wine, and then, outside my hostel, I let him put his hand on my waist again. It is that same light touch, gentler than I might have expected. There is no one around. The darkness is warm and buzzes with insects, with the rustling of leaves, with the red wine in our blood. I touch Raphael; his shirt is damp, and he smells like wine and bike.

"I can't do any more," I say.

He takes his hand from my waist, drawing away, the smell of sulfur and jungle and red wine receding.

We sit without speaking at breakfast, watching the sun rise, whitening the river's broad stones. After, while Raphael revs his bike, I wonder whether I might climb on too and ride north with him to

Colombia. I imagine all the roads we might see, jungled roads lined with waterfalls, and desert roads, sprawling with cactus. Farmfields and flowers; snow and ice. I shake my head to clear it, and now I am kissing Raphael's cheek, closing my eyes, inhaling his coffee and sweat. Now I am pulling away. This journey has only been mine for a little while, and it isn't time to give up the solitude. I want him; of that there is no question. It would be so easy to step into his open arms and follow him. But then the journey would be his and not mine—his bike, his route. "No," I say aloud, and my voice is high and sad. He reaches for my hand, squeezes it.

"Good luck," he says, then puts his helmet on. Bumping down the street, he looks back once and raises his arm.

To kill the time before my bus goes, I walk to the park. There are paintings leaning against fences and statues, artists who lounge or smoke or sit on fold-up stools, staring off into space. They putter around as they did in Quito, admiring each other's canvases, counting their money, checking the sky for rain. Summer is coming; the days here will lengthen, the sky will swell with sun, the city will blossom and then sink in the heat. I rest on a bench beside an old woman who is drinking juice from a plastic cup. Tiny yellow birds hop around us. If I listen carefully, I can hear the river water, white and roiling over the stones. *Goodbye, place*, I think another time, waiting for the hour of my departure to come.

CUENCA, ECUADOR

"You'll find what you need there," Carlos had said of Cuenca. I ride overnight, watching the stars and the dark forests and the towns, and when I arrive in the morning, I go searching. I leave my bag in a darkened dorm filled with travelers sleeping off their hangovers; I pay three dollars for the bed, then stroll along, waiting for the river to darken at nighttime, just as he had said it would. Soon, strings of glittering lights flicker on.

I wait for the air to fill me, and for the thing that I need to come. The ornate buildings, the cobblestone streets, the huge, white churches—all reflect the sky, patched with inflated clouds, the sun breaking through intermittently. I have forgotten already that when the bus stopped in Cuenca, the light of morning just cracking open, I had been afraid. I hadn't wanted to get off, because this was another place I'd never seen. Buses have four walls and a narrow aisle and seats you make, over many hours, your own. A bus lulls, but when the ride ends, your mind is returned to you, your senses jolted awake, your skin and brain spun alert once more.

"You'll find what you need," Carlos had said. "Whatever it is, you will find it."

The friendly man who runs my hostel gives me bread and tea in the late afternoon, and as we sit eating at a heavy wooden table by the window, lazily watching the muted TV, he tells me things about Cuenca.

"The tourists won't get here until June," he says. "Until then, we've got the place to ourselves."

He tells me that this week is Septenario, a seven-day festival to mark the solstice. Each morning, families will arrive to the plaza with trucks filled with sweets: cookies, chocolate marshmallows, biscotti, and jelly candy, all lined up in piles beneath white tents pitched against the churches. The man who runs the hostel tells me that the families will sell sweets in the plaza each day until Septenario ends, and in the nighttime I will hear fireworks until morning.

Outside, jackhammers pound at the sidewalk; still, the hostel owner is able to doze off in his chair.

In the city, I find four-story buildings with delicate molding on the sides of steep hills, and the winding, muddy river, churning and grass-lined and sparkling in the sun. I find little cobblestone paths that lead to crumbling galleries, and everywhere there are churches, this one blue, this one white, the one at the top of the hill painted a thick, knobby gold. I find a *tienda* crammed with raisin rolls and stacked bottles of ginger ale and the scent of cheese empanadas. The owners live upstairs in a sort of rickety loft, and they look down at me when I enter by glancing up at the mirror they've tacked to the ceiling.

I wait in the park, alone. No book, no friend, no phone—just the clouds that darken one half of the sky. I watch the tiles on the roof of the whitewashed building in front of me; some are amber, some are copper, some are dusted with yellow, and some are bleached white. The tiled roof sits beneath the blue half of the sky, and I think that I'll remember these clear colors forever. I let Cuenca soothe me, let the steady murmur of it loosen my mind, let the river that leads to the mountains and the fruit for sale on the sidewalk remind me of my exquisite freedom. My thoughts run rich beneath the half-and-half sky.

In the days to come, clouds move in, darkening the streets and damp-ening the sun, which before poured over the cathedrals, turning those white walls blinding. The clouds filter through the plazas and settle on the cobblestone streets, and Cuenca grows dreary. I bring my laptop to a café at the corner of a nondescript plaza beside a large, plain-looking church. There, through the window, I watch as people form a line from the church's massive door across the plaza, around the corner, and up the street. It's obvious that they've both come from a distance and are used to waiting here. They are poor and most are old, their clothes and shoes speckled with mud, their umbrellas bent and misshapen. They stand with their things, which they've bundled in canvas sacks and tattered *costals*. They chat with each other and glare at the meandering tourists, who have ventured out with their Gore-Tex raincoats and fancy cameras to see Cuenca.

This is a modern, stylish café, with good service and decent pastries. My coffee cup is kept filled. There are many cafés like this one in Cuenca. I remember Riobamba, another Ecuador altogether, where the old women crouched with their carrots, rearranged their piles of onions, and counted their coins, every task done beneath dark clouds. I remember San Roque, void of sleek cafés but rich in produce, in color, in sound. Here in this café, I feel sealed off somehow, overly protected, the coffee in my cup too hot, the cream swirling through it too rich.

A balding white guy comes in and sets up his laptop on a table near mine. I listen to him speak in a mix of English and Spanish to the waitress, and cringe at the unmistakable American pronunciations. He types for a while, I sip my coffee, and eventually we begin talking.

"I'm Matt," he says, holding out a hand. He's got tiny blue eyes and a forehead that bulges, and his nose is pointy and small. He's very pale; his skin and hair are nearly white, and his eyebrows are nonexistent. He doesn't smile when he talks. He likes Cuenca, he tells me. He much prefers it to Guayaquil, where he lives during the week. He's quick to mention that he owns a tech company, and that his main client is the United States government. Then he nods toward my open laptop and grimaces.

"That's about the most dangerous thing you can do," he says. "Carrying that thing around with you like that. Tons of thieves around here."

He gestures outside, toward the rain, the line of waiters, the women hustling past, sharing an umbrella.

"It's like the Wild West out here, it really is," he says. "You might not see the crime, but it's everywhere."

I want to tell him that so far my strategy has been not to listen to such talk, to move quickly and move smart, going out alone only in daytime. Instead, I let him change the subject.

He tells me there are spots around here where you can stop on the lakeside and catch trout, and the locals will cook them up right there on the spot. I think of my parents, who traveled once to Alaska to catch fish and had them packed and shipped home to eat all winter.

"Do you think it's safe to go alone?" I ask Matt. He grimaces. "Probably not," he admits. "There are people getting killed up there, people getting robbed."

The rain endures outside, and so I listen while he tells me about the time he was carjacked, right in the middle of Guayaquil daytime traffic. Matt was sitting in his Tahoe, listening to music while the sun beat down, when two cars pulled up behind him. I do not ask how he thought he could expect *not* to stand out in a car so massive. Matt says that a couple of guys got out, and they had guns. They beat on Matt's windows; he locked the doors just in time. His windows didn't break. There was nowhere to go, as stopped cars surrounded him. Dozens of people looked on.

"I just, you know, plowed ahead," Matt says, his eyes suddenly bright and wide. I cannot tell whether he's lying. Supposedly, he flew over a car, drove through the traffic, and finally escaped, then kept on driving until he got his totaled Tahoe to a government building where one of his buddies worked.

"I bet I did about ten thousand dollars worth of damage," he admits. "I didn't report it to anyone." He grins; it is the first time he's smiled. "No one ever came after me," he says. "It's the Wild West here, I'm telling you."

Another time, on a corner near this very café, he tells me, he was almost robbed by a short man and a tall man. The two walked past him while Matt stood against the wall of his hotel, waiting for a taxi. He'd leaned his backpack against his leg, careful not to let it out of his sight. But when the two men walked past, the short one faked a seizure and Matt leaned forward to help him stand. Quick as lightening, the tall man grabbed Matt's pack and took off running. Matt chased him. He caught him and grabbed the bag back. "Something you never do," he tells me. "You never chase a thief; just let him go. Sometimes, they got guns."

Matt dragged the tall guy to the police, but the short one got away.

"Still," Matt says, "you can't trust the cops here. They aren't well-trained, and they really don't care about the criminals." He drains his cup of coffee and signals for another. "One week in jail, these guys might spend, and then they're out again. The jails are just too packed for petty crime."

He leans back in his seat, his laptop still open to the coding. The rain has stopped, and I begin to pack up my things.

"Maybe tomorrow I can show you around," Matt suggests. "We could go to the lake, see the trout?"

He looks down after making the offer, like he thinks I'll refuse. In the days to come I will wonder how much I chose not to see. Maybe it's the rain, the gray sky, the empty hostel, the thought of her. Matt's not my type, but he's nice enough, and I could use some time out of Cuenca, away from this rain. We exchange e-mail addresses and agree to meet the next day at this café, after lunch.

Matt shows up two hours late.

"Sorry," he tells me, a couple of times. I haven't much minded the wait; the rain has continued, and I have my book to read. He pulls up to the coffee shop in his souped-up Jeep, the Tahoe replacement.

"See?" he says after I'm buckled in. He's pointing to the ceiling and floors, new camouflage padding and carpet. I can smell the chemicals of the installation. The Jeep sits four feet up from the ground, with huge tires and suspension and a roof rack with giant headlights. He seems not to notice the stares from other motorists and instead chats to me about his friends in government jobs, and about how the drug war is a lost one. He tells me about one DEA friend who caught a guy with a boatful of cocaine and seized his rig, only to see it drifting past a week later.

"It's a big, fat waste of taxpayer dollars, if you ask me," Matt says.

Now that we're climbing out of Cuenca and into the hills, the Jeep won't go as fast. Matt tells me that this is the road to Guayaquil, and between the two cities there is nothing else, just a few houses, a few dirt roads, jungle and trees. When I look down into the valley, past where the road drops steeply off, I can see tiny, rocky rivers and stands of eucalyptus. Milling cows, broken fences, huts clinging to the hillside.

At first I don't hear the horn. Car horns, after all, are a familiar sound, and alarms erupt all day and night in downtown Quito. Matt checks the rearview, and when I turn my head to look back, I see that a car has drawn up behind us, a small white car with a woman driving. There's another woman beside her in the passenger seat. We can't hear them, but I can tell that they're screaming, their mouths opening and closing, their arms flapping.

"We'd better stop," I tell Matt. "What if something's wrong with their car?"

Matt shakes his head. "You never stop," he adds. "God," he says, striking his forehead with his palm, "this is just like Guayaquil!"

He steps hard on the gas, but the Jeep won't go much faster. It's an ancient, clunky thing, despite the new carpet and fresh coat of paint. I turn back again; the woman isn't giving up. She's just a few feet behind us now. We continue like this for a few hundred yards. When Matt speeds up, the car behind us does, too. Finally, it inches past us, and the driver leans over the passenger, whose window is rolled down, to scream at us. We still can't tell what she's saying, but her eyes are desperate. The woman beside her looks terrified. Matt doesn't glance over; he keeps his eyes on the road ahead. The woman passes us and tears up the road, and for a moment I'm relieved. She's gone, I think.

"Let's pull over now, okay?" I beg. "There must be something wrong."

But there's no time. The woman is turning the car around, and now she's flying down the hill, straight at us. In this moment, I learn how it is to see your life pass before you. It is just as they show in the movies, for there are my parents, standing in the garden. There is my brother, in the front seat of his car. There is my dog, a little black lab, and there is my cat, sleeping on the windowsill. There is the house I grew up in, with the long side yard and the woods that stretch behind it. I close my eyes but I still see the images, and I'm barely aware of my blood hissing in my head, beating a pulse at my hands and the back of my neck.

The woman narrowly misses us, blowing past. When I look back, I see that she's turning around once more.

"Look for a side road," Matt is saying. "We've got to lose this crazy."

My eyes dart to the left, then to the right, but there's nothing except the mountains rising up on one side and spilling straight down on the other. There's nowhere to turn.

"What's ahead?" I ask Matt, but he just shakes his head grimly.

"Nothing," he says. "We're six hours from Guayaquil, and in between, there's nothing."

The woman won't give up, and I ask Matt what two women can possibly do.

"There could be someone in the trunk," he replies.

He spots a tiny dirt road to the left, off the side of the main strip. He swerves and takes it, and I see blots of my past again. There is my lover, asleep in my arms. There is my apartment with its cream-colored walls. There is my bed. There is the swimming hole and the stand of princess pines across from my childhood home. The Jeep lurches and swerves and now we're racing down the narrow road, past little huts with broken gates, past men in rubber boots who stand in the river. Past brown stalks of corn and barbed-wire gates. I beg Matt to pull over at one of the houses, but he won't.

"They won't help us," he says. And so we drive and drive, swerving and curving, and when I turn my head again I see the white car behind us, keeping up, the driver's mouth still open in a scream we cannot hear.

I pray. I close my eyes and say the words in my head, try not to imagine my body, bullet-ridden, on the side of this beautiful road. *Please, God, keep me alive. Please keep me alive. Don't let this be it. Don't let me die here. I won't do this again, God. Just keep me alive.* I keep my eyes closed, keep my parents' faces in my mind and my hand tight around the oh-shit bar beside me.

"Don't worry," Matt says, but I keep praying.

Finally, we see a gate.

"It's the national park," Matt says. I can hear the relief in his voice; it enters my own body, calming just slightly my heart. There's a little shack by the gate, and inside I can see a guard. Matt drives up to the gate and the Jeep comes to a shuddering stop. I grab my backpack and push the heavy door of the Jeep open and run to the shack. I duck under the gate, ignoring the guard's protests, and pound on his door. He lets me in. My voice shakes as I try to explain, but I cannot remember the word right now for "chase." I can't even remember how to tell him I'm scared. He peers out the open window of the shack to see for himself.

"It's just two women," he says calmly, as the white car stops behind Matt's Jeep. "It's nothing," he says.

"I'm not leaving," I tell him.

"Fine," he says, and leans back in his chair. "It's two dollars to enter the park," he tells me, and holds out his hand. I root in my pocket for the money.

The female driver is out of her car by now, too. She's parked sideways, so I can see her passenger, a young woman who leans her head over her arms against the window and is crying. There's a child in the backseat, too. It's a baby, really, in a car seat set backwards, so the baby faces the trunk. *Who would drive like that with a baby?* I think, remembering the woman screaming, the way she turned the car around in the middle of the curving road and then drove straight for us. I realize that being inside that car must have been even more terrifying than being in Matt's. Matt jumps out of his own seat and runs toward the driver, who is trying to beat him with her fists. He puts his arms around her to restrain her. She's screaming something I can just barely hear, and it takes me a minute to realize she's speaking English.

"That's my husband," she is saying, in a voice with a thick Spanish accent. "This is his child! This is his kid!" But Matt is shaking his head. He pushes the woman away, then jumps back into his Jeep and pulls right up to the window.

"Two dollars," the man tells him, unfazed, and Matt digs around in his backpack for the change. Eventually, the woman gets back in the white car, defeated, and drives off.

Afterwards, Matt tells me it was a scam. He says he should really get a gun. We wait for thirty minutes at the edge of the park, making sure the white car is gone. I want to walk, to find the lakes where fish swim and mountains rise up, reflecting blue onto the silver water, but I realize that, with Matt, I am afraid. I think that I'm in shock. I try to remember exactly what the woman looked like, but all I can see is the small white car and the outline of her passenger. I ask Matt if he knew the lady, and he says no, over and over again.

"It's a scam," he repeats, peering down the road through a pair of binoculars. The guard at the gate has lost interest in us and is checking his cell phone. He does not watch us when we leave. As soon as we enter Cuenca again, grocery stores and sidewalks appearing, I tell Matt to let me off.

"No," he says.

"Yes," I tell him. *Two women*, I am thinking. When he finally pulls over, I jump out, not saying goodbye, not looking back, cursing myself for having trusted him. With Matt, I felt more afraid than I ever have. I saw my whole life, but in the end there were two women and a baby behind us, nothing more.

In the morning, I open my laptop to check my e-mail. There is a message from Matt's e-mail address.

I am the woman in the white car. I am Matt's wife. He's always doing this. Please help me…we could meet.

On my last day in Cuenca, I see a dead man. He's lying on the cobblestone plaza in front of one of Cuenca's huge white cathedrals, just as the rain is starting to fall. I am running to the nearest café without an umbrella when I see him there, flat on his back, his arms spread out beside him. It isn't uncommon to see men passed out on the street here; they get drunk and sleep it off. But the rain isn't waking him up. It picks up and then starts to pour, soaking him, soaking the streets and the trees, but still he doesn't move. A short man in an old suit and a navy baseball hat comes over and tries to lift the dead man up by pulling on his arm, but he can't move him. The dead man's head slumps back, and the short guy lifts his limp wrist and holds it in his hand.

Two men are drinking beer and smoking cigarettes in the café, watching. At first they are laughing; how drunk can you get in the middle of the day? But then they see that the short man can't make the man on the ground move. They see the way he raises his head and looks around, the dead man's limp wrist in his hand, and so they run out into the rain, leaving their cigarettes smoking in the ashtray. The three of them struggle with the dead man's body, and I can see when they lift him that his gray hair is combed back and he's wearing a dark, elegant suit. His shoes are shined. He's no bum. The men stagger across the plaza and disappear into the library across the street. A few minutes later, I hear the sound of a siren screaming, and then the ambulance appears and the medics jump out and run through the library's open door while a guard stands watch, a huge gun strapped across his chest. The two guys come into the café now, shuddering, and one of them has tears in his eyes.

I replay the images in my mind: the princess pines, my brother driving his car, my mother in the garden, her pail filling with peas. I think of the two women in the car, the baby in the backseat, Matt's face unchanged as they chased us, unchanged as we flew off onto the side road and tore through the little village. *We are all going to follow that man in the suit*, I think.

"You will find what you need," Carlos had said. Without E—'s voice in my mind, her next e-mail waiting to be read in the Internet café, her next phone call to be scheduled—without her, I can see my route more clearly. I am looking for places to imprint onto me; I am filling pages with words. At night, I type on my beat-up laptop, recounting the afternoon with Matt, scarcely believing it happened at all: the frantic, jolting ride, and then the e-mail that explained everything. I write it down, but I show the words to no one. No one knows, and that freedom has its cost. Today I saw an old man lying on the cold street, and I learned that your life can change with a drop of rain. I vow to be more cautious, for life is like thread, so easily broken.

VILCABAMBA, ECUADOR

Besides me in the cab, the taxi driver also has his two daughters, who sit with backpacks on their laps and ribbons in their hair. Their uniforms match. We ride quietly through waking Cuenca, the girls murmuring questions to their father. They each lean forward and give him kisses when he pulls up to their school, and then they bundle out and for the rest of the ride we are quiet.

In the bus station, a young family sits on an unwrapped mattress, surrounded by their possessions. The four of them don't have much—a few over-packed *costals*, a rickety bicycle, a couple of taped-up boxes. They all sit, shoulders hunched, and the little boy fiddles with something on the ground. There's one other foreigner standing around, a tall boy with curly hair and a very old, very patched backpack resting on his bony shoulders. He boards the same bus I do, flashing me a grin as he eases himself into his seat. I smile back, turn my head, watch as we slowly leave the lot and begin to inch through town. My next stop will be Vilcabamba, one of Ecuador's southernmost towns, and from there I'll cross into Peru.

Goodbye, place, I say in my mind to Cuenca, beautiful with its churches and cobblestones, its emerald national park. This city left a sour taste in my mouth, but I cannot blame the land. I think of Matt's wife bawling at him and wonder how he'll ever let himself face her again. He'd pretended not to know her. I feel sick all over again, remembering that I waited for him, I got into his car, I listened to his stories, I did not trust myself when two women pulled up behind us, frantic. "You'll find what you need there," Carlos had said, and I will his words to be true.

"If you have any questions about Vilcabamba, let me know," the curly-haired boy beside me is saying. The two young women in the seat next to ours are watching attentively, bouncing their babies on their knees.

"I lived there for a year," he adds, sticking out his hand. "I'm Isaac."

Isaac taught English in this valley for a year, and it's been four since he returned. He can't wait: his host family is waiting for him, he explains, and a few of his students, maybe even one of his fellow teachers. He's practically bouncing in his seat. I remember the white car, the frantic ride, the panic in the passenger's eyes, and am grateful again for this bus, this landscape that rolls, these peaks, smaller than in Cuenca and reminiscent of home: rounded ridges, overgrown hillsides, mountain farms. Isaac points out the little towns, explaining that they never got famous like Vilcabamba did, even though, in his opinion, they're just as beautiful. Vilcabamba is the one known for longevity, but Isaac says all these places offer that. He shows me the pretty blue church at the edge of one village, and the valley that's sprung up with houses since he was last here. "Vilca*bamba*," he keeps saying. As the bus pulls into town, he claps his hands.

He points me toward the hostel he remembers and gives me a hug.

"Good luck," he says, grinning, and then he's jogging down the hill, around the bend and out of sight.

Once a retreat for Incan royalty, Vilcabamba is now one of dozens of towns scattered in this fertile, mild south-central region of Ecuador. Mandango Mountain—otherwise known as 'The Sleeping Inca'—is said to watch over the town, cradling it against natural disasters. In the past few decades, Vilcabamba has gained notoriety for the longevity of its inhabitants—some claim to be as old as a hundred and thirty-five.

Researchers have attributed the long lifespans to the high altitude, the mineral-rich water and soil, the abundance of fruits and vegetables, and the vigorous walking a Vilcabamba life entails.

The hostel Isaac recommends is inexpensive and pretty: adobe cottages built around a garden. As he points out the breakfast room and the place to hang laundry, the owner explains that everything grows here: honeysuckle and hollyhock and Queen of the Night, which winds around the big laundry basin and creeps off toward the hammocks.

"Enjoy," the owner says after he's shown me my small, spotless room. He's left the window open, and after he shuts the door I sit on one of the two firm beds and close my eyes. The wind through the curtains is warm and holds the faintest hint of rain. Besides that and the birds and the sound of the owner's footsteps, though, there is silence. This is the marvel of travel; I have gone from rain to sun, from city to country. I have met someone who helped me. I have forgotten Matt just a little. I have forgotten to think about her. I discover that I'm ravenous, and I try to count back to the time I last ate a real meal.

In town, at a table on the sidewalk, a waitress serves me sliced chicken, big brown beans, warm tortillas, a pile of guacamole, and a hot cup of coffee with milk. The town's healthy air has done its work, and I eat and eat of the lunch. As the waitress clears my empty plates, a truck passes with Isaac in back, perched in the open bed. He catches my eye, grins as he did before, and flashes a peace sign.

In the morning, Isaac comes by.

"I thought you might want to hike," he explains, peering all around at the place, inspecting.

"Last time I was here," he says, "we drank red wine with Coke! All night!"

He takes the seat across from me at the breakfast table and glances at the basket of toast.

"Have some," I say. He picks up a slice and butters it, putting it away in two bites. He moves on to the second, then polishes off the third as I finish my coffee. Isaac's presence feels easy and light, and again I am struck by the contrast: Matt and Isaac are, in a sense, opposites of each other, and their accent is all they appear to have in common. Whereas Matt seemed to hide a darkness and a fear of everything, finding protection in his weapons and vehicles, Isaac pins his heart to his sleeve with every conversation. He has come for me, plain and simple. It's before eight o'clock, and he looks a little sleepy. He banters with the woman who comes to clear the dishes, and she brings him more toast. He's got crumbs on his mouth and an overlooked smear of sunscreen on his nose. I lace up my hiking boots and pack my camera while Isaac inspects the garden and the laundry room, and introduces himself to the couple who drove here all the way from Ontario.

We cross a river as stubby, steep hills rise up alongside us, forming jungled valleys. The river curves to sidle the road. We pass a barn with animal skins tacked to the outside walls, and a group of men laying cement for a new house. Isaac notes that many homes have gone up since he was last here.

"The *gringos* love it," he says. "For twenty thousand, they can buy a nice piece of land, and for another fifty, they can build their dream house." He gazes up the valley, where the roofs of new homes glint in the sun, and stone gates keep intruders out.

He tells me about the hippies, the way they flock from the States and Argentina and Europe to buy up land where they can grow whatever they want.

"It's easy to live off the map," Isaac says. "But," he adds, "there are a lot of crazies too, guys who come and live as hermits, or go into the town square to get drunk every day before lunch."

Still, Isaac's love for Vilcabamba is clear. Every man who passes us, Isaac knows. His Spanish is still good after four years in Berkeley, and he chats with men in dusty rubber boots, machetes slung at their hips.

"Sorry," he apologizes after each eager, lengthy conversation, but he beams.

We climb up out of the valley and traverse the ridge, and you can see that the hills around us were stripped bare long ago. We look down to where the river divides the land and see that houses have sprung up, and fresh roads. "Those weren't there before," Isaac says many times. He talks steadily as we walk, keeping me entertained, stopping periodically to look around, his hand shading his eyes.

"God," he keeps saying. "*Vilcabamba.*"

We pass an old man with a long white beard and round spectacles, and his wizened, gray-haired wife. They're hiking to visit a friend, they tell us in Spanish, even though their accents beneath are American. We pass a hippie girl with rosaries around her neck and no bra who asks us about the purple flowers we keep passing.

"What are they called?" she asks, squinting in the sun, but we don't know. Two men are cutting the brush on the sides of the hill with machetes—"food for the cows," Isaac says.

"How's it going?" he asks them cheerfully.

"Working," the men grumble without looking up.

We never end up finding the waterfall Isaac was sure existed down in one of the valleys, but we stumble along the rocky river, stopping once to sit and eat cookies. Isaac tells me about his girlfriend, who he calls his partner. They met a year ago. She's a professor at Berkeley, and he believes she is the one.

"That's hard," he says when I tell him about E—. "I know how that is. Distance is basically impossible." He passes me a Ziploc bag filled with M&Ms he brought from home. We get lost several times, but not very, and eventually clouds come and fill the sky, cooling the afternoon. We pass a tree with wide leaves the colors of pale stone. We see birds— little yellow ones, iridescent blue ones, once a toucan sitting perfectly still in a tree, its beak long and curved. It doesn't stir when we call and clap to it. On our walk back toward the village, we pass the same men, hacking at the hillside brush. An orange-brown mutt sits perched above them, looking down, and this time Isaac doesn't say a word.

Later, I figure I can see why the hippies come, why the old people hold onto their years, and why these little hotels spring up and fill every season. In the morning the sun will almost certainly shine, and in the late afternoon there are almost always rainstorms. Here is eternal summer, monsoons washed out by sunshine. I sit beneath the awning of my clean adobe room while the rain comes, first spilling over the earth gently, then breaking and pouring with such force it turns to hail. The smell of the earth rises; the sky right above me blackens. Still, a blue streak on the horizon holds on. In a moment, the clouds will turn pink.

I'll sleep one more night in my Vilcabamba bed, where outside my window spicy clover grows thick. Although I might dream of staying, I'll board a bus and keep traveling south, propelled by the route Theroux sketched so many years ago. His map is mine now, and his mission belongs to me: Make it south, write it down. Shuck the monotony that clouded your other life. Try and really see things. Worship every moment as if nothing matters more. In the morning I'll check out of my hostel, and then someone else will come, and sleep in this bed, and walk the Vilcabamba mountains to be amazed.

LIMA, PERU

I find in the morning a thermos of hot water, a tea bag, a sandwich wrapped in paper, and an orange, all stacked on a saucer filled with water to discourage ants. I prepare the tea, toast the bread, peel the orange and separate each section to eat. I wash the dishes, thinking of the practiced ants, and then hoist my pack up onto my shoulders. All the while, the darkness hangs outside, thick over the flowers, who have closed their blooms against the night. The gate to the hostel is unlocked, and I step out onto the empty street.

Everyone in Vilcabamba sleeps, everyone except the roosters, whose caws I hear from the end of every street. The darkness is ink black, warm as blood. At the station, a few men standing around in cowboy hats ask me politely where I'm headed. The tallest, youngest one says a shared taxi will come any moment.

"We're all going to Loja," he says. The other two men are old, with stooped backs and old clothes. While the young guy peers at the green light of his cell phone, tapping out messages, the old men close their eyes and sway. An old, brown Sedan pulls up, a clean-shaven man behind the wheel and a pregnant woman in a white blouse beside him.

"This is it," the young guy says, and I squeeze in between the three men in the back seat. They discuss the price with the driver and agree on six dollars.

"Is that okay?" the young guy asks me, and the driver glances in his rearview to catch my nod. We'll each pay just over a dollar for an hour's ride.

The young guy and the oldest man fall asleep immediately. The rest of us watch out the window at the sleeping cornfields. At silent, darkened churches, the driver and the woman beside him cross themselves. We pass a couple with a young child between them; the three stumble along the roadside in the darkness. In the tiny towns that we drive through, the lights of the *tiendas* are already coming on, and a man in a cowboy hat smokes on the porch of his house, tipping his cap as we pass. The driver toots his horn. He rolls his window down, and warm wind pours in.

We are deposited on a side street in downtown Loja. The sky is still dark, and the shared-taxi driver won't take me to the terminal.

"Sorry," he says with a shrug. "I always stop here." He points toward the corner, where the cabs come, then takes my money, closes the car door, and tips his seat back for a nap.

I buy a cup of sugary coffee at the Loja bus terminal. My ticket to Piura costs ten dollars, and the ride will take all day. The other passengers are mostly poor, with second-hand clothes and *costals* full of their things. The men, bored, buy cups of coffee and mill about in dirty baseball hats and oversized fleece jackets printed with fish and game club insignia or the names of North American church groups. There's one other foreigner on board; I imagine she's European, a little older than I am, and has been traveling for a while. She's got a pierced nose and earrings made from pieces of sharpened wood. Her hair is long and sun-bleached blonde, and she sits cross-legged in the very first seat on the bus while ladies with big bags and small children pile in beside her. A little boy runs on, barefoot, and asks if the bus goes to Cariamanga. A few people nod, one man shouts that it does, and half a dozen women follow the little boy on, urging him back so they can all sit together.

The elderly woman next to me plucks strands of my hair from my purse and drops them into the aisle, then smiles at me. When I offer her a stick of gum, she murmurs gracias, unwraps it slowly, puts it in her mouth as if it is a delicacy, and sucks on it. I wonder how many teeth she has. A vendor comes on selling Spanish-English dictionaries, small paper-bound books he claims cost two dollars in the store, but he's selling them for just fifty cents. The woman beside me touches the man's arm after he's given his speech, buys a book, examines it briefly, then slides it into her purse.

In the next town, a different man comes aboard selling pens that light up at the end.

"They're best for nighttime," he tells his audience. "For when you need some light," he adds, demonstrating by pointing the laser around the bus. The woman beside me buys a pen, selecting a red one from the bunch the salesman holds in his hand. She takes a dollar coin from her little coin purse and pays him, then slides the pen into her purse alongside the dictionary. Then she jostles her seat back with some effort and goes to sleep.

The landscape, green when we leave Loja, grows progressively drier. The grassy hills become dry like burial mounds, and we can see into deep valleys where riverbeds wind, scattered with stones and sand and smooth, wind-worn branches. We pass tiny adobe huts built camouflaged into the hills, where shepherds herd goats, the color of the earth, and thirsty-looking cows, their ribs visible. There are tacked-together *tiendas* with bags of potato chips for sale. And then it is emptiness, just these clay-colored hills and burnt-looking shrubs.

The sky is a hot, hazy blue, and we drive through the desert for hours. When we reach Cariamanga, the last town before the Peruvian border, most of the passengers disembark. One of the women getting off notices that my neighbor still sleeps. She prods her gently.

"Mama," she says, and the old woman nods awake.

"It's time?" she asks, and the younger woman helps her to stand. And then it's just me and the white girl up front and a young couple behind me, pale-skinned and dark-haired, who whisper to each other in Portuguese.

We come to a gate and a dusty shack. The driver pulls over, turns off the engine, pulls his cap down over his eyes, and leans back. The four of us passengers look at each other, shrug our shoulders, and trundle off the bus. A guard comes out of the shack and takes down our information, one by one, writing our passport numbers and expiration dates painstakingly down into a ledger. All around us is desert: hills eroded by sun and wind and layered with dust. It is much hotter here than in Loja, whose clouds caught Cuenca's leftover rain and deposited it over the city. Climbing back onto the bus, the blonde girl with the pieces of wood in her earlobes catches my eye and smiles. Now we're in Peru, though out our window, nothing changes. The desert rolls on, the jungles of Vilcabamba and her inky nights erased.

Our next rest stop is a one-street town with a school, a fruit-juice *tienda*, and a restaurant, which offers bowls of rice with meat and vegetables and plastic cups of sugary hibiscus juice. I eat hungrily, though the food is not particularly good, overly seasoned with salt and sugar. I don't know when I'll eat again. Afterwards, I look for a bathroom and find, eventually, a toilet behind the school. There aren't doors on the stalls, and the floor is flooded. I remember the bathroom in San Roque and try to imagine my high-school bathroom ever looking like this. No water comes from the tap when I turn it on, and I wipe my hands on my skirt and hurry back to the bus. The blonde-haired girl sits on the curb, peeling a mango.

Through the long afternoon we drive, and after the rest stop the land becomes even truer desert. Everything seems barren—the sand-colored road and sky, the spindly trees, the shacks that line the road. I notice that each hamlet has matching outhouses, all with the same lime-green corrugated roofs and the same plywood walls; they all seem to have been built by the same hand. I imagine the government or some NGO swooping down and distributing the outhouses, and the people receiving them, replacing their old systems with these, gifts like the stoves in Uspantán. After many hours we do finally come to a city. It appears on the horizon as a dirty mirage, and though eventually there are many buildings, there still isn't color. Everything is dust brown beneath the gauzy sun. No one walks in the street; the cars drive noisily past, their headlights just now coming on. We pull into a bus station and I make to stand and gather my things. But the Brazilians behind me shake their heads. "We're not there yet," they say. The blonde girl cranes her head around to look at us. She, too, has been gathering up her stuff.

"This isn't Piura?" she asks, and then I know she's North American. We both get off to buy bottles of juice, and when we get back on, she takes the seat across from mine.

And how easy it is to talk to her, Kerry from Arizona. She tells me about the farm she's been working at, up in Quito.

"It was crazy," she says, grinning. She describes the lesbian couple who ran the farm. One night, all the volunteers drank tea made from San Pedro cactus and then vomited into bags. They'd wept, sang, and stayed up all night. Kerry slept with one of the other volunteers that night, she tells me, as if we're already friends.

"It was horrible," she admits. "Plus, the condom broke." He'd gone to buy her a morning-after pill, but that was his only acknowledgement of their night together, and after that, whenever she saw him, she always tasted something bad at the tip of her tongue. There was something about the farm, something lawless, not just because of the pot that grew at the edge of the property or the way the San Pedro, that tribal drug which is said to induce mild hallucinations, came so easily. There was something about the way the lesbian couple fought, Kerry tells me, and then there came the night one when of them slept with the guy Kerry had been with. She tells me all of this with her body turned to face me, her eyes resting on me. She's beautiful, blue-eyed and blonde-haired with long, angular bones.

"I had to get out of there," she says, and reaches into her bag for another mango, which she begins, carefully, to peel.

We reach Piura just before the sun sets. We aren't far from the sea, but there's no scent of it on the wind. An orange-gold glow casts itself over the roofs of cars and the dusty streets, and the busy roads remind me of India. There is a near-tropical quality to the city; tall, tired-looking palm trees line the streets, and in the central plaza there is water, which springs up out of a fountain and spatters onto the street. Looking at the map, Piura doesn't seem so far, just a few thumbnail lengths from Vilcabamba. But the hours on the bus make the distance palpable, and Piura feels a world apart. The people look different than in Ecuador—smaller somehow, without the high cheekbones and broad foreheads of the Andean indigenous. With their darkened skin and smaller bones, these Peruvians seem to have adapted to the desert sun. Piura receives less than three inches of rain annually, and outside these city limits, sand stretches, broken only by those windswept hamlets we passed, and by the sea.

Kerry's in a rush to get to Lima. She's signed on for a week-long yoga retreat and needs to be there tomorrow afternoon, so she's headed now to the bus terminal. I think of searching for a hotel room and spending the night there, alone, and I wonder whether I'll be able to bear the silence after such a long and guzzling drink of conversation. So when she invites me to travel with her there, I accept. We'll cross Peru through the night, and reach Lima by morning.

Those raised in the United States are trained, I think, to see Latin America as a disjointed place, many small countries within one triangular landmass. It isn't true. Each of Latin America's countries, especially those of South America, seem massive once you're there, the cities so huge, the distances between them so vast. This is true especially with Peru; I'd always heard of Machu Picchu and bustling Lima, but never realized that in between those there was desert. We're driving through it now, the hours turning over themselves, ten hours turning into twelve turning into fifteen. More than half of Peru's population lives on these deserts, while most of the country is uninhabited jungle. The society is split between a white and mestizo middle class and the poor indigenous. A Chinese presence is strong, and Quechua is a national language. Like Ecuador, Peru offers some of the world's highest peaks, mightiest rivers, and most diverse jungles.

We board another bus and ride through the night. In the terminal, we paid for tickets with our credit cards. They cost more than any bus fare I've paid since leaving Boston. But the air conditioning circulates evenly, and the generous seats recline. The bus leaves exactly on time. A steward goes up and down the aisles, offering soft drinks, then dinner, then coffee or tea. A movie plays, and then, around midnight, the lights in the cabin go off and the steward distributes blankets and pillows. We've paid twenty-eight dollars for this fifteen-hour ride to Lima, and I think, leaning back as we rumble through the night, that every penny was worth it. We sleep, and when we open our eyes again the sky is bright and the steward is coming around with tea. Soft music plays from the speakers, and we wait for the condensation on the windows to bead and run so we can see out.

We are flanked to the left by massive dirty-gray dunes flecked with clusters of shacks. A thin mist has formed, and I'll learn that Peru's coast nearly always has this fog where the desert meets the sea. The ocean is to our right, and at first we're enchanted by it, the way it sprawls massive, nearly the color of the dunes. But after several hours we grow used to its expanse. I wonder whether anyone chooses to live here, for I see no green, barely any traces of life. I wonder where the fresh water comes from, and imagine that the people who live here, so close to the sea, must spend much of their time obtaining water to drink.

We drive through Lima's outskirts for an hour. How ugly it is here, with the repair shops and car dealerships and dirty walls along the road, spray-painted with advertisements for the two presidential candidates. The race is between Ollanta Humala, a left-wing, nation-alistic ex-army officer, and Keiko Fujimori, the daughter of previous president Alberto Fujimori, who now waits in prison while the elec-tion draws closer. I will learn that Fujimori was accused of embezzle-ment and of human rights violations. Still, many in this country favor his legacy, and the name Keiko, spelled out in block letters on the walls of buildings and on the strips of billboards that crawl over this city, becomes ubiquitous.

Quito was surrounded by mountains, which filtered the air. Any-where you looked, you could see the peaks. For this, Quito is a beautiful city, crammed with cheap cement houses and flimsy plaster walls, but clean somehow, always. Lima, at first glance, is the opposite. The sea does not filter the air; instead, it seems to clench it, weighing it down. The dense mist clouds the streets, and when we finally climb off the climate-controlled bus, the humidity nearly chokes us.

Kerry decides she has a few hours to spare before she needs to leave for the yoga center, so we take a taxi to the Miraflores district, a neighbor-hood recommended by the guidebook. We give the driver the address of a hostel listed in the book. From the outside, the hostel could be any building; with the exception of the color variances—white or peach, cream, pale yellow—every house on this street is identical. Each res-idence has a metal gate, and we hear the sound of three keys in three locks. Finally, a young Peruvian man pushes the door open.

"Welcome," he tells us, as though he knows us already. "I'm Antonio." He gives us both brief, perfunctory kisses on the cheek and leads us onto a tiny patio crammed with potted plants and mosaiced tables, ash-trays and black folding chairs. Antonio wears tight black jeans, black flip-flops, a black sweatshirt, and a white collared shirt beneath it. His hair looks wet, slicked back, and he smells crisply of cologne. But after he's shown us to our room—four low walls with just enough space for a double bed and a chair set beside it for a bedside table—he pours us cups of coffee in the communal kitchen and admits with a small and guilty smile that he is very hung over. He rolls his eyes.

"Welcome to Lima," he says, his voice low and cigarette-scrawled. "It's crazy here," he says.

Kerry and I finish our coffee and venture out into the misting city. We cannot see the ends of streets for the fog. We follow our noses to the ocean—salty, dirty, and huge—and then stand at the edge of it. The edge of this city slides into the ocean, red cliffs sloping into churning gray water far below us. Behind us rise the most expensive buildings in Lima, modern, airy-looking apartment buildings painted white and turquoise blue, or sided with lightweight steel. Before them, lofty palms wave their arms. And yet there is this constant mist, and it induces a kind of melancholy.

We stumble into the Park of Love, where snippets of poems curl in mosaics over benches and fountains. We meander between the statues, reading each passage:

I always say goodbye, and I stay.

I adore everything that isn't mine, you for example.

"Love," Kerry says, and rolls her eyes. Couples strolling in, hand in hand, don't glance at us as we leave.

This part of town has sleek clothing stores, high-ceilinged galleries, tiny bars in the half-basements of buildings, fish shops whose counters sit stacked with salmon and sea bass and shrimp. We enter a gleaming grocery store, and for a moment I am stunned. Everything is so clean.

"This looks like home," Kerry whispers, and I nod. This *is* home. Handwritten signs, expensive cheese, a room full of wine, produce from all over the world, a bakery at one end. This is a part of home. It's overwhelming, the richness. I feel unsettled, for this grocery store was so familiar to me once, so routine that I never noticed how pristine and how abundant stacks of apples could seem. After much deliberation, we buy chocolate, bread, cheese, and wine, and then fumble with the still-unfamiliar Peruvian bills we pull crumpled from our wallets. A girl before us in line buys cotton balls, tweezers, nail polish, eyebrow wax, and tampons. She pays with a credit card, and I marvel at the fact that she found all of those items in one store.

After that, Kerry decides to stay a night.

"The yoga can wait," she says. "I like it here." We both know the truth, though: we cannot wait to taste the soft cheese, the cold wine, the fine chocolate. At one of the tables in the hostel's patio, we unwrap the food and screw open the bottle. I close my eyes to the savory cheese and the hint of pear in the wine. We tell each other that we'd better leave soon, for too much time here will make us fat and broke.

"We'll never leave!" Kerry sputters, reaching for another slice of brie. "Everyone will wonder where we are!"

This was how my life was, once, but the flavors came so often I forgot to notice. Later, my stomach will turn from the food, food I've grown unused to after so many nights of rice and vegetables dusted with salt, of bread in the morning and of fruit sliced into plastic bowls, of instant coffee, of cheap canned beer, and of squeaky homemade cheese, sliced from a wheel.

Kerry leaves in the morning, guiltily.

"The yogis won't mind!" the Australian owner exclaims, but Kerry refuses another cup of coffee. We embrace and kiss on the cheek, automatically, for we've both been here long enough to know. And then she shoulders her pack, waves one last time, and crosses the street to hail a cab. She'll take one bus and then another, and will arrive at the ashram, she thinks, by late afternoon.

I never told her that Lima was where E— wanted to go. She'd taken a college course on urban design in Latin America; Cusco and Lima had been two of the cities the class had focused on. The backbones of these cities are ancient, thousands of years older than any modern North American metropolis. These were the ports, the centers, the places that were recognized for their proximity to water or the way they were cupped, protected, by the mountains; they were cities built long before the colonists ever started trickling in.

I take the shiny train that cuts through the center of the city and runs along the main highway. Here, Lima is all pavement and traffic, and the city is a map I cannot read. I want out. But I get off the sleek train, dutifully, and climb up the stairs into the city's main plaza, massive and dirty. The buildings, at least, are molded and interesting, stretching to the sky. The gray humidity presses onto me. I go into an empty museum, pay a little money to see a few modern paintings on the wall. It's cool in this museum, but even the paintings, to me, are grayscale and uninteresting. I miss the hibiscus in Vilcabamba and the rolling, windy climb.

Here, paint peels off every wall, and there comes the near-constant smell of urine. Reeking piles of trash lean torn against the curb. Cars pull up next to me and slow down. The drivers click their tongues. On a curving one-way street lined with hostels and narrow apartment buildings, gardens, and trees, I see two cats behind the barred window of a home. They're cleaning themselves, and they blink slowly at me as I pass. I am nothing more than another passerby, the places I've been invisible to them, and irrelevant.

HUANCAYO, PERU

I miss the first bus to Huancayo by ten minutes, so there's time to get a coffee from the snack shop, where the chef behind the counter is busy frying eggs and laying ham and cheese over them, then heating up corn tamales in the microwave, then toasting bread on the griddle. Finally, he makes my coffee on the espresso machine.

"Strong or soft?" he asks. I tell him strong, and when I take my first sip, I burn my mouth. And then my bus is here. The people have queued, and an older man in a cowboy hat helps me stow my pack in the bus's belly. We settle in our seats, rustling with our purses and lunches. Someone turns the music up, then abruptly off. The bus grows quiet, and we pull out of the station, exactly on time.

We drive down the main highway, thick with cars, and alongside us the buildings get shorter and shorter, poorer and poorer, now constructed of plywood, now of ribbed metal sheets. I don't see Humala's name anywhere as we pass bicycle shops and *tiendas* and a factory that puffs huge plumes of smoke the same color as the sky. There are just the block letters: KEIKO. The buildings are gray or brown as the treeless earth, and on the scrubby charcoal hills houses are built in stacks, like blocks, and painted bright colors—lime green, citrusy orange, teal, and pink—in an effort to defy the drab place.

I think of the homes beside the road. I picture dirt floors, families sleeping in one room, maybe even sharing one bed. The family in Loja waited with all their possessions: the three of them—father, mother, young child—perched on a bare mattress, waiting, while their duffels and beaten suitcases and plastic bags waited with them.

"Look at them," a man had said, a man who I suspected was drunk, though the sky had just barely grown light. "They've got their whole house with them," he had cried, mockingly. The family on the mattress crouched closer together and the father wrapped his arm around his small son's shoulders. Eventually, the loud man stumbled away, complaining that his hot chocolate was only water before dumping the contents onto the ground. I think again of their bed, their satchels, their possessions limited to what they can pack and load onto a bus.

Farther east, the city erodes, and the land becomes suddenly, startlingly green. A blue sky peers down through white-gray clouds; crops patch the hillside. A river cuts through the deep valley, and on either side of us, jagged hills rise up, treeless and brown. The dunes behind us are already gone, and I glance back. *Goodbye, place,* I tell Lima silently, and then look straight ahead once more. There is water here; there is green. The moment of travel is merciful, and Lima is behind me now.

The road winds through the river valley for a while, and eventually I catch glimpses of snow on the peaks in the distance. The villages grow smaller and barer the higher we climb. Built along the roads, the little towns are nothing more than a few houses, a *tienda*, and a church in the city's center. I wonder whether I've seen more a beautiful countryside so far. Costa Rica's expansive green pastures, northern Guatemala's stretches of mountains, Ecuador's rolling road toward Vilcabamba—none were like this, so barren and beautiful both. There are snippets of rugged lives: a man herds goats in the road, and schoolchildren in uniforms run to the side to make way for the bus.

We come to a mountain pass, and my ears pop. It's impossible to remember anything else being this dramatic, especially after those days beneath Lima's gray sky. How jagged the peaks are, and how white, with stretches of glacial lake at their bases. The lakes reflect the blue-white of the sky and glow nearly green. And then the snow begins to fall, shrouding our view, and I wish for my father. He's dreamed of seeing the Andes, and now I'm among them.

I see the place for him. I watch out the window as the exquisite landscape unfolds, as we ascend, as the homes grow simpler and the landscape more dramatic. I take pictures in my mind and send them to him. The sky widens, and clouds darken the bus's interior. I feel something latch into place, deep inside me. I am ready for the peaks and the rainy trails. I will be alone, but I'm not afraid. There's no Kerry, no Isaac, but there will be others. Something has loosened. I don't know what it will look like when I get there, but I'll get off of this bus and find somewhere to go. People will help me along, and hours from now, somewhere in Huancayo, I will sleep beneath this now-familiar sky.

In Huancayo, an old woman answers the door when I ring the bell. She leads me inside, brushing dirt from her clothes and straightening the kerchief knotted around her hair.

"I've been in the garden," she explains, folding her gloves and setting them on the stair.

"There's no one else here," she says. "How many nights do you need?" She looks at me finally, her eyes blue and black both, her mouth wrinkled but dark so that her lips seem those of a much younger woman.

"Just one night," I say, and she frowns. With just one guest, one night, she won't be able to turn on the hot water. "It's just too expensive," she explains.

"Okay," I say, and turn to leave. But on my way out, as she's unlocking the front door, she asks me if I really need hot water. I tell her I don't. Her house reminds me of my grandmother's, the same whiffs of cleaning products and mothballs and the underlying scent of dried flowers. The same blocky windows and clean floors. The doors are made of the same light wood as my grandmother's doors, panels narrow and long in the Finnish way. The woman gives me a towel and the key and then goes back outside, where her garden awaits. I sit a while, marveling, inhaling.

I've come all this way, but maybe it hasn't been so very far.

Constructed at an elevation of over ten thousand feet, Huancayo is known as the cultural and economic center of the Peruvian Andes. For a thousand years a part of the Wari empire, the district was officially deemed Spanish by Pizarro in 1534. Today, the Mercado Mayorista stretches over many blocks: truck drivers unloading crates of oranges, ladies stretching umbrellas out over tables of river fish, heaps of brown dates, open sacks of rice and dried beans, buckets of dried red chilies. When you buy a fish, the woman behind the counter chops off the head and the tail for you, so that before her lie a row of fish heads, their empty eyes gleaming. Whole chickens hang by their veiny legs, their bodies plucked bare and their eyes shut tight. There are buckets of calla lilies and hydrangeas and baby's breath alongside long, purply plantains and blotchy green peppers.

One man has huge bags of dried green leaves on display.

"Coca?" I ask him.

"Coca," he says, scooping a few leaves up onto the scale then into a plastic sack. "Chew," he instructs, folding one in half and putting it into the corner of his mouth. When I ask how much, he shakes his head. I try to offer him two soles. He shakes his head again, insistent.

"It's a gift!" he cries, and then cranes his neck around me to attend to the next customer. I thank him and get out of the way.

The coca leaves have no effect on me. I read later that they should be chewed with a catalyst, like lime, but I chew them up raw and then let them sit in my mouth, and then I spit them out onto the ground. I notice that many people carry the little sacks of leaves at their hips; they pluck leaves out, one at a time, and place them on their tongues as they wait for someone to buy their oranges, their bananas, their batteries, a belt from their handful of belts. All day I imagine they chew the leaves, which are a stimulant and an appetite suppressant both. Eduardo Galeano describes his 1970 encounter with Bolivian miners: "They all chew coca-leaf and ash [...] and this too is part of the annihilation process."

Coca leaves had been cultivated in South America for centuries, but when the Europeans came, they used the coca as a tool of enslavement, paying laborers with leaves instead of money, using the addictive coca to deprive the workers of food and to simultaneously keep them awake.

Now, though, the people seem sleepy and busy both, the munching of their jaws automatic.

The man at the café where I sit and drink a coffee has lived in New York before. "The Big Apple," hey says in English when I tell him where I'm from. He shows off his first granddaughter, who is just six months old and sits perched on her weary mother's lap. The baby points at my dish of yogurt.

"She wants some!" the man teases, reaching for her and jiggling her on his hip.

"How do you like my country?" he asks in his plucky English, and I tell him that it's very nice so far.

"And the people?" he asks eagerly. "The people are nice?"

"Yes," I tell him. "They're very nice." He grins. Then he hands the baby back to her mother and walks around to the back of the register to write out my receipt.

"Aren't you afraid?" the man asks in English, just as I'm leaving. He is watching me, waiting, and I imagine he wants to say more, as I often do, but cannot find the words in his second language.

"I'm not afraid," I say quietly, in Spanish. "It's been wonderful here." For I have come this far, after all, and every night I've had a meal and a bed in which I've slept unafraid. Oh, there have been nights, there have

been bus rides, and there have been cities whose maps I could not decipher. But I don't tell all of this to the man behind the counter, for I don't
have the words in my second language.

But I think: every place so far has caught me. I have learned that
in the nighttime, or at the ends of silent streets, or at the very back of
a crowded bus, you must watch yourself. But if you're aware, I have
learned, you will pick up on both the good and the bad. Yes, people will
help you, and this, at least, I can say to the man behind the counter.

"You're brave," he says in Spanish. The baby's mother looks up at
this, glancing first at him and then at me before turning her head down
again to her baby. He follows me to the door, leans in, and whispers in
English, "Be careful."

I cover my purse with my hand to show him I'm starting now.

"It's dangerous here," he says, glancing out the open door as if
checking for thieves already. As I turn to leave, he calls my Spanish name.

"Katy!" he is saying. I turn.

"Come back soon!" he calls out in English, grinning at the line he's
remembered from somewhere, some movie, some sitcom, some street
corner in New York many years ago.

"You can go to Cochas," the woman at the hostel tells me, "to see the
gourds." Her husband points to his collection, displayed in a glass case
behind the front desk; the apple-sized gourds are stained mahogany,
then carved with a tiny, sharp tool. They have the shape of wooden Rus-
sian nesting dolls: softly pear-shaped and arranged in graduating sizes.
The designs, too, remind me of the dolls, not the content but the intri-
cacy, the craftsmanship implicit, each pattern slightly different, reflective of the artist's hand at a moment in time.

The gourds tell stories, the husband explains, pointing out the way
pictures wrap around and around: a man leaving home at the bottom,
then the man meeting a woman, then the woman pregnant with child,

then the couple at the top of the gourd, their new baby in their arms. The bell at the door tinkles just then; the wife has come in from shopping, and she needs help in the kitchen. The husband locks the glass case behind the front desk and follows her back. They click the door shut behind them, but their voices still come through the wood, muffled and quick, the edge of their banter unworn by the years.

The road to Cochas quickly turns to gravel, then sand. We drive slowly to make way for the numerous pedestrians, mostly schoolchildren walking in groups, eating ice creams and shoving each other. More schoolchildren and a nun climb on, and two indigenous ladies in front of me draw coca leaves from a plastic bag to chew. They hold the leaves in their cheeks, practiced at speaking with their mouths full. Both wear their hair in long and glossy braids with hats perched atop, rounded ladies' derby hats in pink and pale green with faded flowers of ribbon sewn to the bands. Both wear heavy woolen sweaters; when they climb off, I admire through the window their knee-length skirts, the lace of their petticoats visible. Their woolen tights bunch at the ankles.

Finally, it's just me in the van and a uniformed schoolgirl with plastic clips in her hair. The driver pulls over, cuts the engine, and tips his seat back. The girl gets out and passes him a coin through the window. From there, I walk one way, she goes the other, and the driver closes his eyes to nap.

A bright sign by the road lists Big Cochas and Little Cochas. On the sign, someone's tacked a tiny map for tourists. "You are here," the map says, a finger on the dot that is Little. There's no one about and nothing to do but walk, and so up the road I go, past adobe houses and cement block garages, past men trying to fix a motorcycle on the roadside and dogs sleeping in the sun. On either side of the road, the hills scoop upwards, where pale yellow grass is broken by stands of creaking eucalyptus. In the center of Little Cochas, there's a festival; from within a huge, old-fashioned red-and-white tent, kids emerge with plastic bags of popcorn, and they all watch me as I pass.

As my hostel owner said, these twin towns are famous for their gourds. I pass houses with huge gourds painted on their outside walls, thick lines of blue and black and tan. One home has a sign above it: *Gourd Factory, Step Right In.* I wander into the little courtyard, poking cautiously about, until a girl comes out a door with a stack of pots in her hand.

"Come right in," she tells me, and sets down the pots to lead me to the showroom, where hundreds of gourds are displayed on blankets and tables. There are pots, jars, Christmas ornaments, earrings, bracelets, and one massive gourd, too heavy to lift, the detail etched upon it like a book with dense lettering.

"That one's eight-hundred soles," the girl says proudly. "It took the artist two months to make."

I think of how many hours go into two months of work. Eight hundred soles is two-hundred fifty dollars. I peer carefully at the artisans and trees, the babies and houses, all carefully, finely imagined onto the gourd's massive surface.

"Thank you," I tell the girl when I'm done looking, and she nods and follows me back outside to collect her pots.

A woman passes with a herd of sheep, which she shouts at and prods with a long, crooked stick. She wears an embroidered skirt, again with the petticoat visible, and olive green tights. Upon her braids, her derby hat sits jauntily. She looks sturdy, her face unlined, her hair salted with gray, the bones in her nose and cheeks prominent. A few tiny children are playing in the street, and a woman yawns and hunches over a tiny table spread with gum and cookies and loose cigarettes for sale. A man walks past with tall rubber boots and a dusty sweater; he tips his hat as he passes me and winks.

The church at the end of the road is locked, but one of the panes of the front window is smashed, so I peer inside. The pews are made of plywood, the walls bare and smudged, the altar adorned with a few fake flowers and a plastic Christ. The church itself is built of adobe and painted a rusty orange, and the steeple is constructed of wire.

A man wishes me *buenos tardes* as I turn the bend on my way back toward the main road. He asks me if I'm looking for the gourds.

"I'm looking," I tell him, "but just to see." He nods and clasps his hands behind his back.

"I have some," he says. "If you like, I can show you."

A little girl is standing beside him, one hand on his pant leg, and he rummages in his pocket for a few coins and gives them to her. "Go now," he tells her, and pats her on the head. She runs down the road toward Big Cochas.

"Right this way," he says, swinging open a creaking gate.

His property angles down toward the river; he's got a little plot of dusty land with corn growing. A few chickens cluck about and a couple of cows graze in the stubby grass. The man goes into a little shed attached to his house—the kitchen, I assume, because of the pots he's got hanging on the walls—and brings out a chair, which he sets in the dirt.

"Have a seat," he tells me, "and I'll get the gourds." I sit and wait while his dogs come over and sniff my boots and then try to jump up on me. He can't see us from where he's rummaging, but it's as if he knows just what they're doing—"Come here now," he calls to them. "Don't bother her." The chickens have followed him inside through the door he's left open, and now they're pecking at crumbs on the rough cement floor.

He comes out with a canvas sack full of gourds. When he sets them down before me, I can see that some are old, having been finished and then handled many times, and some have just been started. Those new ones are pale and sweet-smelling, with penciled lines marking the etchings still to come. He pulls an older one from the sack and hands it to me.

"Every gourd has a story," he says. He tips the gourd bottom up and shows me where he's drawn an arrow to mark the start. "This is a story of birth," he says. The first tiny picture is a couple in bed, the man on top of the woman. "This is the conception," he tells me easily, with nothing to be ashamed of. As the story continues, the woman gets sick, and the people in town must make medicine. They give her the medicine. The little pictures tell the story of the medicine being made, a room for the unborn child being built, blankets being woven, a bed being fashioned. Finally, there's the birth. The story rings the gourd, so that I must turn it many times in my hand to read the whole thing. He's included tiny captions, too, for each chapter. Most of the words are incorrectly spelled— *haser* for *hacer*, *durmir* for *dormir*.

"It's beautiful," I tell him truthfully, for the gourd, worn smooth by many hands, seems to glow with the light the story produces.

He shows me another gourd, stained red and etched with the story of a house being built. Again, the first chapter begins at the base, beside the little arrow. It winds and winds around the gourd, telling of the boards being gathered, the design being drawn, the community coming to help. I ask how long it takes to etch a gourd. He tells me that he has other work to do, with his animals and his vegetables and his house; he gestures to the outside wall, which he has recently painted blue.

"I have lots of projects," he admits, "but finishing a gourd might take two weeks."

He asks me where I'm from. He hasn't seen the United States yet, he says, but he wants to go there. Meanwhile, he's alone in this big house, both of his children studying in Huancayo. I don't ask about a wife or about the little girl who took the coins. I ask him the price of the gourd with the house. He stands up, touches the blue wall, thinking.

"Five soles," he says, after a moment. It's the price of my hostel bed. I take five soles from my purse and hand it to him. He takes the money without looking at it, puts it into his pocket, and wraps the red-hued gourd in two layers of newspaper, tying the package with brown string.

"Good luck," he says, placing the gourd in my hand. He watches me a while from the gate while I walk down the road, but eventually, when I turn back for the third time, ready to wave, he is gone, and I'm alone again in the lengthening shadows of the afternoon.

On the pebbled bedspread that reminds me of my grandmother's own spreads, I unwrap the gourd from its paper and string. I remember the hot road, the straw-colored hills, the adobe church with its simple pews, the man giving coins to the girl whom he called "little daughter," the fresh blue paint on the wall. The burnt-red surface of the gourd gleams, and the etched lines that tell the story have darkened with time. I hold the gourd to my nose and inhale nut and stain. I rewrap it and pack it deep, buried against the green feathered pen and the woven cap, gifts passed to me only weeks ago in a hillside school in Ecuador, gifts which I hold in my hands and feel I have had for many years. I cross my legs on the pebbled bedspread and open Theroux's book to his map.

And I realize: I had forgotten. I look at his map and remember: Theroux skipped the trains between Lima and Cusco. He had planned to take the mountain route, passing first through Huancayo, but mudslides had washed out the tracks. He had flown.

I am alone.

But it doesn't take long to realize: it doesn't matter. He's never been with me, not really. He is a man in a book, thirty years ago, and his experience of this route was nothing like mine. I laugh at myself, for thinking it mattered, and then open my guidebook to Central Peru.

Ayacucho is the next city south; tomorrow, I will go there.

AYACUCHO, PERU

In Huancayo, the woman at the ticket counter told me, with no expression on her face, that the journey to Ayacucho takes ten hours. Ten hours to cover the distance of thumbnails on my guidebook's map. Beside me on the bus, a teenage boy checks his cell phone and then falls asleep, smelling faintly of cologne.

The crescendo of farm fields is flecked with cows and hay bales. At first, the grasses are green, but they quickly shorten, turning brown and then pale yellow and finally gray and lunar. The mountains are always present, now stubby and brown, now bald and blue, and farmers till their rocky soil or rest with their lunches and lie on their bellies, their kids running around them. Always there are women in braids and long skirts leading flocks of sheep or herds of goats along the roadside, and always, too, there are sleeping dogs on the side of the road.

When we reach the river, the road changes permanently from pavement to dirt. Here, the water erupts from a trickle into full-blown white rapids, changing colors as we go, reflecting the shifting sky and the minerals in the ground: iron, copper, sulfur. Evidence of mining, one of Peru's most significant income sources, is everywhere; each hill is stripped almost in half to reveal its insides—rusty red, chalky white, slate gray.

For decades, Peruvians have relied on mines. The country is the sixth-largest gold producer in the world, yet the practice has stripped parts of Peru bare, forests and rivers destroyed. The waste a mine produces is enormous—mountains of sand, dead forests, stagnant water—

and rarely is the environment restored. Mining has begun to encroach upon Peruvian World Heritage sites and national parks. Mercury is used to extract gold, and a lot of it ends up in community water supplies. Hundreds of thousands of Peruvian acres have been destroyed for unsustainable mines. We drive past the mines, and then across blank, rolling expanses of barren land that resemble the surface of the moon, craters and odd boulders, dirt and sky for miles and miles.

I'm in the first seat—a poor choice, as it turns out, because in the other seats you can stretch your legs forward, beneath the seats in front of you. My legs just hit the wall that divides the passengers from the driver; to get to him, you have to pound on the door he keeps latched. Thus, the driver has control of who goes in and who goes out, and behind that latched door, he sits watching the road. My front seat, at least, allows me to see the various ways people try to get out; salespeople and passengers who have reached their stop mostly jiggle the lock first, step back, then try jiggling the lock again. The three little boys who ran on to sell ice cream don't even try with the lock; they just pound on the door and yell, "Open up!"

At the first lush, overgrown rest stop, one elderly woman uproots flowers and herbs, shakes dirt from the roots, and slides the plants into a canvas bag. Behind an old stone house surrounded by garden and set on a cliff that drops straight into the river, we wait in a line for the outhouses. At least, the women wait; the men go around back and use the bushes. The driver doesn't blink as the woman with the canvas bag boards again.

"Everyone on?" he shouts, waiting a moment, and then we pull away from the empty stone house. The bus fills for a while with the scent of the flowers the woman took.

"Best to travel to Ayacucho in the day," the old woman at my hostel in Huancayo had advised. She'd stood in the hall outside my room and asked me where I planned on going next.

"The roads to Ayacucho are this thin," she had said, running her finger along the doorjamb. "So thin," she'd said again, shaking her head. She told me buses tipped over the sides of the roads all the time, but during the day I'd be all right.

"There are thieves at night," she had said, looking at me with worried eyes. Still, she'd left bread and butter and water on the table for me that night, so that in the morning I'd have something to eat before the long ride. She'd shown me where I could best catch a cab, and she and the old man had both wished me luck before turning in. I would leave in the darkness, when they'd still be sleeping.

Now, I look down and see the edge of the road and, inches beyond, the cliff falling into the river. Our height above the water varies; sometimes, we drive level to it, but for most of the ride we're many feet above, and there are moments when I look down and can't even see the roadside. When another car comes, we have to slow to the side and find a place to pull over, and once, an eighteen-wheeler approaches us, coming from the south. There is no room for anyone to pass, and the *ayudante* jumps out and directs our driver back, curving along the perilous road, until there's enough space. Meanwhile, the passengers on my side all lean way over to watch the process, to see how close we are to falling, and those who don't have a window seat stand up and lean over, too. I wonder whether it's a good idea, all of this shifting to one side; might the bus topple? But no one else seems concerned, and advice is shouted in the direction of the driver. Finally the truck chugs slowly past us, tooting its horn, and the passengers break into a shaky, giggly applause.

At another rest stop in a tiny, nameless hamlet, Queen of the Night drops white trumpets onto the road. There's only one other foreigner on board, a spindly, middle-aged woman with a backpack and Tevas who stretches and walks back and forth up the road, munching on bread she bought from one of the vendors who came on board way back in Huancayo. I eat cheese, long grown warm, and raisins Isaac left in my pack.

So long ago, Isaac, Vilcabamba in summer while now the wind whips through the canyon and snow flecks the peaks just above my head. The buses have carried me through seasons, changing the way time has flowed. Months have passed, or weeks; both calculations are correct.

Erected in a valley, the city of Ayacucho climbs up the surrounding brown winter hills, dotted densely with houses, which are also brown, as is the grass and road. Only the sky offers color: a clear, dry blue speckled with brown-white clouds. On my first morning, I climb to the city's highest point, marked by a lookout and a narrow white monument. A winding, crumbling set of stone stairs takes me up, past two drunk men who sit outside of *tiendas* close to the lookout. Sloppy and leering, they call me *gringa* as I walk by. I ask two ladies perched nearby whether it's safe to keep going up. I tilt my head toward the drunks. "Sure," the women say, rolling their eyes. They hike up their skirts to begin their descent back into town. "Good luck!" they call, ignoring the drunks who cackle at them now instead.

Ayacucho is known among travelers for having thirty-three churches, one for each of the years of Jesus's life. Even before Ayacucho was "founded" in 1540, also by Pizarro, the city was a religious and cultural mecca. For 15,000 years people have inhabited this valley, flanked on either side by the ripples of the Andean foothills. During the Peruvian war of independence in 1825, Ayacucho hosted arguably the most pivotal battle. In the 1980's, the Sendero Luminoso, or "Lighted Path," put Ayacucho on the international map a second time when the terrorist group of communist guerrillas set about establishing "a dictatorship of the proletariat" through central Peru. Ironically, the proletariat suffered the most during the years of the Sendero, most notably in the district of Ayacucho, where the organization held its meetings. Sendero sympathizers, mostly in the form of poor, terrified peasants, were tortured and slaughtered by the Peruvian military in an effort to curb the Sendero's influence.

Members of the military wore black ski masks to protect their identities, and ski masks became a symbol of death and terror in the hearts of citizens. Tens of thousands died in the conflict, which finally came to a bloodstained close in the late nineties. An on-and-off border war with Ecuador compounded the trauma of those decades. Bouts of rampant inflation shattered the economy, and worker unrest still plagues Peru.

"Gringa," a little girl mutters as I pass, and her mother shushes her. As I climb, buildings dwindle and disappear at the top of the scrubbed-off hill, and I can see all around, all of a sudden, past the city to the hills and eventual Andes. I turn in a circle and watch the loop of the horizon, craggy on all sides, stretching for miles. The ground is littered with trash, which has its own life in the wind. There are a few *tiendas* around, closed for the morning, the bars over their windows padlocked. The little girl and her mother disappear over the other side, and then I am alone, the monument a testament to a history I do not know, have never been taught, and so this place means only wind and mountains to me, a cool spot over the brown and busy city. I close my eyes and listen for what Guayasamín had called the gun scream, but nothing comes.

From where I stand on the mound, I can see a bright white church at the top of the hill to the east, a white structure with a very high steeple. I pass through tiny alleys on the way down and empty, narrow spaces on the way back up. I keep my hand on my purse. A woman calls out to me as I reach the scoop of the valley and start climbing again. Her hair is white, her face deeply lined, but she walks sturdily.

"Gringa," she calls, and I slow down. "Gringa, gringa, gringita," she sings as she walks, holding her skirt out of her way with one hand. The word seems not to be an insult; I'm merely a rarity here. A *gringa* is what I am, after all.

"Where do you come from," she says, stopping to catch her breath. I tell her. She peers up at me with clear brown eyes.

"And where are you going now?" she asks, folding her hands, taking a seat on the low stone wall.

"I'm going up," I tell her, "up to the church." She nods and mutters something, and I lean closer to listen, but it's Quechua she's speaking now, and I shake my head. She shrugs.

"Nice church up there," she says. She stands again, and we walk companionably together for a moment, taking our time up the sun-baked steps. She sees a friend, another woman wearing a knee-length skirt, a derby hat, and a woven sack strapped to her back. They stop to chat, and I bid them goodbye and keep walking.

I think: it doesn't matter where I'm going. This year is a gift. I am making my slow way south through the mountains; that is all. This is who I am now. I board a bus and ride for hours, and then I find a place to sleep. I walk through cities and forests and into churches during the day. When I read over my notes from Xela, Granada, even Quito, I'm amazed at how far I have travelled.

And in the evenings, I see all of the places again and write them down. That way, each turns to a written photograph; years from now, I imagine, they'll remind me of the wide-open way I once lived.

I walk past the place where the pavement ends and the roads turn to dirt the color of corn, past houses of plywood and bamboo poles, or rocky adobe flecked with hay. There are no more *tiendas*, only women crouching on the street selling oranges and short, squat bananas on blankets, or gum and cigarettes from baskets. Men lean against the church wall before rows of belts and rope and remote controls, but no one beckons. This isn't like Guatemala, or Ecuador, or Nicaragua, where the vendors called out, their wheedling so practiced it came automatically. I pause to inspect a pair of earrings on a plaid blanket. The stones are white as bone, and the woman sitting beyond her items doesn't say a word.

"Thank you," I say, moving away, and she doesn't reply.

The top of the hill reveals a clean, new-looking white church with a health center attached. People flock in and out; the church is the nicest

building around, and the only one with two stories. Beside this place
there's an old swing set, well-used, once red, most of the paint long peeled
away to reveal its metal foundation, which glints before the sanded hills.

A little boy who sits on the floor of his mother's *tienda* looks up at me
and calmly says, "Gringa." He shouts it again as I'm walking away, and
I turn my head. He is waving at me though, and I raise my own hand.
My hotel room has a balcony that looks out over a tiny parking lot, the
table-strewn patio of a small restaurant, and someone's miniscule yard,
where a small, yipping dog lives. The room is high enough that the wind
blows over the city and comes right to me. I sip tea, wake when the sun
comes in, and sleep when the sky turns pitch. On my second or third
morning, I find that I do not know the date. I cannot even guess at it. I
wonder when I last forgot to measure the time as it passed, to count the
days and hours I had left, and the ones I'd already used up.

In this hard-to-reach place, they call me *gringa*. In the market, I sit
on a stool in a noisy *caféteria* and drink fruit shakes made in blenders
by aproned ladies. I walk up the hills in morning and evening, sidestepping the drunks who jeer. I forget to unpack my clock. In this way, my
days begin to feel like they are secrets. I write letters to myself, so I won't
forget how Ayacucho is, but I tell no one I am here.

On my second morning, I share a taxi with seven others to Wari, a
sprawling hillside of mostly unrestored pre-Incan ruins. Two men are
in front, three in the backseat, and two in the way back. We ride out of
Ayacucho, and the earth turns pink, the homes built tight to the earth as
they were in New Mexico. We pass through little towns built in river valleys, where children walk along the road in packs on their way to school,
screeching to each other and kicking balls into the road. We take on
another passenger, a tall man who makes his body small to fit alongside

the other men in the way back, but still no one speaks. We drive with the windows open. Our driver swerves to avoid cows that amble across the road. The cacti grow in prickly fields, stretching their spiky, paddle-like hands and bulbous yellow blooms toward the sky.

I've been seeing ruins everywhere: along the roadside, behind gas stations, in people's yards. It's as if ruins are part of the natural landscape, not something to be gawked at or studied but simply ignored—or else used. The ruins seem still to serve as boundary lines or garden plots. Contrary to popular belief (mine, at least, and that of many *estadounidenses* I know), the Incans were not the largest or necessarily the most powerful of pre-colonial empires in South America—they were simply the ones the Europeans encountered. Before the Incans, many more civilizations had come and gone. The first South American civilization dates back millennia before the sixteenth century—the Norte Chico is believed to have originated three thousand years before Christ, followed hundreds of years later by the Chavin, the Moche, the Nazca, and the Wari. Yet history so often begins, I've come to realize, when the white people say it does, and so although Ayacucho was "officially" founded in 1540, these ruins represent a civilization epochs older.

Today, the ruins are busy with school groups who arrive on tour buses, bringing with them portable radios, cell phones, and bottles of Inca Cola. Both the girls and the boys wear tight jeans. They're all lined up and waiting to enter when the cab drops me off. For a while I stand behind the students, waiting to pay my three soles to enter, until I realize they're all stealing glances at me and giggling.

"Am I supposed to wait here, too?" I ask, but nobody replies. I wonder whether I've used the wrong words, and I repeat the question differently. "Can I pass?" I ask, knowing I am stupid at the mercy of their fluency. They just titter and poke each other and stare at me, until one of them pipes up in English: "Hello!"

"Hello," I mutter back. Now their voices rise in a piping chorus: "Hello! Hello gringa! How are you!" I push past them toward the entrance while they hold up their camera-phones and cry, "Photito!" The uniformed man at the museum door ushers me in like a celebrity. "Right this way," he says.

Inside, it's as though I've passed into a different realm: the dark rooms, the squares cut into walls where old things are displayed through glass, the thick silence—all a contrast to the jabbering brightness outside. Inside a glass box in the center of the room, beneath a low light that makes a pool on the floor, a mummy crouches in the fetal position, bones brittle, clothes the color of uniform clay, moth-eaten. The teeth are still mostly there, and the collarbones, and the hands and feet that seem disproportionately large, the bones in the toes thick and long and curved. The uniformed man sticks his head through the propped-open door.

"Go on," he says. Then there is brightness again, but quiet this time with the rustling and chirping of insects, and the wind feeling its way over the cactus field.

The ruins resemble stone walls I've seen from bus windows since Lima: thinning lines of falling-down piles of rocks that run up and down hills, across farmland and alongside rivers. This country abounds with rows of stones that still divide properties or else are haphazardly pulled apart to make space for farmland and livestock. Peru is crisscrossed with the architecture of ancient civilizations. No one monitors these ruins, and I imagine that people pluck stones from the storied walls for keepsakes, slipping them into their bags and taking them back to their homes, where they'll sit and gather dust and, eventually, be thrown outside again, their origins lost.

Trails lead all around the ruins, up over the hills and into a massive field. Suddenly, I feel very far from the school groups, the ticket counter, the crammed parking lot; the space stretches before me, a field speckled with clusters of cacti and blue peaks in the distance. The wind hurtles, and short cliffs rise up, lavender with chalk. The trail opens at one point and becomes a circle-shaped patch of dirt. I see the remains of a fire; stepping closer, I realize the ashes and charcoal form the deliberate shape of a cross.

I'm suddenly chilled, though the sun reflects off the stone and grass and intensifies. I take a tentative step toward the cross. I cannot tell whether it's old or new. Rain may not have fallen for weeks. This blackened grass, these ashes, this empty place. I remember the candles and petals in the hills above Xela, the scent of the recent ceremony there, how quiet it felt, just as it feels now. I turn back and walk away from the field, eventually passing again the students, hearing them—their tinny cell-phone music and their chatter—long before they appear through the cacti. "Hola, gringa," the boys murmur at me to make their girlfriends laugh.

Outside the ruins and across the road, an old couple sells drinks beneath a wooden structure made up of four poles and a thatched roof. "Water, water," they say quietly as I walk over. They hold out the bottles they have for sale: sodas with US labels, the green and clear plastic sheathed in dust. I buy a Coke, and the woman wipes it off on the hem of her skirt.

"Two soles, mamacita," she says.

"Has there been any traffic?" I ask. I will need a ride if I want to see Quinua, the town ten miles to the north, up the road.

"Yes, mamí," she says, "yes, mamacita, I'll tell you when they come." Then she walks down the road a little ways and squats down to pee. She flicks her two long braids behind her back and then stands, ruffling her skirts a little, absently watching the grazing cows. The old man is still sitting behind the drink stand, and he hasn't said a word. Two taxis pass by. "There, mamacita," the old woman says, urging me to step up to flag them down, but both times the driver waggles his hand from side to side. Full.

I wait for a long while beside the drink stand. When I finish the Coke, the woman offers to take my bottle, tucking it behind the cooler with the other empties. Finally, a taxi pulls out of the ruins' parking lot across the street and turns onto the main road. I flag it down.

"Can I get a ride?" I ask the woman in the front seat. She is friend-ly-faced, tanned, and wears a lavender-colored silk scarf knotted on one side of her neck.

"Claro!" she replies, and her driver snaps his door open, jumps out, and runs to pop the trunk. I start to climb into the way back of the stationwagon after my pack, which the driver takes from me and tucks beside the an old tire and an opened toolkit, overflowing with tubes and nails and a short saw.

"No, no," someone cries in English from the backseat. "Get in with us!" Three bodies squeeze together to make space, and the driver helps me back out of the trunk. They're teenagers, dark-haired and well-dressed and smelling of fresh shampoo. "Thank you so much," I say in English, and the woman in the front seat turns to look at me, adjusting the knot of her scarf so it lies exactly between her collarbones.

"You're from the States?" she asks in English. I nod. As we roar away from the little stand, I wave at the old man and woman, who don't notice.

"We're from California," she announces. The teenagers beside me say nothing and smile sleepily.

"These are my rotten kids," the woman says, smiling at the three of them. She has dyed her hair red, and her gray roots show at her crown. Her kids have bony noses and full mouths, and the boy wears a baseball cap embedded with sequins. The woman has a scar on her chin, which she seems, with her angled haircut, to be trying to conceal. She explains to me that she's from Lima, but left in the seventies to attend high school in Mexico.

"Things got bad in Peru," she tells me, and then her English slips to Spanish. "Bermudez was in charge," she says. "You know? Bermudez?" She peers at me, waiting. I shake my head, and she sighs.

"The young people never know," she says, but I am thinking that we were never taught; my high-school history classes covered only the his-tory of the Tigris and the Euphrates, and the march of wars that defined Europe, and last the slaves in America and the life of George Washington.

The car bounces up the road. The cacti cast long shadows and my mind softens. The car is so warm.

E— comes just then, inexplicably. Maybe it's something about the woman's perfume, but I think I can smell her: shampoo and coconut and something deeper, something indescribably her. I hear the sound of her name in my mind, and feel hate and desire simultaneously. *Don't come to me now*, I think, letting my eyes settle on the teenagers' hands, folded on their laps. *Don't come to me now*, I tell her again, and I'm surprised at how quickly she's gone.

At a bend in the road, a couple of cops stand around beside their motorbikes. They wave us down, and the driver slows. They ask to see our passports, and there's a rustling of clothing and purses until the small blue books are produced. The woman's kids all have crisp-looking passports, but the woman's, like mine, is beat up, bent, and taped with stickers, old customs notices, and baggage receipts—proof that we have gone through many checkpoints, many times.

"Don't say anything," the woman in the front seat says, turning the knot in her scarf back to one side. We watch through the windows as the cops review our passports, taking the most time with the woman's, handing them to each other, holding them close to their faces. Eventually, one comes back, leans down, whispers something to the driver, and then opens the door for him. After a second's hesitation, the driver steps out, leaving the door open.

Through the window, I can see that he's a young guy, maybe eighteen or twenty, the age of the kids beside me. The cops produce paperwork on clipboards, and one of them jots down things that we can see but not hear the driver say. The other cop comes over to the passenger side, and the woman rolls her window down halfway. The cop explains that nothing is wrong. The cab driver doesn't have a license to leave Ayacucho, that's all. He was supposed to stay in the city and as we can see—the cop chuckles a little—now he's here.

"We must issue a ticket," the cop is saying now.

After he steps away from the car, the woman turns her head to us and rolls her eyes. The kids next to me continue to stare out the window, their arms crossed over their bodies, their knees pressed tight together. An old beggar man hobbles up to the car and asks for money, for bread, but the woman tells him we have nothing and rolls her window up all the way.

"He's a clever one," she says in English, "waiting here for the cops to stop people." Still, her children say nothing. She pulls a little compact from her purse and checks her mouth, her eyes, and then, satisfied with her reflection, snaps the mirror down and sighs. Finally, the driver gets back in his seat. "Everything's fine," he mumbles. "Don't worry."

THE ROAD

The bus to Andahuaylas, the next big town on my way to Cusco, is running late. Everyone's on board, but still the driver mills around in the dusty parking lot, smoking and talking to a toothless old man who was there the day before, too, when I came to buy my ticket. I don't much mind the delay, as long as we arrive before nightfall, but the man beside me is getting angry.

"Let's go!" he shouts for the third time, and ten more minutes pass.

"Come *on!*" he cries, but the driver, as I do, pretends not to have heard, taking his time with the last of his cigarette, shaking the toothless man's hand, climbing into his seat and adjusting the mirror, finally cranking the engine. The man beside me leans back, triumphant, and grunts, but I've learned that a running engine isn't always a sign that we're going. On this day, there's no exception to that rule. The driver chats through his open window to an old woman selling bread, while girls with bottled drinks and bags of chips push through the aisles to make last-minute sales. I watch the sun on the ground turn to copper.

Finally, we chug out of the station, down the narrow streets of Ayacucho and through the suburbs. We pick up speed through the hills that take us east, and the mountains change from scruffy brown to pale gold, the color of the shifting hay that covers the treeless hills. For miles it is like this, just gold and the blue of the sky, and I do not think about how the man beside me is taking up far more than his share of our seats; he's falling asleep, his head is bobbing onto my shoulder, and his legs are splayed, but it doesn't matter. Women lead goats to water in the fields, and the passengers in the bus are quiet, rustling their food wrappers and shushing their babies and watching their land pass us by. I have been on this bus before, many times, and I saw these fields in Honduras, in southern Ecuador, in eastern Guatemala. I suspect I will see them again: in this way, my route loops over itself, remembering.

We stop before lunch where there's space to pull over, and almost everyone gets out to pee. The men just stand right by the road, but the women push a little ways into the brush and squat there. I follow. One lady generously tears some toilet paper off the roll she's brought with her and passes it to me. Tiny children lean against the bus to pee. Then we all climb back aboard. "Let's go, let's go!" the *ayudante* urges, clapping his hands as if some might wish to stay at this jungled curve in the road. A few people eye me as we board; today, I'm the only foreigner, the only one with a North American backpack, light eyes, light hair, freckled arms.

Much later, we stop for lunch. Most passengers crowd into the nearest restaurant, a tent stretched over rickety tables and a grill, and so I walk across the dusty plaza, past kids playing foosball beneath plastic tarps, past ladies selling woven blankets, to the *tienda* on the opposite corner. I duck inside; three men in dirty t-shirts are sitting on stools, drinking beer.

"Come right in," they tell me, as if they are the shopkeepers themselves. In fact, a woman behind the counter helps me draw a juice box from a pack of six, then charges me one sole and beckons me to sit on the bench outside. She joins me there. The three men with the beers come out and ask to take a picture, then produce a camera and take turns standing beside me, their arms around my shoulder, grinning. They ask me the usual things: what is my country, where is my husband, how do I like Peru. The tallest man pours beer from his bottle, little by little, into his friends' cups before taking a swig himself. He spots a girl he knows walking past and sputters a little. She's holding her jacket over her head to keep the sun off her face.

"Come here," he calls to her.

"No," she says.

"Come on," he says, "meet my new friend at least." She rolls her eyes and walks over.

"Give her a kiss," he tells the girl, and she obediently pecks me on the cheek. Everyone is quiet for a moment, and then I ask, stupidly, whether it gets cold at night in this town. I want to say something to break the funny tension between this drunken man and this pretty girl. But the girl just giggles and mutters something indiscernible to me, then walks away.

In Andahuaylas, I sleep in a hostel run by an old woman who shuffles to the front door when I ring the bell and washes peaches in the kitchen while I wait for her to give me my key. The rooms are set around a long balcony that looks down over a dried-out garden of crushed leaves and a labyrinth of vines, silver with age and the cold. There's a well-used *pila*, where I wash my pants with the brush I bought so many months ago in Guatemala. The pants don't dry in the night, even though they're lightweight and the wind is blowing and I hang them over the rail of the balcony, because it gets so cold that the stars gleam brittle through my window. I wake to the sound of footsteps above my head, and outside my door, I hear someone running water in the *pila*. A man spits and coughs nearby. The clock in the center of town tolls three slow times. I lie in bed and marvel at where I am tonight: the dried-out garden, the freezing specks of stars, this tiny room with peeling paint, a mattress stuffed with straw. A cup of water by the bed, and a marigold in a jar. No one knows where to find me now; what fragile, quiet freedom I have found.

236 – KATE McCAHILL

I'm at the bus terminal by six. I bought my full passage to Cusco back in Ayacucho, where the dog had lifted its leg to the walls, where we'd waited while the driver smoked and the man beside me had scratched himself and shouted. But the woman at this ticket window in this frosty Andahuaylas morning looks at me grimly and hands the ticket back.

"This bus doesn't exist," she says. "It only runs Tuesdays." She pauses while I search my mind for an anchoring date; was Monday the day I arrived in Ayacucho?

"Today is Thursday," the woman tells me, counting out twenty-five soles, the price of the worthless ticket, from her black lockbox. She hands it over, businesslike and unapologetic, turning away from me before I can ask any more questions.

It's a sharp morning, colder than any I've stood in since leaving Boston. I close my eyes, inhale, exhale. There are many buses, and it's early. I remind myself not to be afraid. I can't feel my toes now, and my fingertips are starting to dull. I jump up and down on the frozen road and clap my hands.

I hear footsteps, close, and turn to see a girl behind me, a young woman with curly, messy black hair and heavily lined eyes, a big pack like mine and a guitar case slung over her shoulder. Here we both stand, stomping and inhaling the crisp air, alive together in this high-up town. We both traveled on treacherous roads to get here, dirt roads along crashing white rivers. "Hi," I say, and now we're both smiling. She eases her pack off her shoulders to the ground.

I ask her in Spanish if she's going to Cusco. I guess that she's from Argentina, because her hair and eyes are dark but her skin is pale, her nose bony and narrow. She nods, explaining in breathy, fluent Spanish that she had a ticket, but the bus had been cancelled.

"Or something," she adds, sighing and drawing a packet of cigarettes from a pouch at her hip.

"Me too," I say, waving my rejected ticket, and as she blows smoke through her mouth, her long lips curve upwards at the edges.

In the station, we buy tea, sticky with honey, from a woman with a cart. She sells us bread, too, split open and stuffed with fried eggs. While we eat, we talk. Her name is Gaby. She's from Belgium, not Argentina, and she switches to perfect English after I tell her I'm from the States. Her mother is Guatemalan, she tells me. "That should explain the darkness," she says, twisting her mouth and twirling a ring of black hair with her finger.

She's been traveling for one year, she tells me, having worked in Guatemala and Colombia as a teacher. She hitchhiked through Mexico, too, with an English girl she met in Costa Rica. We sip our *maté*, and I ask whether anything bad ever happened, hitching.

"Only once," Gaby says. "We found a ride with a couple of guys, and I knew they were drunk, but it was late, and we needed a ride. They were drinking beer, and they hadn't slept in two days, they told us." Gaby drains the tea from her cup and says, "After a while, they started wanting sex, and I kept telling them I had a boyfriend." She draws another cigarette from her pouch. "I was lying." Her lighter snaps a few times before spitting out a flame. "I told him I was Catholic," she says, rolling her eyes.

"But I couldn't get those guys to back off. Alice was crying, but I knew I had to..." she trails off. "What do you Americans say?" she asks. "Keep my shit together?"

"Finally," she says, "we stopped in this city, some city, I don't even know which one, and while the guys went to get more beer we jumped out and ran. We stayed in a hotel that night, a hotel by the road, and the whole night I could hear the trucks on the highway. The sound of them made me sick all night," she says.

We manage to get seats on a minivan that will take us to Abancay, four hours from Andahuaylas. From there, we are told, we can go on to Cusco, no problem. In the van, Gaby chats easily with the other passengers. They ask about her Spanish, and she tells them again that her *mami* is Guatemalan. They smile at her, approving. Then Gaby reclines her seat and closes her eyes and sleeps instantly, a blanket over her knees, the whole way to Abancay. I envy her for that—the ability to sleep so easily. I watch the landscape out the window, thinking that I have seen these same pale hills already, covered in wheat, and these same herds of goats, led by a boy with a stick and a dog. Was it in Ecuador that I saw this stretching place? Was it just the day before? There are the same jagged blue peaks in the distance, the same stands of eucalyptus, and always the dark brown of the adobe huts, pillowcases tacked over windows and sullen dogs in yards.

At the bus terminal in Abancay, a city three hours from Cusco, we cross the street to enter a small restaurant—both for lunch and for a place to wait for our connection. In the bathroom, there's no paper, no sink, and no light, just a toilet and a bucket and one small window, cracked open. We eat rice, pork, and vegetables and drink watery hibiscus juice. While we eat, she tells me she spent the first three months in Guatemala with her mother's family, then eight more in Medellin, Colombia. In Brussels, she's a certified psychologist, and her qualifications earned her a paid internship abroad. In addition, she's given a small monthly stipend from her employer while she's on sabbatical.

"It's a good life," she says, drawling out the words, batting her lashes, pushing her plate from her, and crossing her hands over her belly. When it's time to pay, Gaby insists we split the check exactly. It should always be fair, she says, and I suspect she's been cheated by fellow travelers before. Her nails are a chipped strawberry red.

Outside the restaurant, she smokes a cigarette. We sit on the curb and watch the traffic go by, lazy and thin at lunchtime. Buses roll out of the station, men bicycle past, and a woman clutches a man's waist as they speed past on a motorbike.

"I've sat on so many of these," Gaby remarks.

"So many of what?" I ask. She touches with one finger the edge of the sidewalk. "Sidewalks?" I ask. "Curbs?"

"Curbs," she says, testing the word in her mouth. "Curbs, *curbs.*"

This curb is spattered with old spots of oil but is otherwise clean, hosed off in the morning and brushed in the afternoon.

"Like *curves*," Gaby says, and I nod. "I like it," she says, her long lips turning up again, the smile of a cat, the smile of a gypsy, slow and sly.

At an elevation of higher than 11,000 feet, Cusco served as the seat of the Incan empire from the 13th century into the 16th and was declared a World Heritage Site in 1983. Millions visit Cusco each year, drawn to its historical stonework, its folk art and food and nightlife, and its proximity to Machu Picchu and other, less famous ruins dotting the Sacred Valley. Rebuilt dozens of times since its Incan glory days, Cusco's inhabitants now endure busloads of tourists, chilly temperatures, and the occasional earthquake.

When Cusco comes, it is a brick-colored city cast with soft light: red roofs and steeples flanked by russet mountains and the lavender sky. The bus goes quiet, for all of the looking. It's as if we're all seeing the place for the first time, even those who have been here before. This is the city whose center is said to hum, whose bricks were hauled and erected long before the Inca came.

"Breathe," Gaby says, reminding us both.

CUSCO, PERU

Outside of the bus station, where flat, round loaves of bread are sold and cab drivers call to us and amble over, Gaby sits on the curb and smokes a cigarette. She bats the cab drivers away, telling them she needs to think and smoke. "I've been on buses all day!" she shouts to them, and they chuckle at her and light their own cigarettes, smoking and wiping dust from their cabs with the tips of their fingers. I reach for my guidebook, as I always do when the time comes to find a bed, but Gaby shakes her head. She puts out her cigarette on the sole of her shoe and flicks it into the street, then digs in her pack for her own book. It's a tattered English-language edition of *Let's Go: South America*.

"I've got the real dirt," she says, her eyes flashing, the cat-smile shaping her face into a heart. As she pages through the book, I see that copious notes have been made by different hands and different colored pens, here and there the old tracings of a pencil. The pages are soft from having been turned so many times.

"It was a gift," she explains, running her finger over the print. "Two guys in Colombia gave it to me." She pauses, stops her finger, looks at me. "It's been *passed down*," she says. "Passed down, right?"

"Passed down," I say, "passed right on down."

"Passed right on down," she says.

In the end, Gaby decides on the hostels at the north end of town, up from the Artist's Park. The notes in the margins of her guidebook direct us into the city center and then up the northern edge of the valley. Gaby insists we walk, though I complain, my pack heavy on my shoulders and my computer bag banging against my leg. We walk for miles, it seems, her a few steps ahead and teasing me.

"How did you get this far?" she says, laughing at me, sweat forming at her temples. "With all those taxis you take, how do you have any money left at all?"

We stagger along, stumbling over the stones and broken pavement, past enormous, silent, rigid-faced men dressed as Incan priests. Pans of coins sit before them on the ground. We pass through a walkway lined with massive stones, stones which I will learn are almost all original and date back to the Incan construction of this city. A couple of guys in tight, black woolen hats and loose jackets huddle toward the end of the walkway, passing a cigarette between them. They glance at us as we heft our packs past, and one smiles. The sun is setting.

Her hostel parameters, Gaby explains as we trundle along, are a good communal kitchen and good vibrations.

"Good vibes?" I ask.

"Good vibes," she agrees.

And then I think that, across this continent, there must be thousands of solo female travelers just like us, joining together and breaking apart, picking their ways into and out of cities, shaping their own systems, setting their own rhythms and then matching them up against each other's.

After the first four hostels are vetoed (No kitchen! No books in the lobby! No music playing! *Too clean!*), I tell Gaby we need to decide soon, or else I'm setting up camp right here on the road. I stop and point to the ground. A boy selling bananas sits down near us and stares.

"Hi," Gaby says to him. "Those are nice bananas." He grins, then jumps up, grabs his bananas, and darts off down the street.

"Just one more," Gaby begs, marching ahead, her guidebook in hand. "I have got a feeling!" She continues to sing as she walks, a song she half makes up, half remembers from somewhere: *I gotta feeling, yeah, I have got a feeling.* The song is tuneless and joyful. We pass an old man hauling his bike up steep stone stairs. He stops to applaud, his mouth cracking at the sight of Gaby: wild hair, gypsy makeup, glittered skirt, pack strapped with sandals and a bouncing water bottle. Keychains and lanyards blackened by the bellies of buses. My shoulders are aching, the night is falling, and I feel so happy, so strangely rich, as if the city belongs only to us. How bright the stars are tonight, and people crowd the sidewalks and parks. I follow Gaby up the hill; we are companions, backpackers flung.

At the top of the hill, we come to a gate with a sign: Inca House. Gaby turns to me, triumphant, her finger on the buzzer, her eyes round, her skin gleaming.

A young blonde girl holding a teacup opens the door, and we can see that this property is built on the hillside, a view of the city and the mountains to the south. The girl leads us in, chatting; she has come from Seattle and pays ten soles a night here. No heat, bucket showers, breakfast in the morning. She sits down at a table made out of a tree stump, and sets her teacup on its mismatched saucer alongside a broken roll of bread. Eventually, the owner, a small, neatly dressed man with thick glasses and dark hair salted with white, comes out of the main house and shows us to an unlocked room in a long building at the edge of the property. It's freezing cold, with two thin beds, high ceilings, and stone floors. There's no door to the bathroom, which contains a low toilet, a spigot in the wall, and a bucket on the floor. The wind blows in; we can see our breath. From behind me, I hear Gaby inhale deeply, then ease her pack from her shoulders to the floor.

"We'll take it," she says.

"I'm not a fool," Gaby declares at the market. She knows the price of peppers and rolls and chunks of cheese. When a young girl, a child, asks two soles for a head of broccoli, Gaby scoffs.

"I would have paid it," I tell Gaby. She snorts, tosses her head. "That's not the point."

We visit the women's weaving cooperative and examine the delicate, elaborate work on display: ponchos of indigo blue or crimson, and thick, black blankets stitched with lines of pink and green and white. At night, we drink beer and stir-fry vegetables from the market. Another man from Belgium is staying in the room next to ours, and Gaby learns through their conversation that he, too, is a psychologist. "We're both shrinks!" she crows. The Belgian guy invites us to a bar, but Gaby declines. After he's combed his hair and spritzed himself with cologne and gone out the front gate, Gaby winks at me. "We can make our own fun," she says.

In the room we share, she changes into a black dress, purple tights, and little red shoes that point at the toes. She slides clips into her hair, and darkens the lines around her eyes.

"Don't you have anything?" she asks, facing me with her hands on her hips. I've put a jacket on over my t-shirt and exchanged my sandals for sneakers. I shrug, gaping at the costume trunk that is her backpack. She frowns and then leans forward to darken the rims of my eyes with her kohl, to brush pale green shadow over my eyelids. She leans back, examining me, and her breath smells of beer and tomatoes.

On the way into town, Gaby ducks into a small, bright *tienda*. The man behind the counter gives us two cups with our wine and compliments Gaby on her accent.

"They'd think I was native if it weren't for you," she tells me outside, good-naturedly. "You Americans," she adds, "with your North Face and your hiking boots." She looks me up and down, nodding at my fulfillment of the stereotype, then perches at the edge of the plaza's empty fountain and inhales deeply. It is as if she wants to breathe in moments that she likes, places where the vibrations are good. She pours the wine, toasting our journeys as the artisans around us whisper to passersby, holding out the things they have made, the cuffs and necklaces of wire and shell, the earrings made of bone collected from all over this land.

I, too, feel the urge to breathe deeply. The air is cold, scented with leaves and grass, with cigarette smoke and roasting sausage, with the thin berry-colored wine that spills onto our fingers, with the perfume Gaby wears, heavy with lilies and vanilla. I sip from my cup again and again, letting the liquid and Gaby's conversation warm me, watching as men wander over to introduce themselves and bum cigarettes from the pack Gaby draws from the pouch at her hip. They compliment her again and again on her accent.

Mi mamí es de Guatemala.

They offer us handfuls of chips from bags—Lays, salty and crisp, just as they've always tasted. The men pour rum into cups of Coke and we toast to all of our journeys, to this beautiful night, to the good vibrations here in this city. Church bells sound ten, eleven, twelve times. Still there is wine in the box. Still there are musicians wandering over with guitars and a flute. Still there are artisans unwrapping jewelry from heavy pieces of black velveteen. Still there are people asking where we are from and what are our names.

There's an old homeless man with a long wizard's beard. Everyone seems to know him, and he enters the plaza trailed by six or eight small, rough-looking dogs. He allows them to hop onto his lap and perch on his duffel. He asks many times for cigarettes. Each time, Gaby passes him one and holds up her lighter, sparking the metal, and he leans close to inhale.

The clock strikes one. I still am not tired. Gaby is flushed, and strands of hair have loosened at her temples and curled. We've been invited to a club. "Free drinks!" one man says in English.

"Let's go!" cheers the crowd that has formed around Gaby, and we clamor in a pack down the hill toward the center of the city.

And then: a thick bouncer at the door with tattoos on his neck, a slim woman in a tight blue dress patting my body down, a low-ceilinged room with pulsing lights, red and green, red and white, gold and red. Now the room is pitch and the music is swelling. I can feel the bodies around me but cannot see them. Gaby is taking my jacket and showing me where she's hiding it with hers, underneath a stubby chair in the corner. Now we are dancing. My body remembers how to do it, and the wine has turned my limbs to liquid. The hands at my waist are not Gaby's, and the hips moving against mine aren't hers. I don't care. Something I do not want is leaving me now. I'm lifting my arms up and my fingers are dancing on their own. My body is turning, and the lights make everyone visible, but just for a flash.

Then: we are climbing some stairs; no one watches, no one follows. I am not afraid of him. The music fades as we move up, and he holds my hand. He doesn't go too quickly. In a darkened room I am turning to him, this man whose name I did not hear when he shouted it to me, this man with hair that smells of dried flowers and wax, this man whose hands are strong and light at the same time on my body, this man whose mouth is on mine now, not too heavy, not too much. It has been so long, and I am desired.

I think that I don't care what he does. He tastes delicious. He is not pushing. He is not forcing. *What is your name? Marcus. What is your name? Katy.*

"Katy," he whispers, then says it again. Someone opens the curtain and comes in beside us, allowing a slice of light to enter. There is another person with us now. It doesn't matter. The smell of red wine, the taste of it now, those cigarettes drawn from a pouch at her hip.

It won't be until much later that I'll think of E—: her hair, the smell of her, not wax, not flowers, musk maybe, a whiff of coconut lingering. I will grieve, as I have so many times, for the place her body had against mine, but this grief will have a slightly different shape, a finality. I will wonder whether she's already left me as I leave her on this night behind the curtain. The next morning, I will reach for her, and she will not be there. I will remind myself that I did not betray her. I'll lie there in my bed, in the cold, and I will tell her again goodbye. There are so many stages of leaving: the last kiss, the last e-mail, the last phone call, the last joke. The last time you lie down together. The first time you lie down with someone else.

The hands on my waist are getting warmer now. They're moving beneath my clothes; they're on my skin; the sound I make is not a sound I've heard before. In the morning we will wake and be strangers again, but in this velvet darkness, we are in love.

For a few more days, Gaby and I will stroll the streets together, looking into the dark interiors of churches, into stores selling sell alpaca wool, or girls' barrettes, or cell phones. We will eat lunch in the market as we did before, paying fifty cents at a counter for a bowl of hot noodles and broth, carrots and peppers and potatoes. When we finish our bowls, the woman ladles more—"It's included," Gaby explained the first time.

Only once, Gaby asks if I want to talk about it. I turn red and stammer. I tell her I wasn't ready. "Do you feel guilty?" she asks. When I shrug, she says, "You shouldn't."

She reaches toward me and takes my hand. "It was just one drunken night," she says. She has painted her lips a burnt red. "It was only a few kisses."

Gaby's touch was nothing like hers. From now on, I realize, the skin will always be a different shade, the hair a different length, the stroke of the fingertips different. Every time we start over, we learn this again.

SUMMER

Travel is a vanishing act.

—Paul Theroux, *The Old Patagonian Express*

MACHU PICCHU

The route, as it does every time, starts with buses. This time, it's the Hippie Trail, the alternative route to Machu Picchu.

"Skip the train," the hostel owner in Cuenca had said. "Buses and your legs will get you there."

And so I begin the four-day trip, which starts with a bus out of Cusco. We leave the city's adobe bricks, its base of Inca blocks and its terra cotta roofs, and then we climb to the place where snow covers the peaks. They are jagged, these mountains, all covered in white.

"I'm scared," I tell the small Peruvian man beside me. He wears a pressed white shirt and a woolen vest.

"Don't worry," he tells me, placing a fatherly hand on my arm. "It gets warmer from here."

To get to Machu Picchu from Cusco, travelers have several options. The train is the easiest, the most direct, and the most expensive. Package tours on some of the famous treks, including the Inca trail, take tourists down a well-trodden, ancient route, but this method is also expensive. The Hippie Trail—the backpackers' option—is low-cost, low-technology, and perfect for me. I'll splurge and take the train on the way back.

At the road's highest point, the snow-capped peaks surround us, and then we begin to descend. The man in the woolen vest leans over me to look out the window.

"We'll go down three thousand meters," he says, "by the time this is over." My ears pop; we wind around bends, crisscrossing the mountain on red roads, zigzagging down and down until the alpine shrubs are replaced by green grass, calla lilies, eucalyptus, and finally the flat, lime-colored fronds of banana trees. The man unbuttons his vest and peels it off. By the time we all unload in Santa Maria, I am sweating and can hear the river beyond the crops of coffee and plantain that the locals grow behind their *tienda*-homes. I sleep the night in this tiny town, in a hostel where the doors to the rooms don't lock. All night I can hear men drinking; they start off quietly, talking together, their radios crooning and their bottles clinking, but by midnight they're singing themselves, and this is the sound I finally sleep to.

On the second day, I hike to Santa Teresa, across floodplains littered with round, white stones and occasional smacking waterfalls. The track isn't hard to follow; this is the Hippie Trail, after all, and all of us hippies get to know each other fast. There's a group of students from Chile, a couple of skinny guys from France who wear their expensive cameras around their necks, and a mother from Argentina with her twelve-year-old son. His name is Andreas; he sidles up to me and suggests we practice English together. We chat slowly, using simple words, telling each other about our travels.

"I'm writing a book," I say.

"What will you call it?" he asks me. When I tell him I haven't decided, he pauses.

"You're kidding me, right?" he finally says, cackling, then asks me my name. He thinks for a second, then looks up at me. "You could call it *Kate's Adventures*," he suggests.

We start early this day and end late. Walking along the river is tough going; now it is sandy, now it grows rocky, now the path is steep and clings to the riverbank, now I pass through water and must jump from stone to stone. It is dark by the time I reach Santa Teresa, and again I find a hostel without locks on the doors. The owner is kind and makes me a cup of tea stuffed with coca leaves. At night, Santa Teresa is silent, and I wake only once, to the sound of a brief, hard rain on the roof.

On the third day, I trace the river once more, and again I see the Chilean students, the Argentine family, the French guys with their cameras. We follow the trail over rocks with rounded edges, past water that churns out of manmade caves, past crops of plantain. We climb out of the floodplain by lunchtime and follow a dirt road. The Chilean students offer me almonds; I share my raisins. We sip at our water and watch the white sun cross the sky. Even after the rain in the night, the road is clouded with dust, and each time a truck rumbles past we close our eyes tight, shield our faces with our arms.

And then, "Look," someone says as we turn a bend. And before us is the mountain, the great Machu Picchu, with its little hump and its rainbow flag, the flag of the Inca, a tiny speck that flaps high above us.

"There it is," we say to each other. "There it is." I am cold, all of a sudden, even with the sun beating down. Closer and closer we come, plodding past the hydroelectric power station, past the Machu Picchu entrance gate, past the start of the railroad.

I sleep my last night on the trail in Aguas Calientes, a town the hostel owner in Cuenca deemed the worst in all of Peru. I can't say I agree; though overpriced, over-paved, and hyper-clean, Aguas Calientes, set as it is in the crook of two green mountains, is decidedly better than the crumbling desert shacks I passed on the way to Lima, whole villages swathed in trash and gray sky. I sleep lightly in expensive Aguas Calientes, waking in darkness to walk my final stretch with the other sleepy hippies.

It's raining, and we hike without speaking. No one has a light; we stumble along the stony path that rises steeply up. We're all sweating, walking in a line, and glancing up every few moments. Slowly, daylight emerges, lightening the sky, casting a glow over our faces and hands, but still the sun doesn't quite show its face, and the rain doesn't weaken. We walk and walk, comrades by now, but when we finally reach the entrance to the park, we're disappointed.

For this is not what we expected. We had hoped, I suppose, for the ruins to sprawl before us, for the gates to open, welcoming us, but we never imagined this endless line of tourists waiting to enter. We didn't expect these buses that line up and pump exhaust into the sky, or these guides who saunter around with little flags in their hands, or this rain. None of us have rain jackets, and the second we reach the gate it starts to really pour. The silence of the climb is gone, replaced by the sound of water hitting the ground and of tourists complaining in every language. I don't have enough clothes; I'm shivering. We all are. We stand in the line, in the rain, blinking our eyes and frowning.

Through the press of the tourists, we inch forward. All must show their passports; we hold our documents close to our bodies to try and keep them dry. Everyone is soaking; water drips from the brim of my baseball cap, from my shirt sleeves and pant legs and shoelaces and nose. I think of the sunny days we've had, trekking here, and search the sky for a glimmer of blue. The minutes tick past, and then, finally, we are in, past the passport control, and I feel a surge of something good.

But there's more waiting. Everyone's huddled under a shelter just past the checkpoint, and I push and push, but no one budges. Police come, blowing their whistles and shoving through the crowd, past the patient guides and grouchy tourists and crying children. This line is wet raincoats, dripping hair, and the water that slides off the branches of pine trees right down into our collars. I won't get there, I think, and just then there's a break in the crowd. I spot a path, and push through.

In the end, my first glimpse of the Lost City isn't the sweet moment I'd hoped for. I'm jostled and shoved as I look out at the ruins, which are partially shrouded in fog. I cannot see the famous peaks that surround the terraces and columns and crumbling bricks; the clouds move in and out, concealing the city from view. I climb up, past the tourists taking drippy pictures, past the tour guides with their umbrellas. I climb along the terraces, and finally the people dwindle. Now there is silence, and when I turn around again, I see my second glimpse of the city. The clouds ebb a fraction, and the city is revealed, mystical in the fog, the ruins like old writing and beyond them those famous, jagged peaks.

And here they all are, every person who taught me to love the mountains. There is the face of my father, walking beside me, and there are his friends, the Big Fellas, men who dragged their daughters up and down peaks in every season, teaching them to ski, teaching them not to whine. There is the face of my very first lover, and although I don't know where he lives now, haven't spoken to him in years, he is beside me, his hair fluttering in the wind and the mountains all around him.

"No city will choke you," he told me once, "as long as you remember where you're from." He's the one who said to me, when I wept in the Boston night for how far the mountains felt, that they'd always be waiting for me, whenever I decided to return.

And so all of them are with me as I climb, all of the ones who showed me that the mountains are my home. I don't have pictures, or strands of their hair, or letters that they wrote to be scattered to the wind, but I have the memory of their footsteps on the trail. I have the touch of a hand in my mind, my dad reaching down to help me climb. It's the smell of bodies as they sweat, lightly, and it's the way skin glistens with rain.

Later, I will wonder: did they feel something as I stood over that city, looking out? Did they glance up from a desk, from a garden, out the window, and think of me? Did they see them in their dreams, these peaks like ghosts?

I hike in the drizzle back down the stone stairs, past tourists in bright anoraks. Some smile; most say nothing and keep their heads down. Many tourists are huddled in the Temple of the Sun, shivering beneath umbrellas and peering at the watery sky. A couple of light-haired *estadounidenses* in expensive workout gear snap pictures of the ruins in the fog.

"We're going to have a fuck-ton of pictures of this shit," one girl says loudly to the other. I can see only the backs of their heads, the blonde

highlights in their pert ponytails. One has a tattoo of a whimsical butterfly on her neck.

"A fuck-ton," the friend agrees cheerfully, snapping the button on
her own digital camera. "Wish we got Facebook up here," she adds,
taking her iPhone from her pocket and looking at it dismally.

Here, the voices of the girls sound sharp, like a knife slashing through
air. Higher up, the wind would have stolen their voices, smashing them
against the ancient bricks and tossing the shards for the clouds to consume. The drops of rain might have wrung out their accents, so similar
to mine, so that all we emitted was our breath, breath that matched the
wind in the trees and the settling earth.

An old guide sits beneath an umbrella, a little apart from the Sun
Temple group. I go over and sit down beside him and open my water
bottle to drink. I root around in my pocket for a packet of cookies and
offer him one. This guide has skin like the skin of a nut, brown and
slightly wrinkled but not veined. His eyes, when he turns to me and
looks me over, are surprising: green flecked with shards of burnt gold.
He looks at the cookies for a few seconds before taking one and putting
it in his mouth quickly. He holds it there, sucking on it.

"You're not supposed to bring food up here," he tells me, once he's
drawn the last fleck of cookie from his tooth with his tongue. "But for
you," he says, lowering his voice and wiping his mouth on his sleeve, "I
make an exception."

I barely make the train back to Cusco, having run all the way from the
Temple of the Sun to the Aguas Calientes station.

In the train's tiny washroom, my breath steams the mirror. Condensation collects on the small porcelain sink. I change out of my wet
clothes into dry, dirty ones. My hands turn from white to red, and my
hair, I discover when I glance at my reflection in the tiny mirror, hangs
in ratty, knotted strings. The other passengers are stylishly dressed and

sip coffee from Styrofoam cups. The women beside me don't touch the cookies the steward brings around. I devour mine; they offer their extras and then beam at me when I graciously accept. I know how I look: like a mean cat just in from the rain. I eat all of the cookies with relish.

For six hours, the bus creeps south from Cusco towards Lake Titicaca, crossing arid, wintered plains and sprawling Peruvian cities littered with plastic bags in a hundred colors. It's late afternoon before we reach marshland, and then we round a bend and here is the lake, ocean-blue and ocean-huge. The road tips down into Puno, a rippling, clay-colored city pinched into the shore. The woman beside me says that you can see Bolivia from here.

In the bus terminal, I get in line to buy my ticket for the morning, a one-way to Copacabana. The old man in line in front of me speaks in stumbling Spanish to the woman selling tickets. He is tall and thin, with long ears and a white beard. She is telling him when his bus leaves; he shakes his head and switches to English. Now, she is shaking her head. He unzips his pack, roots around, removes a battered dictionary.

I step forward and translate the woman's message for the old man: his bus leaves at eight, he should arrive fifteen minutes before, and his fare, to a destination I didn't catch, is thirty soles. The woman waits, her hand outstretched, while he counts out the bills.

Outside on the sidewalk, the old man thanks me and suggests we split a taxi into the city center.

"Do you have a hotel already?" he asks, and I shake my head, hold up my guidebook and shrug.

The woman at the ticket counter gave him a flier for a hotel in town advertising rooms with lime-green walls and fuzzy sunlight leaking through the windows.

"There's breakfast," he says, pointing to a picture of toast and a fork and knife at the bottom of the flier. The driver has his window cracked and the lake smells salty, gamy, the sharp cries of looping gulls piercing the air.

We check into the hotel, taking rooms opposite each other, and then the long-eared old man comes and taps on my door and invites me to dinner. I am grateful for the invitation, for in a near-empty hotel room, I have learned, a buzzing bulb can sound so loud. A night can last so long. Outside, the sky has already grown dark. We walk through Puno, past tour agencies and pharmacies and bakeries, past the three-story market as it is closing for the night, women packing up raw chickens and steaks and wiping down white counters. A massive cathedral dominates the plaza, and the old man says, "Let's go inside."

So we slip through the heavy double doors. The cathedral is dim and gorgeous, with old wooden floorboards and an arched, whitewashed ceiling. We admire the shrines of Mary Magdalene, of the Virgin, of Jesus on the cross and then again, bleeding, in Mary Magdalene's arms. Behind glass panes, we see figures of the saints, the doctors of the church, the disciples. The air is thick with incense. Candles flicker before every statue. Our feet creak over the floor, and a few people in pews turn their heads. Their eyes move past me and settle on the old man, whose legs and arms cast long shadows against the church's soaring beams.

We eat our dinner at an upstairs café on Puno's main drag. We order trout with avocado and salad and French fries, and the old man invites me to share a bottle of wine. He orders red and the wine tastes thick and good, warming us.

"Tell me about yourself," he says, and so I say that my journey began eight months ago in Guatemala. I tell him my pack gets heavier every time I leave a place, and then, after a second glass of wine, I admit that sometimes I miss home so badly I can't think. I've come this far, I say to him, yet sometimes all I want is a familiar face, a familiar room, a meal I've had before. I miss my mom, I admit. The old man listens gently, taking tiny bites and savoring his wine in little sips. He refills our glasses, mine first.

When his turn comes to talk, he explains that he is German and has traveled much: he rode his bicycle for seven months from China to Athens a few years ago. He's seen all of Europe, much of North America, some of Asia, a little of Australia. He's been in Peru since May, with another two months scheduled in South America.

"In my previous life, I was a civil engineer," he tells me, but he never mentions kids, or a wife, or a house. He says only that his German home is near the Black Forest, and that it is very beautiful there.

He tells me that he spent one night on the Isla del Sol, the most sacred island on Lake Titicaca. He woke early in the morning, and he couldn't get back to sleep. So he packed his bag and left the hostel and walked.

"How wonderful it felt," he says. "I am an old man, and there I was, walking in the moonlight, alone." He grins, remembering.

"I'm an old man," he says again, "and I was free."

It's hailing as we make our way back to the hotel. This makes the old German man laugh. "Snow!" he exclaims. "Rain!" When we get back to the hotel, he gives me a kiss on the cheek, and then a long, tight hug. "I like to feel you," he says, but I'm not embarrassed for him. It's not so bad, a hug. My hotel room has lurid green walls, a buzzing bulb, traces of stale cigarette smoke leached into the bedcovers and the carpeted floor.

"Good night," I tell the old man, and watch him cross the hall and enter his room, a room identical to mine, and close the door.

COPACABANA, BOLIVIA

Bolivia is considered to be the most indigenous of all the Latin American countries. People I met on the road either loved it—*so beautiful*—or hated it—*so poor.* The country famously celebrates more than one festival for every day of the year, but the festivals, I will discover, are micro-regional. I will learn that Bolivia is ancient, the land inhabited for more than 20,000 years, the country steeped in myriad cultures with different dialects, colors, and holy days for each community. There are thirty-seven official languages in Bolivia, and the population is a mix: indigenous Quechua and Aymaran; German, English and Japanese; Mexican and Balkan. The country is largely Roman Catholic, though what that means differs town to town, as pre-Colombian practices still heavily influence religion, in Bolivia as they did in Guatemala.

And Bolivia is enormous, 400,000 square miles with the Andes running all down through. Bolivia and Peru own Lake Titicaca in a much-disputed joint arrangement. The northeastern part of Bolivia is forest, and in the southwest you'll find some of the largest salt flats in the world. As was Peru, Bolivia is dotted with mines, most of them exhausted of the silver that fueled the sprawling Spanish empire in the sixteenth century. Now, zinc and tin are some of Bolivia's largest exports, though, as in the seventeenth century, the country exports raw materials, while the processing is done in other countries. This practice keeps Bolivians unskilled, valuable only for their country's raw materials. As for the finished products—cars, lithium batteries, processed petroleum—the craftsmanship is invested in elsewhere, and it is there that the markup is applied.

Until the 1880s, Bolivia had its own section of Pacific Coast, wedged into what is now northern Chile. Today's Bolivia is poor and landlocked, exhausted by revolution and border wars, drought, and the price of growing coca against the world's wishes. Bolivia is the third largest cocaine producer in the world after Peru and Colombia, who jostle between first and second places every year. Evo Morales, Bolivia's famously socialist president, is known for putting his foot down against US bans on coca, and in general for being a man of the people. In the past decade, Bolivia has made moves to nationalize agriculture, water, crude petroleum, and natural gas—often with a high price to pay.

In short, the country is known for being impoverished and drug-plagued. The truth is, certain resources mean it has the potential to develop fast, but limits to national investors—not instituted without reason, I suspect, after having seen the damage the United States has done in Latin America—and high rates of poverty keep Bolivia poor. My *estadounidense* friends and family remain fearful. The entry fee for me to enter Bolivia is more than for a person from any other country—$135 more, to be exact. While everyone else on the bus slips from Peru into Bolivia with a nod to customs—not even a visa necessary—I stand at the desk for ten or fifteen minutes answering questions, passing over money, and waiting for my stamp. I apologize to the bus driver afterwards, who grunts at me over the engine's growl.

The Copacabana bus terminal swarms with young men in t-shirts and flip-flops. They clutch the straps of their backpacks and barter with the *ayudantes* for the best prices to La Paz. Copacabana is a lakeside town with stripped brown hills in the distance and a boardwalk flanked by the white-capped lake. I walk the streets, which are narrow and busy, tight with cafés and money exchanges and shops selling inexpensive clothes displayed on bosomy mannequins. I ring the buzzer at a hotel on a side street, and after the sound of much shuffling, a woman comes to the door. She's still in her nightgown; behind her, two children watch me.

"I'll have a room at four," she tells me, and shows me the way through the messy kitchen to a closet where I might stow my pack. The room will cost thirty bolivianos, she tells me, and I calculate the sum in my head. Three dollars, just about.

At the Internet café next door, I send cheerful emails home, assuring everyone I've made it to Bolivia safely. I laugh to myself as I type. Pale-skinned tourists with dreadlocks and bones in their ears are noisily making their way up the street, and through the window, I can see waiters and waitresses waiting for the lunch rush. Through the open door, the air smells of cooking meat and of the lake, salty like the sea. *This is just a place*, I think to myself another time.

Copacabana's main cathedral dates back to the seventeenth century. The whitewash is fresh, the railings wrapped in flower garlands. The cabs and cars parked on the streets are decorated with ribbons, artificial flowers, and confetti. On the hood of one cab, a candle burns. Women sell a dozen varieties of sweets on tables beneath blue tarps, as they did in Cuenca during the week of Septenario, except that these are different sweets, this church is a different church, and these artificial flowers seem to blossom more brightly against the whitewashed walls and brown hills and blue sky. Everything feels so sharp in Bolivia: the air laced with charred corn and spun sugar, urine and cigarette smoke, and an underlying tinge of spilt liquor; the shrieks of children; the bustle of old women in the cathedral, standing at the altar lighting candles; the way, turning a corner, the street goes from light to dark, full to empty, and then, at the next turn, to full and bright again.

Through Copacabana I walk, first down to the little scoop of beach, paddleboats lined up along the shore. I walk the tourist strip, sleepy at siesta time but looking scruffy and funky, colorful. Next, I walk north towards the town's highest point, a rocky outcrop. I'm used to the altitude, and I feel strong. I'm grateful for the sun. I shuck off my sweater and smile at big families making their way down the road the opposite way. At the sound of church bells, I remember that it's Sunday. People glance at me, but their looks are subtle, curious, sidelong glances and little nods but no *gringa* this, *gringita* that. Even the groups of boys say nothing.

A series of crosses like shrines marks the summit, and families snap photos and eat picnic lunches. By the time I get back to town, my room is ready. It's a tiny third-floor room with a window over the street and another looking out onto the balcony and down into the courtyard. A breeze flows between the two windows. The room smells a little dank, and it's a little dirty. It's nothing I haven't seen before; in fact, it is pleasant, very quiet so high up. I can smell the wind off the lake, faintly salty. I sleep immediately and wake only after the sky has grown dark.

On the beachside boardwalk, cafés serve fish and rice, salad and beans, sangria and beer. There are many people wandering and more seated in plastic chairs at plastic tables. Teenagers pass bottles between them and swagger in herds, and a gust of wind brings the scent of marijuana over the sand. I go into one of the cafés, really a cooking shack and four beams with a tarp for a roof. I take a plastic chair. The young waiter comes over and recommends the fish prepared with spices. So far down the beach, this place is quieter than the rest, and I listen to the tinny music playing in the kitchen, the sounds of dishes washed in a bucket, the rattle of coins in the waiter's pocket. When the fish is ready, he brings it over, then comes back with a liter of beer and two squat glasses.

"May I?" he asks, and because his eyes are friendly and the fish and potatoes are heaped high and steaming on my plate, I nod and smile.

He is Flavio, born in La Paz, and has lived here in Copacabana for three years now. I eat the fish while he sips his beer and watches people stumble past outside. He has his eye on Peru, he says, on a restaurant job in Lima where he can make real money, but for now he's living here, saving up and smoking grass. He smiles a sneaky smile then, and glances around the restaurant. The sounds from the kitchen have ceased and, over the water, the moon is low and full. He takes a crooked joint from his breast pocket and winks at me, lights the joint, draws in deeply, and coughs. He draws again, coughs less this time, and sips from his glass of beer. Again, I laugh out loud. Flavio thinks I'm laughing at him. I don't have the Spanish words to explain what's so funny—where I am, how afraid people were, how different tonight's Bolivia must be than any they have in their minds. Or maybe this is just what they imagined—a dark, windy, lusty night and a strange boy with a joint in his hand.

"Want?" Flavio asks. The moon is round over Lake Titicaca, and my belly is full. I take Flavio's joint and inhale.

The ferry, crammed with tourists, chugs out of the Copacabana port fifteen minutes late. In the light of dawn, I can see that the port, more of a beach with a couple of docks, is ugly without the moon. Paddleboats are strewn about, hundreds of them, along with canoes and kayaks and an odd sailboat, turned on its side like a sleeping horse. There's trash here, the sand is blackened in places, and dogs mill around, sniffing and lifting their legs. Tourists lounge in wicker chairs outside of cafés, sunglasses blocking their eyes, coffee cups in their hands.

We're bound for the Isla del Sol—the most sacred island on the lake and the alleged birthplace of the Incan Sun God—and the ferry creeps along. There are a few trees—occasional stands of eucalyptus or imported pine—but mostly the coastline is bare, stripped clean, the vegetation unable to regenerate in such cold nights, and with such little rain. On this ferry, I count only one local, a thin woman with a bony face and shiny black hair who murmurs to the child she holds on her lap. The rest of the passengers are tourists, who speak in loud German or muttery French or the shushing Spanish of Argentina. The surface of Lake Titicaca, my guidebook explains, spans over three thousand square miles and is fed by melted Andean snow.

Eventually, the inside of the ferry fills with the smell of gasoline. People begin to wrap scarves around their noses and mouths, and the windows are opened. A German man sitting with his family gets up and storms to the back of the boat, where the men are working the controls. He screams at the men in a mix of German and Spanish—"Get rid of this gas!" I think he is shouting, though over the motor it's hard to know for sure. "Look at us—we can't breathe!" The men working the rig nod, eyes down.

"Si, si, si," they tell the German man.

"*Si, si, si,*" he mocks them back. "Do something about it!" he says, loudly. Then, flushed, he pushes his way back to his seat and takes up his book, but his eyes remain hot. After a few minutes, though, the smell is all but gone, and the man lets his children stand on his lap to look out the window.

At the ferry's first stop in the port of Yumani, I disembark. Tourists mill about on the grassy shore and the tiny, stony beach, waiting for the boat that will take them back to the mainland. On the hillside, women with long braids and babies strapped to their backs skip down a trail.

"That's the town up there," an old man says to me. He's sitting by the ferry's ticket office with a book of tickets in his hand. He gestures up the stairs, which are made with slabs of flat stone. "Go ahead," he urges me as if I've spent too long on this beach already.

The air is so clear and tight up here that I must pause often to breathe. I stumble up the cobbled path, grateful that I paid the hotel-keeper in Copacabana to store my pack in her bedroom. When I look behind me, I can see the impossible blue of the lake, sharpened by bare hills. Brown and blue, brown and blue; the colors of this island are the colors of the desert. The trees shorten and grow stubby, worn by the wind, branches low to the ground. Brown and blue and hard as a rock.

Yumani is a one-road town. There are no cars, and the street is empty. A few shops advertise pizza and cigarettes or maps of the island, but no one lingers outside smoking or chatting. No motorcycles rev; the only sound is the wind and the occasional yip of a distant dog.

I see a sign at the roadside for a youth hostel and follow a curving stone path, the grass alongside it stubby but remarkably green, to a two-story house with a small porch. At the edge of the scratched lawn, the land tips down into cliff, and the water is directly visible below. I touch the buzzer; a woman answers right away. She opens the door but does not yet invite me in. She is dressed in a full skirt and legwarmers, her long braids woven with yarn. An olive-green derby hat sits perched on her head.

"Si, mama?" she asks, her voice low. I ask for a room.

"We have plenty," she says, making space for me to edge past and then pulling the door shut and locking it behind her. She slips her ring of keys into her apron pocket and looks me up and down, taking in my muddy boots, my faded black jeans, my stringy hair and uneven freckles.

"Where do you come from," she says, not a question in the obligatory way the words fall. It is simply the usual question, the standard thing. I tell her the States; she says nothing. She takes me around the peach-colored house, pointing out the only bathroom, the big white kitchen, and the wooden tables and chairs in the lobby. She shows me the available bedroom, filled with sun. There's a bright yellow woven blanket on the bed, and the floor is made up of creaky, slender boards. The woman takes my money—thirty bolivianos, three dollars again. "There's breakfast in the morning," she says. She fumbles in her apron pocket and produces a single brass key on a chain with a plastic purple tag. "Don't lose the key," she warns me, and then she goes out, pulling the door almost all the way closed behind her.

I lock the door behind me when I go out, though I've left nothing in the room. My pack contains nothing extra, not even pajamas, not even extra shoes. I splash icy water on my face in the bathroom, whose walls exude the scent of cedar. I dry my hands and face on my shirt, and then I go into the lobby, where the woman is sweeping.

There is a trail, she tells me, that runs around the whole of the island. She goes to the window and advises me to walk the eastern side first, continuing through Yumani until I reach the edge, the cliffs. I can come back through the towns along the island's western edge if I have the energy, she says. The whole trip will take seven hours. She points out the delineated route along a yellowed map she's got tacked to the wall. I wish her a nice day, she wishes the same for me, and I leave her in the sunny room to sweep the already spotless floors.

Every house in Yumani seems to double as a restaurant, *tienda*, or hotel. The signs for pizza, for cheap rooms, for cold beer, are all in English. Against the screaming signs, the street remains empty.

Yumani is the color of the land. The owners of the few painted houses have chosen muted tones—dusty marigold, pale peach, chalky tan. It is as if the town has become a part of the faded tonality of the earth. I walk out of Yumani and a new silence comes, sculpted of wind off the water. The stones beneath my feet are replaced with clay and sand. Now come stands of hardy pines, which exude a faint hot scent.

I come to a checkpoint, where an old man with one eye sells me a ticket for fifteen bolivianos. Now I begin to see the tourists: clans of Artentineans, Chileans, French couples and German families. Once, I pass a group of three *estadounidense* girls, their voices clear and loud on the trail, and we greet each other in Spanish. Finally, I can make out the northernmost point of the island, marked by a cresting hill and, at the base of it, the famous remaining ruins of the Isla del Sol. The Sun God was born here, and for decades this place was the mecca for the Inca.

Today, tourists stroll about, snapping pictures of each other between the half-walls. One woman eats lunch alone at the table in the center of the ruins; this table and the chairs surrounding it are made of rounded stone slabs, and I wonder if the largest one is the original. There is no one to ask; a girl in a loose black t-shirt poses while her boyfriend snaps photos, and a redheaded, middle-aged woman in a purple anorak sits on a stone stair and takes out a sandwich.

Beyond the ruins, the shore is a crescent of white, scooping the turquoise water in a half-moon. The tourists zip up their anoraks, and the bright gusts of wind snap. I hike down to the strip of sand, down the steep and even steps built of the soft, light stone, bleached remains of an ancient volcano. The sand is fine, not white up close but gray and gold and pink and tinged with lavender. I remember the old man, the night he slept on this island bright with moonlight.

The route home, winding south along the island's eastern edge, curves alongside clusters of painted buildings all facing the white beach and, beyond, the Isla del Luna, this island's smaller sister. One town has a couple of big pigs that root in the sand while young men without shirts chuck Frisbees. Hippies have pitched tents on the sand and spread jewelry out on blankets; the bracelets and necklaces made of thick, waxy thread accented with silver and stones from all over, I imagine: Argentina and Nicaragua, Venezuela, the nighttime Quito market.

The artisans—wiry, tanned, dark-haired, and dark-eyed—watch the line of white beach through dark glasses. Their clothes are stringy, skimpy, hanging off their bodies like parts of their skin. They don't look at me as I pass. I hear their jabbering Spanish and try to guess where they are from; once, Gaby told me that all artisans come from Argentina.

"Hola," they say without looking up. "Hola." The word, by now, is starting to sound like only its last syllable: *la, la, la.*

Eventually, the beach ends, and the trail turns to rock-studded grass again. Pigs sniff on the hillside for bits of lunchtime bread. The trail climbs steeply again, snaking along the ridge, and the expanse of sky to the west of me matches exactly the color of the sea, scooped into inlets like little slivers of freezing moon.

In one hamlet, sleepy-looking women in chairs along the road wear orange dresses with hats tied below their chins. Their skirts are

fashioned of yellow, gold, and electric-green fabric with silver embroidery. I tell them hello as I pass; they nod and look away. I ask a small
boy with a bicycle what the women are doing dressed like that. "The
festival," he replies without glancing at me, then hops on his bike and
pedals off down the hill.

I come to a plaza at the base of a tiny red and white church. Lively
music blasts from speakers, and a few women sit in folding chairs
and drink orange soda from plastic cups. The women are dressed in
bright blues and fiery reds, white bonnets bow-tied at their chins with
purple sashes.

"Good afternoon," I say to them. "Good afternoon," they mumble
back. Another tourist, I am. I point and ask them the way; they
nod, looking past me toward the men. They refill their plastic cups
of orange soda. The men are wearing sequined pads on their shoulders. Every stitch of their tunics and pants and wide-brimmed hats is
embroidered thickly with sequins, or layered with paint, or glistening
with purple silk.

"What festival is this?" I ask the women as they sip their orange
soda and watch their men. They look quizzically at each other—what
festival *is* this? Finally, the eldest woman pipes up: "San Sebastian,"
she says.

"San Sebastian," the other women say, one after another, nodding
their heads and sipping from their cups.

For a few moments I stand around, watching the men in groups
murmuring to each other. The women remain in their chairs, and a boy
brings around another bottle of orange soda and a bag of potato chips.
I realize that I'm waiting for something that will mark this place, this
festival, some dance or song, and as the thought weaves through me, I'm
embarrassed. Who am I to wait and see how this afternoon will unfold,
what stories will be told, what other days like this will be remembered?
I am a visitor, nothing more, and my face looks the same as all the other
faces of all the other backpackers. Here, I suddenly, palpably feel that

I don't belong. The men stand around, their hands on their hips, their beautiful clothes sparkling. The women sip their drinks. I move on, unnoticed, and am grateful when the emptiness of water and dust fills the space around me again.

LA PAZ, BOLIVIA

This is the ride to La Paz: first the wide lake, bluer than the sky, nearly electric against the constant and unrelenting brownness of the earth, fields, roads, and homes. The bus climbs up out of the hills that surround Copacabana; we catch our last glimpse of that pretty coastal town, and then we crest the hill and it disappears. Now, cows and sheep graze, pigs sniff in the dirt, and donkeys pull at the ropes they're tied to, stomping their hooves and nodding their heads and letting the wind flap their ears. We come to a ferry station where everyone gets off, pays one and a half Bolivian dollars, and rides in a speedboat across the narrow strip of water. The bus goes on a barge all by itself; on the other side of the Copacabana peninsula, we wait for it. I buy oranges and eat them sitting beside the *tienda* in the sun.

Founded in 1548 by the Spanish conquistador Alonso de Mendoza, La Paz is famously known as the world's highest capital. The city, cupped by the Andes, sits at just under 12,000 feet—warm clothes, my guidebook cautions, are essential. Sure enough, from lakeside, sun-baked Copacabana, the wind through the windows of the bus grows steadily colder. We put sweaters on and pull shawls around our shoulders. We yank the windows closed. The Cordillera draws jagged and near, the highest peak glinting pinkish in the evening sun. The only paved road, it seems, is the one we're on; the streets that stretch away are dirt or stone or broken brick. Women have fruit out on the sidewalk, and then come strips of mechanic shops, men on the ground with greasy bikes. Here are the stores that sell kitchenware—wooden spoons, metal spatulas, pots and buckets and pans. Here are the shops with light bulbs and cords and shades and fans, and here are the shops selling wheels of cheese packed close against each other in a yellow rainbow. Every category is clustered, with the products arranged in the same way at every shop.

These are the outskirts of La Paz: the buildings are mostly brick, and everything on this stretch of road seems half-built. Walls stand unfinished, and roofs have been only halfway tiled. Many windows are missing panes and bars, and always there are these dusty roads that run away from the highway. There are many people waiting at corners for buses, standing in lines so long I marvel at the passengers' patient faces. Some are smoking, some are reading, some are looking at cell phones, some are looking down at their children. Night is falling, but no one leans out into the street to watch for the bus. The micros and smallest buses are painted with names and messages: *The Honey of Your Lips* and *Jesus Died for Us; Eva Rosa* and *My Love Bolivia*. The buses are rattling works of art that tear past us and then shudder to stops. They showcase painted flowers, elaborate crosses, or the famous places of Bolivia: the salt flats, the peaks, the massive lake and her sacred islands.

Finally, it comes: the promised valley and then the rippling city, a blanket of clustered, red-roofed buildings, a glowing La Paz in the afternoon light. I hear the sounds of digital cameras and cell phones snapping photos, but other than that the bus is silent.

La Paz city, as far as I can tell, has no tourist-friendly district per se, no cluster of cheap hostels and bars and restaurants like Quito's Mariscal. I get nostalgic for walkable Miraflores in Lima, and I don't even allow myself to imagine bumping Cusco. My La Paz hotel is surprisingly expensive, and the hot water in my room doesn't work, though the bed is large and looks comfortable. The front-desk manager promises to get the water going by morning, and directs me to the market.

I tell the first cheese man I see that I'd like a little cheese. "Ten is the minimum," he says, showing me how much with his knife at the wheel, not looking at me. It's a lot, enough for three days, enough to go bad before I eat it all. "Could I buy five?" I ask, and he just turns away. I stand there for a moment, waiting, but he is ignoring me now and there is no bargaining to be done. "Okay, ten," I say, but he pretends not to hear. I'm stunned and embarrassed.

The next is bread. Bread should be easy, with all the ladies lined up in a row, piles of rolls sitting before them, rolls that will go stale by tomorrow. Surely they'll be happy to unload them. I walk slowly past the bins until I come to a woman who has some nice brown rolls.

"How much?" I ask her.

"For how many?" she asks, not looking at me.

"Two," I say.

"Four?" she says.

"Two!"

"One?" she asks. Finally, a little boy, maybe her son, shakes awake from where he's been leaning against her and says, "Two."

"Oh, two," she says, rolling her eyes.

She doesn't move, nor does she give me a price. I wait for her to reach for a plastic bag and select two rolls, as has been the practice since Guatemala. Finally, she says something to me.

"What was that?" I ask, leaning in. She repeats it; I still don't understand. I don't dare ask her another thing; I just hand her one peso and say a silent prayer. Blessedly, she roots for change and passes it over, and I think the exchange is finally a success, but now she stares off behind me toward the stalls on the other side of the street.

I select two rolls and ask for a bag.

"A what?" she asks, sighing.

"A little bag," I say, but I'm already standing to leave. I knew I should have quit while I was ahead.

"No one gets a bag for just two rolls," she says, loud enough that everyone on the street can hear.

For three days, I talk to the manager at the hotel and no one else. I eat bread for breakfast then walk and walk. Some of these streets remind me of Prague years ago, when I travelled there alone. It was so cold in Prague, with snow on the ground, but there's something so similar about the two places. The bridges, the buildings, not at all the same and yet they share a weathered gray, and the streets a rugged, stony steepness. There is a street of witches, with animal skulls and herbs and teeth for sale. The Coca Museum is a handful of teeny rooms crammed with tourists, the walls pasted with newspaper articles and hand-printed posters and old photographs, tourists snapping pictures of each other beside mannequins bagging cocaine. Massive ravines divide the city, red crevasses dotted deep down with boulders and pine trees. The downtown is sleek, glassed, the parks neat squares, attractive neighborhoods built into hillsides. I walk, take pictures, eat bread and cheese, then go back to my room early and write, and the words on the page always return to the buses that brought me here and will take me away. La Paz is indifferent to my presence, and anyway, I have fallen in love with the ride. I ache for the wheels beneath me, bringing me someplace else.

SUCRE, BOLIVIA

The road south is rolling plains and distant figures stooped in fields. Dogs sleep in the streets. Little shacks with open windows have bags of chips strung on lines and signs advertising gas and cold soda for sale. Occasionally water in the form of low marshes graces the roadside, and the bus reaches Oruro long after the sun sets. The city unfolds out my window: cement-block homes, unpaved streets, dogs on the curb, men sitting on wooden benches, smoking. There are no large grocery stores and no chain restaurants, just stands with fried chicken for sale and a curious abundance of furniture stores with dusty windows.

I find a room on the fourth floor of the third hotel I enter, a tiny room lit by a naked, buzzing bulb. The first two hotels were full. The bathroom has a small barred window that looks out into the night. Freezing air pours in and with it the smell of chicken. I close the window, but I can still hear the low grumble of buses easing into the station, of motorcycles pealing out. The single bed is thin and sunken, and the tiles on the floor have broken in places. This type of room, I know, will turn you sour and sad if you let it, and I remind myself that it is just one room, for only one night. Part of me wishes to lie down on the bed and wait for sleep to come, wait for morning to arrive, wait for my night in this dirty room to end, but my stomach grumbles. My last real meal was breakfast: toast and eggs at the hotel while the man at the front desk watched the television set with sleepy eyes. I go outside and walk past fried chicken stands. In large, brightly lit restaurants, families sit, but they, too, are eating plates of French fries and fried chicken.

I go into a corner restaurant, massive and empty and clean-looking. The menu above the register shows pictures of the dishes—not fried chicken. I suspect that the prices are higher here, and that explains the emptiness. I select a plate of posole and shaved alpaca meat and order a beer. The alcohol settles in my stomach as I sit, alone, by the window. I wait for my food to come, and when it does, I eat and eat of the grainy posole, corn cooked long, turned firm and salty and potato-like in texture. The shaved meat is too salty, but I eat it all, pay my bill, and then go out into the fried-chicken night. The food has made me lighter somehow, and I say good-night cheerfully to the woman at the hotel's front desk. She looks up at me, surprised, as if we both know I'll go back to the tiny, dirty room, and in the morning, I'll be gone.

Once, Sucre was the most important city in Latin America, prized for its access to fine metals, its protected location, its fertile countryside. It was Sucre's bell that rang to mark the start of the Bolivian independence movement in 1809, and Sucre was the judicial and cultural capital of Bolivia until the nineteenth century. Now, it's known best for being the country's colonial gem: Sucre to Bolivia what Antigua is to Guatemala, or Cuenca to Ecuador.

Alongside its sparkling white walls and attractive, grassy center, I can see from the bus that beggars weave amongst blundering tourists. The bus deposits us at a white cement-block station, pleasant and clean with sodas for sale. I turn left at the first corner and walk. There are hours before the sky darkens, and I feel happy. It's nice to be walking; my muscles relax and shed the strain of the jostling seat. The air smells of sweet corn and cigarettes and flowers; I smile, remembering the fried-chicken night, the cramped hotel room, the squeals of traffic all night long. *The moment of travel is merciful.*

I find a two-story hotel with rooms for thirty bolivianos. My room, at the back of the hotel and upstairs, has two beds crammed into the tiny space and a closet with a few bent wire hangers. There is a desk with a chair, and the floorboards are smooth and stained golden. It is a place I imagine was once grand, and I think of the hotel in Cuenca, when it rained and rained and the paint slowly curled from the walls. There, I'd wandered the wet streets. I'd met Matt; I'd taken the ride; I'd left the city jangled and missing E—, glad to be gone.

Here, I take my jacket and sweater from my pack and hang them on the bent wire hangers. I put the rest of my things under the bed, taking with me the old-fashioned brass key to the room and a few bolivianos. *It is August,* I think to myself. The days are slipping past, and each one, I realize, is sweet now. In December, it will have been a year. *A year,* I had promised myself.

Some days, I wonder about staying. How hard would it be, I reason with myself, to find a job? To rent a room, to speak Spanish all the time, to choose one of the places I fall in love with and just stay? And then my thoughts turn to the obvious: It will become another job, and my eyes will dull to the details. I'll grow homesick and bored. I'll yearn for the journey. I'll think of all the places I've seen, places that are blending into each other, one mountain range becoming another, hotels shifting and muddled in my mind. An old man in Puno, a cheerful guy in Vilcabamba, a friendly girl on a desert bus. My mind, like my body, is flung.

Today, though, I am in Sucre, Bolivia, and so I go outside in the sunshine to see.

The churches and museums display the riches of Sucre, glinting metals stripped from the hills and melted into crosses and other products of adoration. There is not much rugged about this downtown; docents abound, visible through the open doors of centuries-old buildings. Rooftops glitter gold, adorned with ancient molding and encrusted crosses. I search for the market, thinking of Gaby, who said markets were a city's heart and the best thing to do in a new place was to find one. I'm grateful to see that the massive place is pulsing, and I walk between the stalls of soup and chocolate, of fruit and cheese and suspended cuts of meat, dripping blood. There is the scent of sugared bread and herbal tea. A plump, friendly woman in a ruffled pink apron serves me a corn drink in a plastic glass while her scrawny male dishwasher eyes me warily. "Do you like it?" the plump woman asks, and I nod, for it is sweet and nutty both. I drink the whole glass and she pours more, laughing at my gratitude. She gives me flaky, airy *sopapillas*, and waits before I've eaten my fill before charging me less than one boliviano.

On the street outside, an old man in tattered clothes sits on the curb, eating Jell-O with his hands. I have seen how Jell-O is sold—on trays, in paper cups, hawked by young men who sidestep through crowds and shout. I remember being very sick in my childhood only once. I might have had the flu, or maybe food poisoning, but I lay on the couch for days, unable to drink even water. The only food I could swallow was Jell-O, and after a few days of the lime-colored stuff I recovered and never ate Jell-O again. I look at the Jell-O in the old man's hands, then up at the gleaming whitewash of the cathedral, the glinting gold of the domed roof.

I sleep three nights in Sucre, speaking to no one but the women in the market. I climb the hillsides to look out over the city. One day, I go to the market and purchase a razor. It's the first razor I've had since Quito, and when I get back to my rented room, I take it from my purse and examine it. It's shiny and sleek, the plastic and metal different shades of blue, the double blades sharp and unmarred. I know it will be destroyed in one shower; it's been uncountable days—weeks, after all—since I've shaved my legs or underarms.

And I've taken to stealing napkins from tables in restaurants, and from the little plastic holder in the breakfast room at this hotel, because there's never any toilet paper, anywhere, and I've learned that a roll takes up space in a pack, but paper napkins fold neatly, conveniently, into my pockets. On my third day in Sucre, I wake up and put on the same shirt I've worn for the past three days, the same sweater I've worn for the past three weeks. My clothes don't smell bad, and who is there to notice, anyhow? I comb my hair with water and check my face in the mirror; I look neat, acceptably clean, and extremely well-rested.

I have taken to carrying around my plastic Guatemalan *costal* full of food: the half-empty bottle of olive oil Kerry bought in Lima and left, a half-eaten loaf of bread, some cut-up avocadoes and pepper, and a head of broccoli. Nothing's moldy or browned. The half-empty bottle of red wine has soured a little, but I'll have it tonight. This way, I reason, the hungry people get lucky, because there are always a couple rolls in there I know I won't finish, or a few green apples I bought in bulk because the big bag cost as much as two or three loose pieces of fruit, and so I've taken to handing out food instead of coins to the people who beg on the sidewalk. Maybe they snort and laugh at the food I give, or maybe they devour it, I don't know. I don't ever look back.

My red watch, purchased in one of Quito's massive underground malls, has begun to fail me; sometimes it will slow and then come to a stop, and I must turn the knob to get it right. Its clear plastic face is permanently waterlogged, making the numbers nearly unreadable anyway. I begin to think that my unreliable watch is a metaphor for my mind; I had forgotten that August came after July, that the weeks had seven days, the weekends two. I eat when I am hungry now. I wake when the sun enters my room or the creaking of floorboards sounds outside my door. I might ask the woman who sells me the ticket to the next town what day it is, and she'll look at me like I'm crazy and roll her eyes. It's Sunday, she'll say, and then I'll remember that the days don't matter to me anyway, and I'll pass my fare over the counter. When I must know the time, I peer at my watch and hope it's not lying. If I miss the bus, I have found that there's always another.

I wonder: How long will it take to sink back into easy laundry, to fresh clothes daily, to clean razors in a hot shower, to towels not permanently soggy? Will I get used to five or six pairs of jeans to choose from, five pairs of shoes, four handbags, two choices of perfume? Will I get used to the way perfume smells, even? Will it stop catching me on the street and making me sneeze? Will I start wearing makeup again, the way I used to every day, carefully applying it before the mirror in the morning before work? Will I get used to the way I look with eyeliner, or from now on will I see myself as whorish for darkening my lids and lashes and mouth? How quickly will I forget what it's like not to care? To have food for the next meal and only that? To have clothes for three days and just that? Will I forget soon enough how it feels to look inside my pack and see the shirts and pants rolled up there and marvel at all that I have?

How fast, I wonder, will I start wanting things again, things beside lunch and a room and a ticket? How long before I start to know the days, the dates, the month, the time down to the minute? How long before I'm rushing, checking, buying, wishing, wanting, saving, fretting? How long before I forget the man with the Jell-O, the woman sweeping cedar boards, the old man wishing for human contact, a young boy bringing me fried fish and beer, a girl with long hair and green jewelry speaking Spanish like a native in the plaza? How long before I start combing my hair, and before I start needing a clock again?

POTOSÍ, BOLIVIA

A guided tour of the silver mine in Potosí, Bolivia costs ten dollars. I buy my ticket for the guided tour in the tiny travel agency just off the main plaza, where sun dapples brick and grass. Music—drums, a keening wail—pours from a high-up open window, and the air smells of instant coffee and woodsmoke. Between brick buildings, I can see El Cerro de Potosí, the clay-colored, triangular mound that looms over the whole sprawling city. Nicknamed El Cerro Rico, the mound is stripped bare: no trees of any kind, no homes, just the zigzagging road, cut jaggedly into the hillside.

Potosí, some twelve hours by bus south of La Paz, is one of Bolivia's largest cities, and was once one of South America's grandest. The elderly bearded travel agent tells me, as he copies my passport number into his record book, that in the seventeenth century, El Cerro Rico made the Spanish rich. He is short, broad-shouldered, and he speaks slowly but without hesitation, as if he has given this information to foreigners many times. The Spanish trekked in manpower, Incan descendants and African slaves by the thousands, to scrape out the glittering veins. The travel agent presses an inked stamp onto my ticket, *Paid*, and then he neatly slides the paper across the desk to me.

"Have a wonderful time," he says without irony, and then he smiles politely and shakes my hand, as if it's been a genuine pleasure to do business with me.

The other people on my tour are a Belgian man and his two teenaged sons. The travel agent introduces us all to our tour guide, a small woman with glossy dark hair. She wears drab gray pants and an olive-colored wool sweater; still, it's easy to see that she's pretty: big brown eyes, and that swing of hair.

"She is also my daughter," the travel agent announces, and they both smile wryly. He says something to her in Spanish too fast for me to understand, and then he is wishing us well and going back into the travel agency. Now we are climbing into a van—sticky sliding door, interior the color of the tour guide's clothes, clean seats with no seatbelts—and now we are off, the three Belgians and the pretty tour guide and I, to enter a Bolivian mine.

Before we ascend the Cerro, we must buy gifts for the miners. This is tradition, our guide explains. She shows us where to purchase coca leaves, bottles of juice, alcohol, cigarettes: this *tienda* at the edge of town has all the items waiting in plastic packets, prices neatly stickered on each one.

I want to bring the miners food, the same packages of cookies and sacks of corn cakes that I always buy for the endless, jolting Bolivian bus rides, but the guide shakes her head.

"They don't eat in the mines," she tells me, and only later I'll find out that the miners don't take lunch in there because of how quickly silica dust and particles of arsenic will coat the food. The grains that float in the caves are tiny shards of poison, and so she holds out plastic bottles of clear liquid, labeled Alcohol Potable, and packages of thick, hand-rolled cigarettes instead. "These are the best gifts for the miners," she says, and I shudder. The healthiest choice, then, seems to be a bag of coca leaves, which the miners chew all day to keep up their energy and stave off hunger. I buy two big bottles of orange juice, too, and my guide gruffly nods her approval.

Once, she tells me, the dried coca leaves were the miners' only payment. Like the travel agent, she gives the facts simply; her expression doesn't ask for a reaction.

As we ride in the clattering van up towards the halfway point of Cerro Rico, where we'll enter the mines, I chat with the Belgians. They've been in Peru, and just got to Bolivia two days ago. "We scrambled down here," the younger son says. "We don't even know why!"

I compliment the Belgians on their English.

"That's the great thing about no dubbing!" the older son crows. "We learn from television!" We discuss the difference between the euro and the dollar: ten bolivianos to the euro, seven to the dollar.

"It's even better for the Swiss," the Belgians say. "They're rich!"

The van comes to a stop and we all pile out, pulling our jackets close around us in the chilly morning wind, remembering again that we are in Bolivia now, atop a bleeding mound. We are issued helmets and rubber boots; we put them on while the miners squatting at the roadside watch. We pass the chutes built of stone and graying plywood where the deposits come through, and the little tin shacks where the tools are stored. A bunch of guys, younger than I am, are punching each other and loading sacks of rock into the back of a pickup. They flirt with our tour guide, who indulges them. I catch a glimpse of her life: the mine a fixture, the tourists today like tourists on any other day—pale-skinned, light-eyed, just passing through. To them, that is who we are, I think, as I have so many times already. That is the plight of the tourist, however well-intentioned she may be: she is always a stranger, an outsider, a source of dollars when you get right down to it. Another mouth to feed.

The guide passes out headlamps; we fasten them on and follow her into the mine. The stone arch of the entrance, she tells us, is original.

It's freezing cold in here, immediately much colder than outside. Icicles drip from the ceiling, and the muddy water at our feet is mixed with slush. We can see our breath. We follow each other gingerly, clumsily into the darkness, and the tunnel gets smaller and smaller so that eventually we're all stooped over, bumping our heads and tripping over the tracks. Several times we all must step aside to make way for the miners who come through, pushing carts laden with stone. They move fast, hunched over and running, and they don't look at us as they pass. Their clothes and skin are covered in a fine layer of white dust. How strange it must seem to them, we tourists who pay money to come into this dark, cold tunnel, where already, in the light of our headlamps, millions of particles float. How strange and how normal both, I imagine; this mine is the town's income source. Even through the mask I've got looped over my ears, covering my nose and mouth, I can smell the acrid dank.

Before too long, the water disappears, the icicles dwindle, and we're enveloped in a cloying dryness. Down we go, climbing ladders, ducking our heads around sharp rocks that jut out at us. Occasionally the walls sparkle yellowy-gold—the lovely vein of a worthless mineral—but mostly they're just a pale, dusty gray. Empty bottles that once held soda, or liquor, have been tossed to the side of the track and appear ancient beneath a coat of white dust. Sometimes I smell urine, or the faint smoke from a cigarette. Often we have to get on our hands and knees and crawl, and in those moments I am afraid, for how close everything seems, and how loose the rocks are beneath my bare hands. You'd never find a tour like this in the States.

The Belgian dad turns around once to ask if I'm okay. I nod, grateful for his presence, a father to his boys and also to me. His voice is muffled behind his mask.

We pass the shrine of a clay figure with an enormous erection; El Tío, our guide tells us. The miners ask Tío every Friday to keep the walls of these tunnels from crumbling, to keep the dynamite from exploding too close to their faces and hands. They ask him, sticking lit cigarettes in his mouth, for the minerals to flourish and for the veins to run sparkling and thick. Empty liquor bottles—*Alcohol Potable*—are littered all around El Tío, piles of them lining this cave's walls. El Tío has marbles for eyes. Our guide lights a cigarette and sticks it between El Tío's waxy lips, and then we leave him there smoking, his eerily lifelike face watching us go.

Our guide tells us that the mine opened in 1651. Millions died in the decades after, either inside the mine or on the way from the campo to the Cerro. *Millions?* I mutter in English to the Belgian dad, not sure whether I've heard her right, but he just raises his eyebrows and shrugs. "I think that's what she said," he tells me, and I wonder how many unmarked graves we're passing, how many ghosts must live in the walls of these impossible tunnels, watching us make our unsteady way through. The dust in the air grows thicker; we start to cough. Most of the miners we pass wear nothing over their mouths.

The tour, we discover, includes conversations with the miners. We stop to talk with one man who tells us he mines alone, without the help of a son or nephew. He looks very old, my grandfather's age, but he tells us he's just fifty-six. He has worked in the mine twenty years. He shows us a vein—a long, crooked black line that runs up the side of the tunnel. He hacks at it with a stone hammer; nothing falls away.

"It's very hard," he says, a round wad of coca in his cheek. He tells us that the silver that's left is cheap silver, and mostly the miners find tin, copper or lead. For one sack of rocks, which he chops from the vein, he earns thirty Bolivianos—sometimes he can fill five bags in one day. "Not lately, though," he admits, and wipes his face with his arm, leaving behind a smear of dust that our headlamps illuminate.

The Belgians have brought bottles of aspirin and rolls of bandages as gifts, which they hand to the old miner. "Aspirin," they explain, and when he looks at them blankly, they add, "For a headache." He inspects the packet of narrow white pills. "Should I take one every day?" he asks. "Every night?" He doesn't understand aspirin, although I can't imagine that he doesn't feel the same throb in his forehead and at the base of his neck that I do, having been in the mine for just an hour. He pockets the aspirin, thanks the Belgians, and resumes his work.

We meet another miner who sits on a rock, chewing coca and spitting the dark mash of leaves onto the ground. He's twenty, he tells us. His face shines with sweat, and he's handsome, muscular, a once-red bandana knotted at his neck. I think of myself at twenty, just graduating from an elite college, spending my afternoons in the library and my evenings with friends, drinking wine or sitting at a dining hall table eating pasta. I remember the part-time job I held, hosting at an elegant restaurant that catered to the wealthy bankers and housewives, professors and lawyers of that ritzy Boston suburb. I'd show our patrons to clean, white tables, then step into the bathrooms to wipe the marble counters and touch up my makeup.

"I have worked in the mines five years already," the young miner says. His uncle runs a cooperative. He grins when we hand him juice and coca leaves, pocketing the latter and taking a long, thirsty swig from the bottle. "Thank you," he tells us in English, and hitches aside so we can pass. "You're welcome," the Belgians say, and it occurs to me that the three of them, the two Belgian boys and this miner, are around the same age. How much younger the Europeans look though, with their translucent skin, and their quick, intelligent mouths. Their striped wool sweaters.

It's only when we start to ascend again that I realize how close the air was down there, how hot it gets deep inside. Now I can feel the cold again, and the icicles reappear; I start searching ahead of us for the literal light at the end of this tunnel. I want to get out of this mine. I can't breathe; my nose and throat are clotted with dust. My head is pounding and the stones have cut my hands; the skin that's exposed—my hands, my face—feels so tight, cracking with dryness. We see, finally, a slice of sunshine before us, and when we emerge into the daylight again, we blink our eyes and smile at each other.

"I never want to do that again," the youngest Belgian declares as his dad leans down to examine a hole he's torn in his travel pants. The same young guys are loading a different truck, still punching at each other, still joking with our guide. Their hands are the pale color of the rock inside, and their eyes jump over us.

TUPIZA, BOLIVIA

I leave at four in the morning on my fourth day at the base of El Cerro, but the hostel owner has put out breakfast anyway: bread, butter, jam, hot water in a thermos, a teabag and cup. I think of an inky Vilcabamba morning months ago, a saucer of water to discourage the ants. This Bolivian dawn holds a different kind of darkness, one so brittle with cold it might shatter. It's Sunday, and I hustle up and down the empty streets, searching for a cab, my breath coming in crisp clouds. A taxi-van turns a corner and slows; I sit up front and we drive down the sleeping streets, listening to the news playing low on the radio.

There are no buses to Tupiza, the closest border town to Argentina and my next planned stop. A few men stand smoking beside a beat-up blue van headed for Sucre, and they shrug their shoulders when I show them the ticket I purchased four days prior. "Try the other terminal," a big man in sweatpants suggests. He puts out his butt on the ground, steps on it, and says to me, "This way." He lumbers inside while the other smoking men observe. I follow the sweatpanted man.

He finds the little office whose sign matches the stamp on my ticket and peers into the tinted window, trying to catch someone's attention. Someone else shoves the window open, and then we see a woman sitting on a cot bouncing a baby on her lap. She nods at the man, looks at me, then comes around, locking the door behind her. She doesn't need, apparently, to see the ticket. "Come this way," she says. Her baby sputters on her hip. I turn to the man and tell him he needn't wait up, that I appreciate his help.

He squints his eyes a little at me, and I can tell that my Spanish is indecipherable to him. I follow the woman with her baby, and he follows me.

As we walk, the woman explains that the bus I've reserved won't be going, after all.

"But we've made other arrangements," she says. We hustle across the terminal to another teeny office, one of a hundred offices, and the woman with the baby takes my ticket and passes it across the counter. The woman there, young and pretty with her long hair twisted into a sleek and elaborate braid, writes out a new ticket, slowly copying the unfamiliar letter combinations of my name.

"Downstairs, to the right," she says, and now the woman with the baby is rushing again, this time down the stairs. "Come on," she is saying, "let's go," and I am following her, and the man in sweatpants is still following us both, puffing a little. When we reach the bus, I shake his hand; he blushes, shrugs. I reach for a bit of money and hold the bill out to him, but he refuses to take it, shaking his head, the blush disappeared, and so I put the money away. I offer him a package of cookies, the ten-cent kind sold at every *tiendita* from Guatemala to Bolivia, the labels varied but the sweet, dry crunch identical. He slips the cookies into his pocket and juts his chin toward the bus. The woman with the baby has already gone. I board and make my slow way down the aisle, and when I look out the window to catch a last glance of the man in sweatpants, I see that he, too, has disappeared.

Families sit behind me—children I can hear but not see and a couple of mothers. They pile their blankets over the back of my seat and chatter to each other, ignoring the screams of their babies. I guess that there are fifty people in total sitting down, plus the half-dozen or so who stand in the aisle. A few more people board, men with big blankets and rosy faces, and then we chug out of the Potosí station, rooftops and white lines on the pavement sparkling in the early sun.

I offer a corn cake to the woman beside me who is bundled as I am in sweater and blanket, scarf, and gloves. She looks to be my age. She smiles and accepts the cake but does not eat it yet. She doesn't speak. Young men ask my name and whether I have a boyfriend; older men and women show concern and point out landmarks. Children tell me things I can't understand, their accents still unformed, their questions murmurs. This woman, though, smiles at me and then looks away, and I am grateful for the quiet, the sunrise, and the crumbly, honeyed bites of cake.

As soon as we leave the roundabouts surrounding the terminal, though, it is awful to be at the back of this bus. The road out of town is dotted with speed bumps, which throw us up into the air; I take care to keep my tongue in my mouth. Each time the bus lurches, the babies scream, the mothers' shushing, and the passengers groan and readjust their bodies. I time my bites between speed bumps. For a while, buildings with tin roofs surround us, the creaking metal weighted down with old tires or cement blocks or pieces of clay. Then the cityscape fades into desert, high-up plains, sand the color of pale gold, stands of cacti that stretch toward the lavender sky.

The road turns from pavement to dirt. We veer off the cement, just before the place where the road has been blocked with a barricade of stones, and then we rumble along the makeshift path. There must be construction, I figure, because for miles we drive beside the paved version of this route. How smooth the pavement looks beside us, how even and comfortable, as we jolt alongside it, crashing up and down in our seats. The baby behind me wails. The boy in front of me opens his window, and dust flies in. I close my eyes, but there's no way I will sleep. I grit my teeth and resist thinking bad things about Bolivia. *Send yourself somewhere*, my mind says, and so I go to Vilcabamba: the muggy hike and then the way the river felt, so cool and paved with stones.

I find a hostel in Tupiza with four stories and a roofdeck. There are two beds in my room and nothing else. In the street, I buy a cup of food from a woman who ladles puffy, soaked corn into a Styrofoam bowl, then adds fried potatoes and a few lean strips of beef. She tops it off with red sauce—"Is it hot?" I ask. "Not so much," she replies, but even so, I need water afterwards.

I find two tall British guys who stay up with me until two in the morning, drinking wine and watching *Butch Cassidy and the Sundance Kid*. They know every line. I find jagged red hills that ring the town and stretch out to the north and south, glowing pink in the morning and violet as the sun sets, and I find the Devil's Door, two narrow, enormous slabs of brick-colored rock that stand two hundred feet high, flanked on either side by red dust and the tallest cacti I've seen since northern Peru. I find dogs who live together at the end of an empty road in a ramshackle house, dogs who bark and bark as I walk past, frightening me so that I pick up stones in case I might need to hurl them, but in the end those dogs are harmless; they just bark and then skulk back toward the half-finished group of adobe houses, the yards scattered with old tires and dried-up trees.

I find a town in the midst of its country's independence day celebration; the parades last from Friday to early Sunday morning, and the music pumps. The ladies in the streets sell chocolate-covered donuts, soaked corn, glasses of *chicha* and paper cups of *papas fritas*. An old man spins a manual merry-go-round while he sips his glass of beer, and the little children perched on the tiny horses scream and demand more. That night I say goodbye to the English guys, who are taking the night train to Uyuni, and then I crawl into bed and sleep to the sound of the celebratory music. When my alarm sounds at 3 a.m., just in time for the bus that will bring me to Bolivia's border, I hear the music again, pumping from the speakers set up in front of the train station. I step out onto the street, hoping that the drunk man screaming shirtless on the corner doesn't notice as I walk by with my pack beneath a bowl of stars. This town is just as busy as it was in the day. The streets are spilling over with people walking home, drunk off the celebrations of their nation's independence.

THE ROAD

"I'm freezing," the girl in front of me whispers to the man beside her. They are English, I can tell from their accents, and I envy them for the way they curl up together in their seats, sharing a blanket. We're waiting for the 4 a.m. bus to leave Tupiza for Villazón, the border town where I'll get my passport stamped and then enter Argentina. I pull my jacket closer around me and wish for my hat, my second jacket, a cup of hot tea. Finally, half an hour late, we pull out of the station, southbound. The driver flicks the interior lights and blasts the radio. I close my eyes and try to sleep, hating him.

In Villazón, the buildings, set evenly along the freezing, empty streets, loom over me, the dark windows like blank eyes. The sidewalks are broken by spindly, leafless trees, and the gray sky hangs close and cold. An Australian girl emerges, shivering, from the Tupiza bus, and we walk together towards the border without speaking, sucking on caramels I bought with my last three bolivianos. The border is marked by a bridge; there's a sign that reads, in antique white lettering, "Bolivia." When I turn and look back, I see that the other side reads "Argentina." Just like that, we've crossed in. I take one last look at Bolivia, and am surprised to find tears in my eyes.

I whisper goodbye to the country with stretching deserts and bare hills, women with wheels of cheese in the streets. The long braids woven with yarn, the jolting roads, the clusters of mud huts and the spindly smoke of fires. The alpaca, the freezing showers, the broken sidewalks. The way I felt, traveling through, like some kind of vagabond in the

296 – KATE McCAHILL

same three-day clothes, lurching along in a bus, the only *gringa*. Already, people who look like me, with big packs and light skin, stand around outside the customs office. I am leaving someplace special, someplace caught in another time, someplace that clings to an ancient, pre-colonial past. I'm leaving that place for one that will remind me of home, one where glass-paned stores will replace street vendors, where paved roads will replace broken ones, where fashionable clothing will make me want what I don't have.

It's a spectacular ride from the border south. I lean back in my seat beside the Australian girl and admire the clean bus, the soft seats, the view from the second level of this double decker. The road feels so smooth beneath us, and the scenery—golden fields, distant mountains, the rainbow colors of the rocks and the blue sky of morning—keeps us silent, looking out. I could get used to this, I think, and then the bus shudders to a stop. I imagine a rest stop, even though we've only driven two hours, and then the driver comes down the aisle. He says something I can't understand, something in the Argentinean accent that crushes the words and merges them together, creating a smooth and unrecognizable sound. He rounds up a couple of guys, and the next thing I know I feel them pushing the bus so that we roll forward, the engine off. Eventually, the bus rumbles to life, the guys come back on, flushed and laughing, and off we go.

"So much for the nice buses," the Australian girl says, grinning. Her name is Else, pronounced *else-eh*. "It's a Dutch name," she says. Together, we remember aloud the rickety buses that took us through Bolivia, the ones with the rattling windows and open grates, and marvel that we ever made it through.

I spend my first Argentinean night in Jujuy, a warm valley city Theroux admired. Else continues on to the larger city of Salta, but I feel compelled to stop. Theroux wrote that Jujuy was "beautiful and damp; it was just high enough to be pleasant without giving one a case of the bends. The rain on the blossoms perfumed the dark air, and a fresh breeze blew from the river."

Anyway, I want to tiptoe into Argentina, savoring these cities that still feed their indigenous roots. Buenos Aires, I know, will resemble every metropolis I've ever known. I will take my time getting there. I stroll up and down Jujuy's sun-baked streets, admiring the tall, elegant doorways, the soft colors of the paint on the aging colonial walls, the cafés that stay open all day and most of the night, serving real coffee with milk. I buy wine and share it with the old woman who runs my hostel; the kitchen smells like chocolate, like the earth, like apples and pine. In the night, the air is soft, warm enough for just a sheet. The shower in the morning is hot, steaming up the white-tiled bathroom as the sunshine floods in. *Riquísimo*, I think as the water pours over me. The body, I realize, instantly remembers things it's gone so long without: hot water on skin, or a slice of hot quiche, or how fresh a glass of white wine can taste.

In Salta, I sleep in a hostel at the end of a whitewashed block south of the center. It is painted inside and out with every imaginable color. A gray cat lives here, a cat who sleeps on my bed at night and races up and down the stairs, and over the connecting roofs during the day. The owners, a twenty-something couple with baggy pants and loose, curly hair, pour me a glass of wine on the first night and then sing together while a guest from Cordoba strums his guitar. The girl is called Madina. The hours ripple past, and I realize that it's been many nights, weeks even, since I've sipped wine this way, chatting with people my age, the smoke of Madina's cigarette curling into the sky. Very late, after midnight, we climb into a taxi and ride to the center of town. Madina sits up front and chews coca leaves with the driver while Salta's night lights fly past. We drink huge plastic cups of beer for very cheap at the crowded bar, and Madina gets drunk and dances with the dark-skinned, dark-eyed guys in the corner. The cup of beer grows warm in my hand as I watch Madina swirl through the room. By the time we get home again, the sun is just beginning to light up the sky, and I collapse into my bed, exhausted, exhilarated, unable for a long while to sleep.

The trip to Rosario, four hours north of Buenos Aires, takes most of a day and one night, and I arrive in the morning. The city blocks contain countless cafés, fruit and vegetable stands, and a few bookshops and mechanic shops. There are grocery stores with Chinese characters on the signs. My driver chats with me as we speed down the streets. He asks me where I'm from, and how I like Argentina. He curses at slow drivers in front of him and toots his horn at a man leaning against his bicycle on one corner. Behind the bicycle, the wall of the restaurant is painted lime green. Rosario flashes past; we make our way across town to the hostel recommended in my guidebook.

We pull up outside, eventually, and the driver points to an elegant, if somewhat unkempt, three-story stone building. The balconies have swirling black bars, and a sycamore bends its branches in the wind against the long windows. I reach in my wallet for a hundred-peso note, the only bill I have besides the twenties I keep folded in a little stack behind my driver's license. The driver fingers the bill for a second, then hands it back.

"Falso," he says.

I hold the bill up to the light and rub the paper between my fingers. The bill is slightly smaller, squarer, I realize, than the other notes I've seen. The paper feels thin, and there's no watermark. I'm embarrassed to have been duped so thoroughly, but in truth, though I'd seen every vendor from Xela to Potosí hold bills to the light and examine the paper with their fingertips, I'd never done it myself. I'd assumed, I guess, that since everyone checked, the money that came into my hands was fine, but now, with this fake note in my hands, I am drained. It's not the sum—a hundred pesos is around twenty dollars. I go back in my mind to the bus station, where I'd handed over a five-hundred peso note for my fare and gotten change. Then, I realize. It was on that Salta day, when the sun had shone so soft, when the park, for wandering, had been so fine.

I offer the driver one of the twenties I withdrew from an ATM in Boston nine months ago, but he refuses.

"Be careful," he tells me, then waits until I've reached the tall, heavy door of the hostel, have pressed the buzzer and pushed open the door, before pulling away.

This, I think, unpacking my bag in the empty dorm of the hostel, where the owner offered me coffee and bread before handing me clean sheets and a towel. *This is the last of it.* These arrivals in new cities, this navigating, these whirling cab rides, this money passing hands, these conversations that get me from one point to the next—these are the things that will fall from my life. I will reach Buenos Aires, where I plan to teach for three months, and then I will go home.

And so the tumble of accents, the stretches of streetside markets, the noonday sun—each glimpse, now, of this new city feels precious. They are honeyed drops to be savored. Each arrival, however different, is also the same. First there's the way a city comes through the window of a bus: suburbs, close clusters of buildings, factories, sometimes, and finally the station. Always there's the feeling of not wanting to disembark after the bus has pulled to a stop. However long the ride takes, there's always, afterwards, the lingering comfort of a familiar seat, especially when compared to the unknown outside.

In Rosario, my rented room has French doors that open to a tiny balcony. A fountain across the street spatters water onto the curved patterns of the cobblestones in the plaza. I walk along the river at sunset and eat pasta very late at an outdoor café. The air tastes sweet, and I don't want to go to bed. I know this place just a little; I love it anyway.

In an e-mail, my mom wishes me luck in Buenos Aires. I picture her and my dad poring over the map, tracking my route based on my own sporadic e-mails home, squinting to find Tupiza, Uyuni, Jujuy, and Salta.

I write back and tell her that tonight I am sleeping in a hostel on the third floor of a Rosario colonial building. The walls in my bedroom are painted lavender. The pale-eyed Brazilian in the room next door invited me to the movies, but I told him no.

That night, dreams come to me like paintings: the crest of a rounded hill in the Peruvian sierra, or an endless stretch of Bolivian salt. Thick jungle in Ecuador, cobblestones in Nicaragua, the smell of coffee on Antigua's streets. A border crossing, dense with night, and an endless red dirt road.

I dream of birds flying in through an open window and pecking at crumbs on the floor. I dream about schools on hills, markets where water flows in the street, bakeries crammed with people. There are men who wear kids' backpacks and kids who can count money better than I can. There's Guatemala on Christmas, Ecuador on Easter, Nicaragua on Valentine's Day, when the sun rose early and hot. I dream about my teachers and my students, and about men who sell orange juice on the corner. Carlos' dark eyes, Gaby's smile, and the way Raphael pulled me to him. I dream of a Buenos Aires I haven't yet met: concerts in the street, a brown and silty river, a crowded Sunday market. Bakeries, bars, and tango on the sidewalk; incense and cigarettes on the wind.

FALL

No good train ever goes far enough.

—Paul Theroux, *The Old Patagonian Express*

BUENOS AIRES, ARGENTINA

Nothing prepares me for Buenos Aires. The suburbs are a sprawl of bargain hardware stores, parking lots, rain-streaked condos, and parks: nothing like what is to come. The skyline is every other city skyline I've ever seen, just a smattering of tall buildings in the distance, sulking beneath the cloudy sky. As for the road, it's the one that has taken me so many places already: into Guatemala City, Quito, and Lima. Into Sucre and La Paz. It's the same road, I know, that brought me for the first time to New York City, through Chappaqua, White Plains, Mount Vernon, and Queens. It can drop hints, this pavement, but it's never going to talk.

The people on the bus start to shift in their seats and whisper. They crane their necks and watch how the lives outside these windows grow tighter and tighter, more and more closely packed. The quickening of breath is how I best can tell. Our hearts beat faster. *This is it*, we're thinking as we wait.

The bus grinds to a stop in a dark, dripping station, and everyone climbs off. No one looks my way. *This is where we are!* I want to tell the woman beside me, but she is packing up her bag and running her fingers through her hair with someone else, someone waiting, on her mind. I collect my bag and comb my hands through my own hair. God, how tired I suddenly feel, with no one outside this bus waiting for me. I had expected to feel so much—this is glittering Buenos Aires, after all—but now, with this press of gray sky, and this sharply nipping wind, all I can feel is dull little stab. Buenos Aires marks the end, and I am not ready.

The man in the taxi doesn't speak to me. He has a hard time understanding me, he says, and that is that. How cold it is, I tell him. He smiles a false smile and doesn't answer. We drive on wide, clean roads past the slums, then past the parks, then past the skyscrapers of Palermo. White statues, cut grass, and even white lines on the road. As the buildings loom silent behind the sealed windows of this car, I see a hundred places I have been already, for these are the cold, remarkable parks that every wealthy part of every city boasts. I wish, suddenly, for a scrap of paper to blow across the windshield, or for a man to stop the car so he can wash it, or for an old woman with a baby in one arm to stumble forward with candies and magazines for sale. All these cars, these planes above, but there's not a single sign of life. I search for a glimpse of the daytime moon, but this city gives me nothing, and so I ride through it, unspeaking, trying to blink away stupid, lonesome tears.

That night, I walk. If I can walk, there's always somewhere I can go, I reason, and nothing chokes the heart like an empty rented room. I walk through Palermo, through the old part, through the new part, and through Soho. The light is turning as the rain fades, and in the distance you can see a pink line in the sky; this is the sun, slicing through the clouds like the knife I used on my breakfast bread. The puddles in the street are glowing now, and the leaves in the trees, because it is spring, are just starting to open over my head. The man who sells me a box of juice in the tiny kiosk on the corner gives it to me for less than it's worth when I scrounge for change but can't find it.

"How do you like my city?" he asks, and shakes my hand.

I stumble across an artisan market, where men in holey jeans and beards stand around with half-smoked cigarettes limp between their fingers, watching me watch them. Ladies knit, sitting beside the hats they've already crafted, the sweaters and vests and shawls. Someone's weaving together a bracelet, and a little girl tugs her mother's hand. Dogs nose through the crowd. Incense floats over everything, and beyond that I can smell the faint and pungent tug of marijuana. Someone's playing a guitar; a girl is singing. An old man with a kind face and light eyes looks up from where he sits behind his stall, a hundred different shells laid out before him on velvet. He doesn't say a word as I pore over them, running my fingers over their polished, spotted backs. "I feel like I'm touching the sea," I tell him, and then regret it; the cab driver thought my Spanish unintelligible. But the man with the light eyes smiles. "Smell them," he says, and I inhale the salt. A woman with long, dark hair walks ahead of me, her heels clicking. A man walks ten dogs on ten leashes. The bricks crumble off a building beside me, and there are glasses of wine on white metal tables outside.

I feel suddenly grateful for all that there is: knit scarves, the scent of rain, the waft of bread, a waiter in a white apron through a window, a car painted pink and green. There are other markets, too, other lives, other streets in this city that change shape and ramble on. There are so many years and so many cracking coats of paint. The veins of this city run deep, and so how could I have thought that those empty parks and sealed-up cars were everything? Sometimes, you must wait for the signs to find you.

The darkness arrives all of a sudden and settles around me, warm with a hint of spring, and though I know I must be getting back to my rented room, I just keep walking, for now I'm craving more than anything to be lost.

On the day I first visit the apartment on Avenida Montes de Oca, jacarandas line the sidewalks. Three months from now, they'll bloom. I check that the number scrawled beneath my map matches the number on the door, then take a shaky breath and touch the buzzer. *You don't*

306 – KATE McCAHILL

have to take it if you don't like it, I remind myself. There are plenty of apartments posted online, plenty of places for a traveler to crash for a couple of months. I don't have to take the first place I see.

But it is because I *already* like it that I'm nervous, I realize: the Bolivian fruit stand right next door and the gelato shop with its employees' paper hats appeal to me. I feel comfortable here amid the casual, working-class bustle. I even like the jacarandas, gray and wintered down. I inhale, exhale, press my finger to the button again.

After a few minutes, a woman appears in the hall. She looks old, but maybe it's just her posture and the way she leans against the rail and shuffles toward me. When she opens the door, I see that something's not right with one of her eyes, so that while one eye focuses on me, the other looks high to the left. *No,* I think to myself immediately, instinctively, though later I'm ashamed to admit it. I had imagined a group of young people sharing a house—a funky musician, maybe, or a young woman my age who might go to cafés with me. But instead this old woman with short white curls and strange eyes is holding the door and inviting me in, saying, "You must be Katy." I had imagined a house like the Quito house—a Raphael down the hall, a Carlos across the hall, a permeating, companionable friendliness. But this is not Quito; this is Buenos Aires, and I must not judge, and I must not hope for anything, because on the road, I never know how things will end up.

The woman smiles at me, a pleasant smile. "I'm Alex," she says, and I follow her into the elevator.

In her second-floor apartment, a small balcony overlooks bank machines and green grocers and tiny delis jammed, I imagine, with cheese and wine. The apartment has a lived-in, crowded feel, but in a comfortable way. There is a warm, smoky stillness to the air. Books and magazines are stacked on the small coffee table and computer desk and shelves. The kitchen is small but contains everything I'll need, if I'd like to move in, Alex assures me, pointing out the set of mixing bowls, the drawer of utensils, the amount of space for me in the fridge, if I should take the place.

A large black cat appears, blinking in the doorway. He leans against the jamb, curls himself around the corner, and emits a sound, something between a cry and a question. "Pirucho," Alex says, and bends down to scoop him up. His legs stand out in all directions when she holds him, but he does not resist. She kisses his head hard. "I hope you like cats," she says, and when I nod, she passes him to me.

In the end, it was mostly Pirucho who convinced me to hand over my deposit. It was everything else, too, though; the street wasn't touristy, but it was historic and vibrant. The apartment was close to the train. My room has one window, a desk and chair, two closets, and two single beds, one more more sunken than the other. A clean, flat light falls onto the wood floor. Alex's sister Vicky has a small bony nose and smart dark eyes, and she returns from work as Alex is showing me the footed tub. Vicky shakes my hand emphatically, hangs up her purse—a woven satchel, something like what I'd seen in Guatemala—and sits down to light a cigarette.

There is something I instantly like about them. They invite me to sit down with them. They heat empanadas and ask me whether I can figure out the MP3 player they bought just yesterday.

"Hijo de puta," Vicky declares, holding the tiny device in her hands, peering at it. *Son of a whore.* Alex hauls Pirucho onto her lap.

"How old is Pirucho?" Alex asks Vicky.

"Stop screaming!" Vicky says, loudly. "He's seven."

Alex snorts. "He's five," she says to me, and Vicky, from where she sits with the tiny MP3 player in her hands, mutters, "Six." Alex nods. "He's six," she tells me, and then kisses Pirucho on his furry black head.

At my new place, I open the door with the key they have given me. I say hello to Alex, who sits peering at the computer, and Vicky, who is opening a bottle of wine in the kitchen. I go into my new rented room with its yellowy-white walls. There's a closet without a door, a set of shelves, mismatched blankets on the beds, and a folded towel.

The window of my rented room watches the overgrown courtyard below, and has tiny cracks that let the wind in. So far from Palermo, I feel. Here the buildings are closer, the people poorer, the grocery stores cheaper and more crowded. Here, Vicky and Alex talk over each other, finishing each other's sentences as we speak. "Puta madre," they shout at the television, as the male politicians of the world parade past. I set my pack down, and I sit down at the table to write.

On weekends, Alex and Vicky take me on walks through Barracas and San Telmo. They have known these Buenos Aires neighborhoods all their lives; they point out old buildings they've inhabited and the places where grand old cafés once stood. They've each been exiled twice, the first time to Europe for political reasons, the second to Mexico for economic ones. Each time, they returned because things were improving in Argentina, and they wanted to be a part of the change. They've rented their spare room to dozens of foreigners over the years, English teachers and language students like me.

Today, we visit the San Telmo market, where produce is piled high and stray dogs sniff and mill around. Beggars cower in corners and women sell clothes on racks and corn on the cob. Here are boxes and boxes of faded postcards from the twenties and warped records to sort through. Here are brooches with fake diamonds and rubies, and ribbon, once white, now faded to golden. Boxes of old shoes that cost more than a new pair in the city center because of how carefully they were crafted years ago, how soft the leather has become. From old record players music spins over us. Old women sell antique plates printed with gold.

Here, time could roll back a hundred years and you wouldn't know. No cell phones cry out. The salesmen wear berets, smoke pipes, and glance over their papers at me as I run my fingers along beaten silver bracelets and pewter spoons. Everything is covered in a thin layer of dust.

Outside, the market runs on up and down the street, encompassing a dozen blocks. Here are the artisans, their bracelets of hemp and waxed thread set out on plywood tables or velvet blankets. Their necklaces, they explain, are accented with stones and shells collected from Nicaragua and Panama, Colombia and Peru, all the far-flung places these artisans have seen. They drag on their cigarettes, their eyes soft.

And then we turn the corner and here is a crowd, huddled tightly around something we cannot see. An old tango recording plays, the even strum of a guitar and over that, a fiddle's mournful melody. The crowd gives way a little, loosening its grasp, and now I can see that it's street tango. An old man, one of the two dancers, is smiling like he's never been so happy as right now. His eyes are closed as he guides a woman around in circles. They have so little space to dance. The woman wears a tasseled red silk dress and heavy makeup.

She bends her knee just so, lifts her leg and then, precisely to the low thrum of a cello, sets it down.

The old man is somewhere far away, perhaps in heaven. But the woman—bright orange hair, white roots visible at the crown—is right here with us, her eyes open wide, her movements crisp and clear.

Now others are taking their places on the sidewalk dance floor. High heels click, and men move rapturously. Buenos Aires-style tango is so intimate: thigh against thigh and hand in hand, mouths whispering words into ears. I can't look away. The women scrape their toes along the ground and stroke their legs up their partners' calves. A woman in jeans moves her hips just a little, making way for her partner's step forward. A man in dark glasses tips his head back. The breathless crowd sways. Alex puts her hand on my arm, but when I look, her eyes are closed.

Oh, the way the dancers listen, hearing each note with their bodies, their movements unbound and deliberate both. The violins are caresses, and the cello's aching chords are a soak for the bones. What dark magic

Buenos Aires holds: what markets, what sidewalks, and what stories, beautiful and bloody both. What inhabitants: a sidestepping old man and his red-haired companion; a group of artisans playing their guitars; two sisters, twice-exiled, who never fell out of love with Buenos Aires.

Since I'm willing to volunteer, I easily find a community center to take me on as an English teacher. I e-mail the organization through their website and get a response within hours. The reply comes in English; a woman named Vera invites me to meet her at an address at the edge of the city. When I tell her I'm coming from Barracas, she writes, "Give yourself an hour and a half to get here." But I'm excited at the prospect of working with adults, and the e-mail exchange is friendly. When I tell Vicky about the center, she grins, but Alex leans back from the computer screen and frowns.

"Not a good part of town," she says.

"Yes a good part," Vicky says. "Now don't scare her."

"Not a great part," Alex says, shrugging, "but you're going, so be careful."

"Just be careful," Vicky says, and Alex nods while Pirucho swirls his great body in a loop around her ankles.

In the end, the bus ride takes an hour and fifteen minutes. I'm to meet Vera at a café on the Avenida Eva Perón. The bus rumbles twenty blocks down that street named after this country's sweetheart before I get off at the gas station across from the Goodyear sign, as instructed. I watch the comings and goings of the neighborhood through the fortified glass of the café's window, thinking that it's not so bad. Working-class, perhaps, with whitewashed cement blocks as walls and wide sidewalks spattered with old gum and bits of paper. But there are trees here and above us a blue sky winks. The café is tiny and immaculate, and I am served coffee with a cookie immediately. Vera arrives a few minutes later; I know right away that it's her, somehow, for she is tall and impressive, with round features and dark wavy hair. She wears a different dangly earring in each ear—one a feather, one a shell—and rings set with stones on each finger. She recognizes me, too, and comes right over, grinning. She has an *estadounidense* accent but kisses me on the cheek the Argentinean way, then tells me that even after a year, she still doesn't walk around this block by herself. All of it, however benevolent it may seem, borders Ciudad Oculta, Buenos Aires' hidden city.

We are in the worst part of town, Vera confirms. Not that anything is going to happen—nothing has so far, she says—but the farther in you get, the more addicts you'll find, the more rabid dogs, the more guns. Fewer and fewer cops. "Those cops," she says, lowering her voice, "will strut up and down Eva Perón with their big steak bellies and the orange jackets they wear over their uniforms. They'll smile at you, check you out as you walk away, and they'll be kind enough to give you directions if you ask. But they're not going to walk down these streets that run off Avenida Eva Perón."

Before leaving the apartment, I'd Googled "Ciudad Oculta" and found a *New York Times* feature on the barrio. The photo-essay followed an unnamed, 45-year-old *paco* user through her neighborhood. The photographer captured the woman as she leaned against dirty walls—she's underdressed, underfed, and holds a crack pipe in her hand. *Paco* is the name for cocaine paste; the drug trickles down from Bolivia, according to the article, and hundreds of thousands of people use it in this city alone. I'd looked at those photos, then shut my computer quickly, guilty almost. I could hear Alex and Vicky bickering in the kitchen. One of them shouted at Pirucho to get off the sink. "I'm going!" I'd called to them, keeping my voice light.

Now, Vera and I turn the corner and ring the bell at a plain white gate. We look farther down the street, which is empty except for a few beat-up cars parked on the curb and a sleeping white dog on the sidewalk. Still, because of what Vera said, because of the article, the warnings, the early-afternoon emptiness of the place, I feel an undercurrent of fear. The sky shifts; a shade of gray crosses over our heads, and wind in the leaves on the trees is eerily soft.

But a kind-faced, red-haired woman opens the door. Her skin looks as if she's spent all her life, every single day, beneath the sun, and she wears a pink ruffled apron, white sneakers, and jeans. She kisses me on the cheek; she smells of bread. "Elisa," Vera says. There seems nothing impure in Elisa's bouncy gait or in the wrinkles by her eyes. She radiates warmth and baking, and my fear dissipates. She locks the gate, and we follow her down the hall and into a small kitchen crammed with boxes and chairs, a big table, and a couple of toaster ovens. There's a utility sink, deep and square, and resting on the oven is a baking sheet of buns, browned and salted. Vera sees me glance over. "Have one," she says, and Elisa goes and gets the pan and brings it to Vera and me. We fill our mouths with the bread, sweet and salty both. For months and years to come, I'll smell bread like this and remember sitting in a warm kitchen at the edge of town, where the roads turn from pavement to dirt.

The community center has a few classrooms, a small courtyard, and two bathrooms with doors that don't lock. "Too many kids have locked themselves in," Vera apologizes. The center offers English classes to students of all ages; each is taught by a volunteer. A few guys come in just then, tall, lanky young guys in collared shirts and khakis. They introduce themselves: Mitch and Nate, on their semester abroad from Middlebury College. They go to the toaster ovens and peer in. "Fried chicken," Mitch says, and Nate grabs plates. The guys eat as if they haven't in days, ravenous at the kitchen table, reaching for roll after salted roll.

"You can have some chicken, too," Vera says to me. "There's lunch all day."

My first English class turns out to be not for adults but for a group of ten eight-year-olds who speak decent English, especially the girls. Most volunteers only stay for three or four months, Vera had said, but I can see that even in their short stints, they've trained their students well. The students take out their notebooks without being asked, and they demand games during the last fifteen minutes of class. They are chatting, eager to answer my questions. We play hangman, and I tell them they can take turns picking the words, as long as they're English ones. We spell *blue, country*, and *Coca-Cola*. They kiss me on the cheek as they're leaving.

A few days later, the same class consists of two fourteen-year-old girls. I wonder where all the eight-year-olds went, but Vera explains that I'm being switched to the adult class and these two women are my first students. They tell me in Spanish that their English is pretty good, but when I ask them their names, they look at me blankly. We review the alphabet, and we review question words, but eventually the class eases into Spanish. They have such thick, lispy accents that I have to ask them to repeat every other sentence, but they are patient with me. I can't believe how young they are. When I was in high school, I didn't know anyone who looked like these fourteen-year-olds do, with hair so long they have to move it to sit down. They've got these curves, these voices, and their fingernails are painted black. They, too, kiss me goodbye when the class ends. "Ciao ciao," they call out, their heels clicking down the cement floor.

I continue to go to the community center four days a week. Eventually, I begin to get the same students each time, although there are days when no one comes, and on those afternoons I go and work with the seven- and eight-year-olds, who have established an easy, teasing rapport with their teacher, Middlebury Nate. Sometimes ten people come to my class, but my best student is Juan, who speaks very slow English, and slow enough Spanish that I understand most everything. He's forty years old, with young-looking hands and a bald spot just starting to show through his dark hair. He wears the same blue pants to every class, the same navy sweater with the same collar beneath it, but everything is always pressed and clean. On the day we learn family words, I ask him how many sisters he has, how many uncles, how many pets. He has too many cousins to count. "I have many cousins," he tells me. "How many?" I ask. "I have many cousins," he tells me again.

Juan tells me he's a chef. Right now, he's studying French cooking, but he wants to learn English so he can take his kids away from the Cuidad Oculta and go to the States. He'll have to leave his dog behind, he tells me, smiling. He's got this little backpack for his things, the same kind of backpack I've seen on grown men all over this continent. It's a kids' pack, and the seams are coming undone; it's been stitched together a dozen times already. *God*, I think, watching him copy the family words from the board into his notebook, *these backpacks*. They kill me every time. All Juan's seems to hold, sitting there, small and flat on the floor, is the notebook he took out for class today. He kisses me on the cheek each day after class. "Ciao ciao," he tells me, then steps out onto the street and walks north, up toward the apartment he shares with his wife and two daughters and three sons and two pets. He walks up toward the barrio we were warned about, the neighborhood where even the cops won't go.

On the bus rides home, I watch closely as musicians and vendors cram on with the men coming home from work, the students returning in uniform from school. Boys with high, sweet voices sing, unashamed and without accompaniment. European expats board with guitars and clarinets, flutes, once an accordion. There are the old men who play tango from ancient stereo systems, singing along, and there was the little girl, that warm afternoon, who sang in such a clear and unfiltered voice that she brought tears. These are the people who bring the music onboard, hauling their instruments and coin-cups on and then heaving them off again, filling their pockets with two-peso notes and fifty-cent pieces, other people's bus fares, other people's useless change. They are like the tango dancers, in love with their craft, and when they perform they close their eyes and fall into the music they're making. I watch all of this, I do not think of my home, I do not remember her. My mind is free to wrap around the present here.

Besides the music, there will always be something to sell. Men with dark skin and clean clothes and swift hands, swift feet, move through the bus in the afternoons, when there's enough room to sit down. They drop pens into our laps, or packets of bobby pins, or plastic cases that hold needles and scissors and thread. They lay pairs of socks down, or paperback guides for all the city's buses, or leather passport holders. Once, bicycle pumps. They are experts at maneuvering these aisles, tracking what they've set down, who moves to get off. Some shout aloud, mechanically, *You'll never find a price like this*, and they'll hold the pen-highlighter combo high. But most don't speak, just take the things from boxes and place them down. We pick the objects up and turn them over in our hands, but mostly we give them back when he comes around again. Of course, there are the guys who offer us something we need, something we've been meaning to buy, and on those rides we pull out our wallets and pay.

Then there are the ones without the music or the black-market pens. They haven't got instruments, they've barely got voices: they've got wilted hair and sallow skin from all those hours beneath the rain and in the wind. There is the homeless person with the long, matted dreads, whose gender I can hardly decipher. I think it's a woman for the size of her bare feet paddling up and down the aisles, and the faint shape of her loose, dirty clothes, which fall from thin shoulders and slap against the jutting bone of a hip. This one moves past the seated lines of us, dropping a scrap of old newspaper into each of our laps. She mumbles, head down, placing the papers down with care, so as not to miss anyone. When she comes back for the scraps, we hand them over as if they are pens, or socks, or leather passport holders. "Poor little one," the woman beside me says, and then the bus pulls to a stop and she gathers up her purse, pushes past the newspaper-woman, and hurries down the stairs.

Today, a boy with a shaved head plays music through his cell phone; it's a crooning duet set to pop, and a few people bob their heads. The windows are open, and the air blows in noisily, nearly drowning out the cell phone tune. Students and grandmothers and tiny children on laps look around at the other faces, and commuters turn their eyes to books in their hands, all of them swaying in time to the jostle of the bus.

One day, a young blind man comes on, eyes squeezed shut, baby strapped to his chest. He is young, younger than I am, and he sits on the portable speaker he's also carried and begins to sing into the microphone. He cannot see, but he has no problem finding a seat on the crowded bus. He does not lose his balance. The baby stays quiet. His girlfriend, who followed him in and stands while he sits, is slight and beautiful and can see. She takes the mike when he's finished his song.

"He's blind," she says, then tells of his love for music, of their new baby, of the importance of public art, and of their desperate need for lunch.

"Thank you, ladies and gentlemen," she says, and then the blind boy takes the mike back and goes on singing. His girlfriend's black hair is long, glossy, and fine, her eyes so wide as she goes around with the plastic cup in hand. Meanwhile, he bounces the baby on his knee and croons. And then the bus slows and it's a rush to get off; there's no time to search my pockets for a coin.

You could ride these buses all your life and never see it all, for its passengers might be those who checked this morning beneath their mattresses and found nothing. Maybe they know the lines better than the drivers themselves; that's how much time they've spent riding. They'll sling their guitars over their shoulders, or else they'll bring their voices or just their open hands. Once, a very little boy gets on with sacks of apples for sale. He looks barely old enough to speak. But these buses are a life force, and here, there is no shame in doing what you must. Those children should not be here, but we can buy what they have to sell. Ten pesos gets you lunch, gets you wine; twenty gets you a bed for a night.

The same blind woman sits outside the Terminal Constitucíon all the time. As commuters and tourists rush by, she calls out the same refrain with a plastic plate in her hand. "I am blind," she tells us, eyes shut tight like the man with the baby and the microphone. "Please, a coin, for I am blind." She listens for the sound of metal clinking on the plate; she listens to the footsteps that hurry past. She sits without seeing, her voice mechanical by now for all of the times she's sang this tune. "Please, a coin, for I am blind. Thank you, a coin." Her voice never wavers, her eyes never open. Her hand holds the plastic plate out, and you never see her pocket the coins. "Please," she says, as the crowds crush past. *I am blind.*

Alex and Vicky take a weekend in Termales, Uruguay, and leave me in charge of Pirucho. "Just make sure he gets fed," Alex said before she left, then she laughed; we all knew that of course the cat would be fed—overfed, even, and spoiled rotten. Alex and Vicky call Pirucho my boy-friend for how fast he comes to me when I enter the apartment. He presses himself up against my legs and purrs. "He is in love with her!" Vicky shrieks when he cries at my bedroom door and then sleeps on my bed all afternoon. "Unfaithful Pirucho!" Alex says from where she sits, squinting, at the computer.

Pirucho works steadily on his food that first day Alex and Vicky are gone, and by evening the little red dish is empty. "Ok, dinner!" I tell him as he cries and swirls, begging. But the door to the pantry won't open; it's jammed and no amount of pushing and pulling and swearing can get it open. "Sorry, Pirucho," I tell him, and he presses himself up against my shins and moans. He doesn't have to cry much longer before I grab my purse and go out for more food.

The next day, when Alex and Vicky come home and see the bag of food I purchased, they explain that it isn't suitable. Vicky pours it out of Pirucho's bowl and into the bag, then rolls the top of the bag and hands it to me. "This kind gives cats kidney problems," Alex explains, jamming her hip against the pantry's door and pounding hard with her palm. The door opens with a wheeze, and she pulls out the right bag and fills Pirucho's bowl. Alex tells me she had a friend whose cat mysteriously died at a young age, and they later found out it was kidney problems. All her life, that poor cat had eaten the type of food I'd purchased.

"Okay, we can just toss it then," I say, practicing the Spanish verb *echar*, which has many meanings, as many as the English verb "to put."

"No, no," Alex laughs. She asks me if I know the church down the block, behind the Plaza Colombia. "Just bring the food there," she says, as if this is the most natural solution in the world. "A mountain of cats lives there; give that food to them."

So I stand up, take my purse and keys, go into the kitchen for the bag of food, and then head out onto busy, late-afternoon Montes de Oca. I cross the street, walk through the plaza, and come to the church, which is massive and has been painted a grainy coral. On this afternoon it looks warm and radiant, surrounded by sweeping palms and ankle-length grass.

And cats.

The cats, if you look closely, are everywhere. They're nestled in the grass, in the crooks of trees, in the corners of doorways. They're perched on steps, and they hide behind rocks. I shake the bag of food and they come inching toward me, stretching, pricking their ears, taking their time. I'm not one of the grandmothers who frequents this place, but they know the sound of food in a bag.

I pour the food out onto the grass through the bars that surround the church; the cats wait until I've gone to approach it. I turn back and there they are, eating steadily and flicking their tails. This afternoon, it's warm enough for a t-shirt and skirt. The air feels slower on this side street, and heavy with late sunshine. The trees shade the cobblestones and the feasting cats.

Alex and Vicky help me with my Spanish immensely. Their accents crush the double-l, normally a silent sound—*llamar*, to call, usually pronounced "yamar" becomes *jamar*, and the words *yo* and *ya* become *show* and *sha*. I grow used to the morphing of words as common as *I* and *already*, and eventually I come to favor the Buenos Aires accent for how familiar it sounds. I begin to use it myself, for Alex and Vicky make fun of me if I pronounce certain words as I learned them in Guatemala.

With Alex and Vicky, I explore Old Barracas, where, on a street called Lanin, every wall of every house is decorated with lines of mosaic. Tiny colored squares are pressed into bright paint to make waves, dots, and abstract swirls that brighten Lanin. Once as we walk, Alex tells me that in high school she jumped on a train with friends and headed north, to Uruguay. Back then, she slept on trains for months, traveling all over, smoking pot and teaching English in stints to survive. "I always loved English," she says in Spanish.

We visit the old train station, now defunct. With its high, elegant ceilings, it's easy to tell that once it bustled. Light still pours in through sloped windows, but now the station is used only by rats and by bums, who come to drink and sleep. We stroll through the old city and Alex and Vicky talk and talk, bickering, bantering; they speak dramatically, especially Vicky, raising her voice and lifting an arm when she's really passionate about something. The two of them fight: "No, Alex!" Vicky might scream. "We paid forty pesos for that dinner, not thirty!" And so their fights aren't really fights; it's just that they've lived together so long, ever since Alex's eye went bad and she had to stop teaching.

Their story unfolds to me in pieces. They've lived twice in exile, as they told me when I moved in. The first time, it was 1983; the Dirty War had begun, and artists, lawyers, business owners, and teachers were disappearing. Alex and Vicky had friends who could incriminate them if tortured long enough, so Alex went to Italy and Vicky to Spain, where she got married. In 1986, they came home. In 2002, the peso crashed, money lost its value, and no one could find work. That time, the two sisters went to Mexico, where they had contacts. They took all the cash they had in suitcases and stayed with family friends for a year. I asked them once how it was to come back, figuring they'd say they'd been fearful, doubtful maybe, less in love with the city then they had been before. Each time, though, they'd returned more committed to Buenos Aires, finding hope and staying to enact change. "We saw that good things were happening," Alex said, "and we wanted to be a part of them."

In the apartment one afternoon, I notice a photograph I hadn't seen before. Vicky and Alex stand beside a short woman with braids and the Guatemalan *huipil*. For a second, my breath catches. "Is that Rigoberta Menchú?" I ask Vicky, and she nods. When Menchú herself was exiled, she came to Argentina, where Vicky and Alex and some other friends got together to host her. I remember the *fincas* I saw in Guatemala, and the ones I didn't. Sometimes, although Vicky told me to stop her when she says a word I don't know, I let her keep talking, missing a word here, a word there, until all I'm doing is watching her, understanding occasional emphatic words between her waving arms, her bright eyes, her fluid hands.

I pace the floor anxiously while Alex and Vicky tease. "She's wearing all black, a low-cut top, and some makeup!" Vicky tells Alex, whose eyes can't decipher such details. "I wonder when she'll come home!" I sit down, blushing, and resist the urge to reach for one of Vicky's cigarettes.

Alfonso is half an hour late. We met the week before, at a tango event I attended with Alex and Vicky. He lived in Vermont for a year; that's how we struck up a conversation, talking while we watched the dancers move across the floor. He flirted, but just a little, and after I gave him my number, he called the next day. We've been out once before, for sushi, and afterwards he dropped me off at home with a chaste kiss. I'd wanted more, just a little. His clothes are white and blue—white pants, blue shirts—and he is tanned. His teeth are square and even and bright. He is sexy and easy to talk to, and he keeps me looking forward instead of back toward her.

He doesn't call to tell me that he's running late tonight, nor does he apologize when he finally shows up. He just smiles, kisses me on the cheek, and then goes to Alex and Vicky for the same. He stoops to pet Pirucho, then straightens and asks me whether I like Arabian food. He asks it in Spanish, and I have to get him to repeat the question two more times while Alex and Vicky, for once, bite their tongues. *Árabe* is the word I'm not getting, not with the way he crushes the *r* and turns the *b* into a *v*.

"Should we be talking in English?" he asks me in English, after the third and final attempt. I pout. "It was just that one word!" I protest, and the three of them laugh at me. We go out onto the street; darkness is just beginning to fall, and the bus lines are long. Alfonso unlocks the door to his car. The door on my side scrapes the edge of the sidewalk as I pull it shut. "You sank the car!" he says, but he's not angry. He's used to the screech of the door against the high curb, and he jokes that if I weighed just a little bit less, the car wouldn't sink so bad. I know he is teasing, though, because he told me the other night that I should eat more, and ordered us both desserts.

I decide, as we drive into Palermo, down Bullrich, past the horseracing track and the massive banyan tree, past the lime-green Chinese restaurant and the tiny gas station, that I won't be mad at him for showing up late. I love riding in his car and find it hard to believe that I, too, had this freedom once. Now, a car is a luxury, and Alfonso tears around expertly. Even if I said something about his lateness, he'd just remind me that it wasn't his fault—"I don't have a watch, remember?" he'd say. And I'd have to admit that I've used the same excuse. *Anyway,* I tell myself, leaning back in my seat and watching the lights of the city flicker past, *isn't the strange slow movement of time the sweetest thing about this place?* I traveled all the way from Guatemala to get to Buenos Aires, yet I found no other place that treated time the way Buenos Aires does. With each mile I crept farther from the States, time loosened—stretching in the dripping heat or altogether ignored, clocks an hour off and watches lost. Yet only here, here in this massive, layered city, can you really let the minutes collect; they sit on your tongue like lemon drops, meant to be drawn out and savored, inhabited fully.

Alfonso enters Palermo and turns up the music as we cruise down Jorge Luis Borges, a street I love for its name and its graying apartment buildings with their green awnings and creeping vines. This street, as it stretches into Palermo Soho, gives way to tiny, dim bars, and to clothing shops with doors propped open late, spilling pink light onto the street. Alfonso tells me that the man's voice coming through the stereo is that of an Alaskan guy who grew up in Buenos Aires. We listen to his raspy, folksy song as we cruise up and down the nighttime streets. "I like the lights," he told me, the first time he took me out. "Buenos Aires is magic at nighttime."

The bars we speed past are crowded with trendy twenty-somethings who smoke and kiss, turning the night sultry. Knee-length stiletto boots, tight jeans, and leather jackets. The girls have such long hair, so straight and shiny, and their boyfriends hold them tight at the waists, drawing out the kisses. We drive down the series of streets named after Central American countries—Nicaragua and Costa Rica, Honduras. I tell Alfonso, in Spanish, that I like this part of town because the streets remind me of where I started my long trip south. "Which one's your favorite?" Alfonso asks, and I tell him, without hesitating, "Nicaragua." I tell him I liked the heat there, I liked the poets, I liked the blue waters of the Corn Islands and the way, in the late Granada evenings, the sun made everything pink.

The Arabian restaurant, when we arrive, is so jammed that we have to add our names to a long list, a list that a bald man holds with importance at the door. He is smoking and ushering couples in and out, and there must be thirty or forty people waiting for him to call their names, standing there beneath the plastic awning in the sweet, unexpected warmth of this springtime night.

"Let's go for a beer," Alfonso suggests, after he puts our name down. "How long is the wait?" I ask, and he tells me it's enough time to have a beer. I don't push it. This is like him ringing the doorbell late and not apologizing; time works like this here. Argentines don't use the word *ahorita*, as the Peruvians do, and the Ecuadorians, and the Central Americans, whose meals are churned out like clockwork at the same time each day. *Ahora* means now; *ahorita* means right now, this very second, let's go, *vamos entonces*. It's a word I've heard a million times, a word I still can't pronounce quite right, not with the way the *ah* becomes *or* becomes *eat*.

The absence of *ahorita* suits Argentina. Nothing ever happens *right now* anyway, and if you even suggest it you'll be met with surprised looks and a possible snort of laughter. "Now?" the person will say, and blink at you. "Right now?" And then everyone will order another drink and the minutes will slip into hours, and when you look at your watch again you won't believe the time it reads. Here, nine o'clock means ten-thirty, breakfast means brunch, coffee means an early dinner, and your bedtime creeps into the *madrugada*. You cannot help but get swept up in the way time advances here; six in the evening ceases to be a viable dinner hour, and you drink coffee at nine without ever worrying about whether you'll sleep that night.

The Argentine clock ticks round and round, twenty-four hours a day, and anything becomes possible at four a.m., at seven a.m. At midnight, eating supper. In the night, my dreams run wild at three, at five: Raphael beside me on the train; a young and beautiful dark-haired woman on the way to Cuba; my brother waking me up to tell me the time, except that he is a little boy, just three or even two, and his hair is so light, his eyes wide open and his cheeks flushed. I sleep when I'm exhausted and wake to the sound of rain, or of Vicky in the shower, getting ready for work.

I wonder whether I'll bring this clock with me when I go, a clock that's warped and slippery like the ones in Dalí's paintings. How long will it take, I wonder, for them to fall from me—these languishing hours of which any interpretation is acceptable? And how long will *right now* stay off limits? The weeks I have left here stretch before me, but because I am now on this country's time, I know not to count them.

Although the Arabian restaurant was jammed inside and out, the streets around here are empty. Alfonso and I peer into the windows of bars that are silent, the stools and counters gleaming and unused. "Spooky," I say. "It's a vicious cycle," he tells me. "The place is empty, so no one goes in. No one goes in, and the place stays empty." I practice saying "vicious cycle" in Spanish; Alfonso makes fun of my accent, then takes my arm. "Here," he says, and points to a little pizza joint with a couple of outdoor tables and a few waiters standing around smoking.

He orders a big bottle of beer, which comes with little dishes of chips and peanuts and crackers. "I'm starving," he admits, pouring the beer into squat jelly jars and then reaching for a handful of peanuts. He asks me if I've eaten, and I tell him I have. "Hours ago," I say. "I can't wait until midnight for dinner," I joke, and he shrugs. "Is it midnight already?" he asks, and checks his wrist for a watch that isn't there. Then he laughs and grabs another handful of peanuts, tossing one at me, aiming for my shirt's v-shaped neckline. We finish our beer, and he chats with our waiter. We sit for a moment. "Our table should be ready now," Alfonso finally says, and he helps me with my coat when I stand.

And it is. We go back to the Arabian place and wait just two minutes at the door, the patio still jammed, until the man with the list and the cigarette calls our name. He doesn't show us in; he just directs us between a row of tables and up the stairs. "Take the table with silverware on it," he says, and checks his list to call out the next name. After we sit, Alfonso orders without consulting the menu. He does this; I like it. He hasn't let me down with his choices yet. He rattles off a list of dishes and orders a bottle of white wine. Hot, thin bread arrives in a napkin-covered basket, then sparkling water, and then the plates come, one after the other, now stuffed grape leaves, now falafel, now a type of meat pie and a type of cheese casserole and a tart, lemony salad. The wine is cold and tastes like flowers and oranges both. We eat and eat, using our fingers, not our forks. After a while baklava arrives for dessert, and with it the best coffee I've ever had. It's sweet without being sugary, grainy and rich without being cloying. Every bite of the baklava requires you to close your eyes, because with them open, your senses are overwhelmed. I am stuffed, I am sleepy. I am in heaven.

Just before we leave, I check my watch. It's 3 a.m. The restaurant remains full; the waiters hurry around. I catch Alfonso looking at me; he shakes his head. I pull my shirtsleeve down over my wrist to cover my watch.

"Time is a different animal here," Alfonso says. "It's another thing altogether than what you know." He pulls me closer as we make our way though the restaurant toward the door, squeezing between tables and chairs, diners and servers and the man with the list. "So forget it," Alfonso whispers, and hustles me out the door.

And he is right. Here, time's a river, and because it moves like water, it would be stupid to try and cling. On the sidewalk, Alfonso stops walking, takes my hand, leans in, and kisses me. I love that he's led me to this night. Above us, one of Palermo's weeping willows drips down, nearly touching the pavement, and the air is sweet with springtime. *Time*, I think, Alfonso's mouth on mine. Here, the sun setting down doesn't mark another hour; the thing is the glimmer, the long shadows of the trees. This night is not the minutes; it's not the morning growing closer. It's the moonlight, it's the coffee, it's the not-so-distant summer on the wind.

Sometimes I am careless, and on one spring night I push my luck. Alfonso offers to walk me home, but I refuse. "It's not far," I tell him. He's yawning and stretching; I don't mind walking the four blocks in peace.

But there is no one on this street, this night, except me. It's too quiet: no birds, no slamming car doors, no honking horns, no windows creaking open and shut. There are a few cars parked up and down the curb, a few more in the street, whipping past. I walk quickly. In a few hundred yards, I'll be on Montes de Oca, and there, I know, shops and bars are always open.

And that's when I see him.

He's riding his bike alongside me. I glance at him once and walk faster. He's looking at me. He's wearing all black: black hat pulled down over his ears, black jacket, black pack, black jeans. "Hey," he says in a low voice. "Chica."

Still I'm not running, just walking fast, and all of a sudden he's off his bike and behind me. "Chica," he says, loudly now, "give me everything."

Now he has me, grabbing me from behind. My body freezes. I cannot move. I cannot speak. *Everything. Everything.* What could that mean? So many times I've walked past dark alleys, dark figures, and every time I've been spared. *So this*, I think, ludicrously, *is how it feels.*

"Give it," he says again, and tightens his grip. I can feel his breath on my neck. I can smell him: cigarettes, faint cologne, an undercurrent of sweat and musk and unwashed clothes. I think that I'll never forget how he smells. "Please," I finally say, in English, because my Spanish, all of a sudden, is lost. I've also forgotten how to move; blessedly, I can at least open my mouth. "Let me go," I croak. I remember the Spanish word for *please*. I use it; I use it again.

Miraculously, he loosens his grasp. My muscles remember, and I take the release and run, for now my body knows how. *Everything. Everything.* We fly, my body and I, down the street toward the bright lights of Montes de Oca. I never look back, not until I've reached the door and have found the key. I am trembling as I fit it into the lock and then, my heart beating fast, I lock it again from inside and run upstairs.

In bed in the dark house, Pirucho's toenails audible on the kitchen floor outside my door, I try to slow my breathing. It takes many long minutes. *Thank you*, I whisper, to whoever kept me safe and might be listening. Maybe I'm thanking the guy, for loosening his grip after all, for not doing to me what every woman fears and no woman can get over, afterwards. I dream that night of a fast dirt road toward the mountains, my hand on the bar at the door, my heart beating fast. When I awaken, I smell blood; it fills my nostrils, the stench of it. But I open my eyes and the smell is erased, and Pirucho's toenails are clicking on the floor outside my door.

You're okay, I remind myself, vowing not to be so stupid again, replaying the moment he released me from his arms and let me run.

In the morning, I take the bus north to the end of the line. Today, the sky is a faultless blue. I have a seat to myself, and all the windows are open. It's so bright I can let myself forget that the night before happened: my heart has finally slowed, and my hands have stopped shaking. I get out in the university parking lot and walk across the campus and along the river. For many, this river is a graveyard. Officially, this grassy strip along the water is the Parque de la Memoria, a space and monument dedicated to anyone detained, disappeared, or murdered by the dictatorships in Argentina between 1969 and 1983.

First comes a series of signs, which I read as the wind ruffles my hair. I take pictures, which years later I'll look at, still not quite trusting the calm of the river and the piercingly blue sky. Now, the silence is fitful, the wind gusty and unsettled. One sign pictures the Ford Falcon, a black outline on a yellow square, the vehicle known for stealing people off the streets and disappearing them. One sign says that there were many pregnant women at the time of the detentions, but being pregnant didn't stop them from experiencing torture. The women were often Disappeared, and the babies were sometimes left in the hands of the military officers and their wives.

One sign pictures white outlines of bodies, and beneath it a number: 30,000.

Halfway down the row of signs, I notice something in the distance, out there in the water. It takes me another second or two to make out a drowning figure, arms raised. I stare at it long enough to confirm that it's a sculpture, a statue, not a survivor but merely a reminder of the actual lives this river disappeared.

I reach the heart of this monument, a wall of nine thousand names. Each name has its own stone, and these stones come from Patagonia. The names are ordered alphabetically and by year, so those who disappeared first are listed first. Ages are listed, and it's noted if a woman was pregnant. There are 30,000 stones but only 9,000 names, and so the memorial is unfinished. New information keeps trickling in, almost twenty years after the memorial was founded.

I stand at the edge of the Rio de la Plata and breathe in salty wind. I close my eyes. I think I can feel something around me, the distinct sense that I am not, in fact, alone. Rays of sunlight beam through puffy clouds, warming my arms. Still, when I open my eyes, the sense of the not-aloneness remains, the hairs on my forearms pricked. I think of the night before: my pounding heart, though in the end I was safe. I think of broken glass on the floor of a Quito school, of an old man eating Jell-O against a golden cathedral, of a pregnant teacher who earns a dollar an hour. I think of the gun scream and of Riobamba: the rows of nail clippers for sale. So much suffering laid bare, from Guatemala to Buenos

Aires. So many sad stories; so many things I never knew. So many things we were never taught; so many things I was given, and took for granted.

I run my fingers over the stones, caressing the names. Flowers are tucked between certain plaques. When the people behind these names were my age, they were poets. They were teachers, doctors, mothers, and fathers. They were the girlfriends or boyfriends, husbands or wives, of other people my age at the time. They were musicians, travelers, readers, and lovers, all of them just starting their lives.

THE ROAD

The day I give my notice, Alex pouts for a few minutes—"You're *leaving* us?"—and then she and Vicky post an ad on Craigslist. Immediately there's a lot of interest, now that summer has begun. They show my room to a couple of Scandinavian beauties, teenagers who speak to us in English and inspect carefully the tub, the fridge, the view from every window. An Indian man comes by in a suit and pointy shoes. He stands in the doorway, his hat in his hands, taking it in. In the end, a girl with long dreadlocks and a stud in her nose rents the room; she's from the States but speaks to us in perfect Spanish. She'll move in the day after I leave.

And so the three of us—Alex, Vicky, and I—find ourselves counting down the final things: the final supper, the last bottle of wine, the last time Alex pulls the dishes I've washed from the drying rack and cleans them again. *The last shower,* I think to myself. *The last time I unlock this door. The last time I open my window. The last time I let Pirucho in.*

Will it fall from me—the ability to walk slowly, to taste fully, to listen with both ears? The ability to see beauty in a crumbling wall or broken glass? I used to think I needed so much, and because I never got all I needed, I couldn't stop wanting. I couldn't stop counting. In my country, we have gadgets, and we tell ourselves they bring us closer to other people, but they really just force us further apart. We legitimize interruptions, hasty choices, jam-packed days and too-short nights. *Take me with you,* Buenos Aires whispers, and I begin touching things—the trunks of trees, the curved wrought-iron bar over a window, the rusted metal on a dented car, the warm wood of tall, glossy shutters. It's as if touching this place will imprint it onto my skin, so that when I leave, the city will come too.

I pack my bags another time and say goodbye. I weep. Alex holds Pirucho up to the window. They wave, and I wave back from the sidewalk. I hail a cab to Retiro Station. I think of my grandmother at the helm of some steamship, hand shading her eyes, the unknown approaching.

That night, I sleep as the bus chugs out of Buenos Aires and into the Pampas. Beneath the stars, huddling with my jacket to keep myself warm against the powerful AC, I dream of nothing.

When we arrive in the bright, blinking morning, I wait until everyone gets off before I stand. I tell the empty seat beside me goodbye, and let the *ayudantes* help me with my backpack. They call me *mi amor* and wish me luck.

In the Cordoba hostel, with its red and yellow walls, its pretty courtyard out back and its long, wooden kitchen tables, I meet an Irish girl called Aifoe. She's got long dreadlocks she winds up behind her head, wrapping the whole mass in a scarf. She's been traveling two weeks, she says. Her eyes are wide and blue. Her companion is her best friend, a French girl called Mariana. Cordoba is Argentina's college town, sun-swept and pleasant with a river running through.

"How do you feel about going home?" Aifoe asks, after the sun goes down and we sit in the courtyard with mugs of red wine. "Are you scared?"

"Let's not talk about it," I say. "Let's be here." Aiofe takes out her guitar and strums and talks. She reminds me of a friend I had in college, a friend who wrapped her hair into dreadlocks and rolled her own cigarettes and listened, carefully, with clear blue eyes, as Aiofe does.

Much later, though, she asks me the question again: "Are you afraid?" And instead of deferring this time, I tell her I am scared that when I go home I will lose something. I'm afraid that I will forget, that my time here will slide away, and I—the carrier of every lesson and each memory—will be responsible.

"No one knows where I've been," I say to Aiofe, and to my surprise she reaches for my hand, naturally, as though we've always talked this way. "I'm holding it all," I explain, "and when I go home, no one else will know. No one there can see me here."

"I know just what you mean," she says. "When you're traveling, you bloom. And then you go home and you are with the people you love the most, and yet there something is missing, something you'll never get back, because you are safe, because you are home." She takes a sip of red wine and closes her eyes. "And that *missing* is the saddest thing in the world."

And then, though she's only been on the road for two weeks and is planning eight months more, she, too, looks about to cry. "You bloom," she says again, and I realize, though I'm nearly penniless, though my clothes are dirty, though I have no job lined up after this—I realize that I'm blooming, unafraid, and I may be as free as I'll ever feel.

We talk long after the rain begins. Inside, through the glass windows, the Porteños sing: two play guitar, and a harmonica wheezes and croons. The members of the group close their eyes and let their voices come together. This group grew up singing for the pleasure it brings, the unity, the ribbon a song can become, wrapping around people and pulling them closer. We listen to the music and the drops of rain on the deck outside, the restless scratch of branches in the wind against the wall. I think of a passage by Rumi I saw posted on the blog of a friend. *Pick up an instrument*, I'd read. *There are a hundred ways to kneel and kiss the earth.*

The next day, I ride buses to Mina Clavera, a town of some thirty thousand people. In this city, a river the color of amber flows. In the sunlight it flickers, and its banks are made of soft, pale sand. Willows dip their long fronds into the coolness, and bridges connect the town, split by the water. I arrive in the early evening, and wander and wander around the little town, grateful for the long summer light. People come out of their houses and sit in the park. I ask a man in a little shop where I might find a hostel, and he directs me to one by the river. There, a beautiful, long-haired woman with a baby on her hip rents me a room. Two cats, orange and big, swirl around her legs as she unlocks the door. Her husband, a dark-skinned, dark-eyed, muscular man, works in the garden, and he smiles at me when we pass.

Later, when we're all chatting in the garden, they give me a beer and tell me to go to Nono, eight kilometers from Mina Clavera. In the morning, I set out. The bus passes through a canyon, at the base of which water flows. Nono's museum, the long-haired woman had said, is the town's main attraction, and it's a pretty walk from the bus station to get there.

I walk along the river for three miles, and no cars pass. The massive museum turns out to be the collection of one man, and I walk inside to find skulls and dolls, crucifixes and car parts, hundreds of lamps, old teeth, old boxes of matches, shells, bones, a two-headed cow. I wander the dusty rooms, which all smell old and different from each other—one smells just like the hot stones in my grandmother's sauna, another like my parents' cellar, a third, the room of playing cards and board games and old paintings, like dried flowers. There are a dozen sets of cutlery fixed to one wall. There are thirty old radios, forty ancient sewing machines, and the taxidermied remains of, the museum claims, the biggest Argentine cow ever recorded—nearly twenty feet long and eight feet high. There are glass boxes of bones, dozens of statues of the Virgin Mary, a hundred spatulas in every conceivable size and color. Indeed, the place is a rainbow of old and new, shiny and dull, red and brown and indigo blue.

On my way back to the bus stop, a car pulls over. "Want a ride?" the driver shouts. He's an older man, and he waits while I run to the car and get in the front seat. I am not afraid, here where the water runs so close to the road, where a thousand skulls live beneath a red roof. In this town, shaded by canyon, I feel at ease, as if I am barefoot. The man drives very, very slowly, and he does not ask me where I'm headed. Cars and buses pass, as do mopeds and one horse. I'm amazed at the sudden traffic. The dust from it rolls up in clouds ahead of us.

He asks me the standard things: Where am I from? What am I doing? I ask him what he does. "Me," he says, "I sell sausage." It takes me a moment to translate *fiambre* in my head, then a moment more to realize that he was the one outside the museum with the strings of sausage in his hands, calling out to the cars that passed, convincing them to stop for just a taste.

"I saw you!" I tell him. "I remember now." And in that moment, he remembers too. "You were the girl all by herself walking in!"

Now we have much to talk about. We discuss the museum, his work (once a pharmacist in Cordoba, now a sausage salesman in Nono). He points out his house as we pass, a little white ranch-style casita with a small, pretty yard, a couple of trees. "What a nice life you have," I say. I put my hand on the spotless dash; the mirrors look recently wiped. "What a nice car," I add.

"How old do you think I am?" he asks. I peer at him, at his ruddy cheeks, his receding hairline, his big belly. He looks at least sixty.

"Forty...two," I tell him. He grins, nods.

"Well," he says, "I've celebrated forty-two years." The conversation shifts to my age—he guesses I'm twenty-seven. We talk about the way life in the city can wear on you, all the dust and pavement, and the sun is setting ahead of us.

"I have to tell you something," he says, after a short silence. He pauses to wave at a family we pass, rolling down his window and then raising it again against the dust. "You know how I said I had celebrated forty-two years?" He glances at me. "I'm much older than that. How old, do you think?"

"Fifty...one," I guess. He laughs.

"Seventy-five!" he cries, slapping his hand against his forehead. "Seventy-five." I tell him again how good his life seems, with the trees that sing here and the river that runs amber around stones. He drops me off at the bus stop and leans over to kiss my cheek.

"Thanks," I tell him.

"You're welcome, daughter," he replies. "All the luck." And then he's gone.

In Mina Clavera, I eat the sweet, enormous blackberries that grow over the bridge in the center of town. At my hotel, I go and sit by the river, and the husband comes over with his baby in a sling. We say hello and then nothing more. The air is heavy with water, and it settles upon us like clothing. I eat rice and beans while the nightshift clerk, a redheaded man from Ireland, tells me how he met a woman here eight years ago and never went home. He brews us cups of tea and tells me he was married a year ago. His family is coming to visit from Ireland in the fall.

"We're expecting," he admits shyly, and his voice holds so much ill-concealed delight that I reach out, spontaneously, and give him a hug.

And when I go to sleep that night, I think, *I must remember this forever.*

I return to the same hostel in Cordoba, where I will sleep and then catch a bus in the morning, back to Buenos Aires. My flight to La Guardia leaves in two days.

After the sun sets, I go out to find the night market; Cordoba's is said to be one of the biggest in Latin America. From a girl with a thick black braid, I buy a woven bracelet with a stone the color of the river in Mina Clavera. The girl with the black braid helps to tie the bracelet around my wrist, then centers the stone just so. It glows gold and yellow and brown, smoke gray, and I turn it beneath the streetlights, both of us admiring the girl's work.

After I pass the money over and she counts it, I turn. There is a woman standing there; she has dark wavy hair threaded with feathers, and she wears a long purple skirt. I take a step closer; she's lined her eyes with black pencil and green shadow. She's talking to a tall boy with blonde hair. She doesn't see me, but I know.

"Gaby," I say, and she looks at me.

And then she shrieks and we run to each other, awkwardly, and my heart is pounding.

"Gaby," I say again. "Where did you go?"

We spend the night together at my hostel, drinking beer late into the evening. She tells me of the months after Cusco, when she went to Bolivia and met a guitarist from Spain. He didn't have any money, but he was so beautiful that Gaby followed him to Santa Cruz, in the east. There, they slept in an abandoned house and made music on the street for money. I notice that Gaby looks thinner.

"I had to ditch him," she admits, laughing. "Next!"

She tells me I look different, reaching out to touch my hair. "It's longer and lighter," she says, and I'm grateful that she doesn't mention the parched, gnarled ends. She examines my face, looks into my eyes, lights a cigarette.

"You're darker and lighter both," she decides. "And the way you walk—it's different." She takes a sip of beer and shrugs. "You seem like you belong."

We walk around the block in the humid night. At one building, a little girl is pushing a baby stroller through her front door. I stop to help. "In or out?" I ask. "In," she says, and together we push the stroller inside.

Back at the hostel, a middle-aged couple is sitting at the table speaking Portuguese. They invite us to eat their cashews and drink some of their wine, and the four of us stay up very late, trying to understand each other. They say things in Portuguese; we answer mostly in Spanish and sometimes in English. They kiss us goodnight when we realize that the sun is beginning to lighten the sky. I cannot believe the time; I don't allow myself to mind. Gaby and I lean on each other, moving sloppily, sleepily, up the stairs and to our beds.

On this night, Gaby asleep beside me, I think of the wind. Right now, it sings through Capilla del Monte, through Mina Clavera, through all the little towns I've seen and all the others I have not. It rolls up and down this continent, through all these wild and spectacular countries, and it seeps inside me also. We all shape our own routes, and sometimes we meet for a second time, guided together by chance like leaves in a river. I'll leave this city alone. I'll fly away, and yet I want this wind forever, this place, these cities and towns and hills that are blending together now. May they come in the night, these images sent by wind. May they slip into my dreams so that when I wake I'll feel them still. May they become tattoos, these places, marks that fade as the years go by but never fully disappear.

BUENOS AIRES, ARGENTINA

In the darkness, I blink around the room, guessing. I know it can't be home—that knowledge has become instinctive—so where am I now, exactly? Which city, which country, is this one? And then something gives the room away—the shape of the table, the light through the window—and so I remember. This is Buenos Aires, this is San Telmo, this is the hotel on Chacabuco where I checked in yesterday and the woman sat smoking in the kitchen, not getting up to hand me the keys. The night before I slept in Cordoba, Gaby in the next bunk over. I am in Buenos Aires again, and that bus was my last. I'm remembering now: I'll be going home soon.

At the beginning of my journey, my dreams were of home, of the deep feet of snow in the woods behind my house and of the smell of my mother's kitchen. In Xela I saw my father's hands, and on Granada's streets I heard my brother's laugh. I dreamed of my lover's skin. I remembered all that I'd left in the night, and in the morning I woke, the memory of home still heavy on my chest. Those dreams left an ache, an empty stillness, and I wept for how far everything felt.

The dreams shifted after a while and turned foreign. Now I was crossing a turquoise sea over fresh coral with strangers. Now I was entering an ancient city; now I was climbing a peak where the air grew thin and my breaths came short and desperate. I stopped thinking, at nighttime, of home, and started dreaming instead of movement. Every possibility came in the night; the whole world arrived. I'd been flung; no one knew me. This was freedom.

In these last dripping days, this room could be any room. I forget my dreams now, remembering only the emotions they held and none of the context. Sometimes I am screaming, sometimes I am crying, and often I am laughing so hard I wake myself up. There are strangers sometimes, although I've heard that every face you see in your dreams is a face you've seen before—on the street, perhaps, years ago, when you looked and barely saw, never knowing you'd remember. I wake and search for a clue: Which city is this? Which country? There have been so many shafts of unfamiliar light through curtain cracks, so many creaking beds, and so many midnight trips for water. My dreams run together like songs, like different colors in a woven cloth, and when morning comes I wake unsure.

The mint-green paint on the door of this last rented room is peeling. Morning glory winds up the banisters, and there's an outdoor *pila* that reminds me of the one Hilary had in Guatemala. We can wash our clothes out here and hang them on the line that stretches over the patio so that they flap against the crumbling cement of the building next door. There are bathrooms with drains in the floors and no shower curtains. There is a little kitchen with a two-burner stovetop and no fridge. There is a single bed in my room, a small table, and two chairs. There is a cup and a plate and a bowl, a fork and a knife and a spoon. A glass, a bar of soap, a folded towel, an open window. It's beautiful here in my last rented room.

No one knows, I think to myself. No one could find me here; no one would know to look for me in room 49. The walls are painted two shades of pink, one old, one new.

No one knows.

On my second-to-last morning, I take my laundry to the place around the corner, the one that is shaded by leafy trees and always locked, so you have to push the bell to be let in. It's the one where the nice man works, the handsome man with kind eyes and worn hands. He has a young son who comes in the afternoons to help him fold.

Today, the man fills out the receipt without asking my name. "You remember?" I ask him, though I've told him only once.

"How could I forget," he replies, handing me my receipt. *Katy*, it says. My Spanish name. He's a beautiful man who smells of detergent, and today he remembered my name. *Don't let this go*, a voice tells me as I step outside, into the sun and the wind that smells so sweet. *Nothing matters more than this moment*, it says, *and right now you have everything you need.*

ACKNOWLEDGMENTS

Many thanks:

To Wellesley College and the Mary Elvira Stevens Traveling Fellowship committee, for making my journey possible.

To Lauren Morgan Whitticom, for your wisdom, your faith, and your loyalty.

To Alicia Erian, Marita Everhart, Sascha Feinsten, Douglas Glover, and Philip Graham—for your insight, your inspiration, and your many administrative favors.

To Lily Balloffet, Elaine Daniels, Julia Deisler, Austin Eichelberger, Richard Hartshorn, Robin MacArthur, Pia Møller, and Angela Smith Kirkman—for your thoughtful, compassionate feedback, draft after draft.

To Kendra Bailey, Kate Broad, Katie Thebeau Burgess, Brook Erenstone Phillips, Raphael Erhard, Samantha Fields, Claire Gilbertsen, Leonardo Fernandez Hermida, Bethany Carson Kilpatric, Daniel Kilpatric, Hilary Kilpatric, Rachael Levitz Wheeler, Alexandra and Vicky Lomban, Gabriella Matton Rodriguez, Elizabeth McCahill, Donigan Merritt, Aoife Ní Mhurchú, Juanse Moncayo, Holly Murten, Carl Pesantz, Katie Rock, Kassidy Rogers, Lynn Sipila, Lavinia Spalding, Donna Tabor, Rachel Levitz Wheeler, and Colleen Youngdahl—for your friendship.

To Pamela Aleta Hill, Miriam Sagan, Saba Sulaiman, and Monika Verma—for your guidance.

To Andrew Gifford—for making this book possible.

To my family: my parents, Pearl and Woods McCahill, and my brother, David McCahill—for your love, encouragement, and support.

And to my husband, David Forrest—for everything.

ABOUT THE AUTHOR

Kate McCahill lives in Santa Fe, New Mexico, where she is a member of the English faculty at the Santa Fe Community College. Her writing has been published in *Vox, The Millions,* and in the *Best Travel Writing* and *Best Women's Travel Writing* anthologies by Travelers' Tales. She holds an MFA from the Vermont College of Fine Arts. *Patagonian Road* is her first book.

www.katemccahill.com

Also from Santa Fe Writers Project

Smoking Cigarettes, Eating Glass
by Annita Perez Sawyer
Annita Sawyer's memoir is a harrowing, heroic, and redeeming story of her battle with mental illness, and her triumph in overcoming it. Hers is a unique voice for this generation, shedding light on an often misunderstood illness.

My Chinese America by Allen Gee
Eloquently written essays about aspects of Asian American life comprise this collection that looks at how Asian-Americans view themselves in light of America's insensitivities, stereotypes, and expectations.

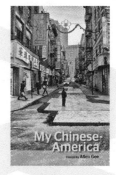

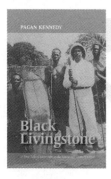

Black Livingstone by Pagan Kennedy
The extraordinary story of William Sheppard, a 19th-century African American who, for more than 20 years, defied segregation and operated a missionary run by black Americans in the Belgian Congo.

About Santa Fe Writers Project
SFWP is an independent press founded in 1998 that embraces a mission of artistic preservation, recognizing exciting new authors, and bringing out of print work back to the shelves.

Find us on Facebook, Twitter @sfwp, and at www.sfwp.com sfWP)